A Fraught Embrace

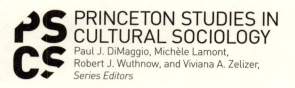

PRINCETON STUDIES IN
CULTURAL SOCIOLOGY
Paul J. DiMaggio, Michèle Lamont,
Robert J. Wuthnow, and Viviana A. Zelizer,
Series Editors

A list of titles in this series appears at the back of the book

A FRAUGHT EMBRACE

The Romance & Reality of
AIDS Altruism in Africa

ANN SWIDLER

SUSAN COTTS WATKINS

Princeton University Press
Princeton and Oxford

Published by Princeton University Press,
41 William Street, Princeton, New Jersey 08540
In the United Kingdom: Princeton University Press,
6 Oxford Street, Woodstock, Oxfordshire OX20 1TR
press.princeton.edu

Jacket photograph by Gerald Cotts

Library of Congress Cataloging-in-Publication Data

Names: Swidler, Ann, 1944–author. | Watkins, Susan Cotts, 1938–author.
Title: A fraught embrace : the romance and reality of AIDS altruism in Africa / Ann
Swidler and Susan Cotts Watkins.
Other titles: Princeton studies in cultural sociology.
Description: Princeton : Princeton University Press, 2017. | Series: Princeton studies in
cultural sociology | Includes bibliographical references and index.
Identifiers: LCCN 2016039899 | ISBN 9780691173924 (hardcover : alk. paper)
Subjects: LCSH: AIDS (Disease)—Malawi. | AIDS (Disease)—Patients—Services for—
Malawi. | HIV infections—Social aspects—Malawi. | Non-governmental organizations—
Malawi. | Antiretroviral agents—Malawi. | Voluntarism—Malawi.
Classification: LCC RA643.86.M3 S95 2017 | DDC 362.1969792096897—dc23
LC record available at https://lccn.loc.gov/2016039899

British Library Cataloging-in-Publication Data is available

This book has been composed in Baskerville 10 Pro

Printed on acid-free paper. ∞

Printed in the United States of America

10 9 8 7 6 5 4 3 2 1

CONTENTS

PREFACE

BEGINNING IN THE LATE 1980S, the horror of the AIDS epidemic in Africa called forth an outpouring of compassion—and of romantic imagination. Governments in wealthy countries created global organizations to fight the disease; church groups sent volunteers; ordinary people sent checks. There was a ferment of altruism in the Western world inspired by a desire to help others in far-away places. We focus on AIDS as the key motivator of the global altruism we study. But altruists also target other issues, such as poverty and women's empowerment, and embrace other transformative goals. Consequently, our analysis of global altruism widens beyond a focus on AIDS interventions alone.

Much good has come from this altruism. Successful efforts to provide drugs that treat, if not cure, AIDS have extended the lives of millions who would otherwise have died. AIDS altruism, however, also inspired powerful fantasies. Donors in wealthy countries, particularly those hoping to prevent, rather than just treat AIDS, have imagined that they can protect Africans by transforming them. Their fantasies have been reciprocated from the African side. Quests for transformation of both self and others constitute the essence of a romance.

The ferment of AIDS altruism has also brought new opportunities to those whom we call "brokers"—educated or unusually entrepreneurial Africans who mediate between foreign altruists and local people who are trying to survive the epidemic and care for those who are ill. Some brokers are employees in the many organizations working to transform Africans' ways so that they can escape infection. Others are brokers-by-chance—locals who often through an accidental contact assist foreign visitors who have come to help orphans or comfort the stricken.

Western altruists and African brokers enact a romance in another sense too. As in a love story, both long for connection, albeit in different ways. They bring to their encounters their own hopes and dreams, and they often suffer disappointment and heartbreak. Sometimes there is an eventual consummation, if not a perfectly happy ending.

To function in such unfamiliar landscapes as Africa's villages or urban slums, both large institutions and individual altruists need local guides—brokers who can connect them with those whom they would help. However unromantic the term "broker" may sound, the foreigner's dependence on the broker as guide, cultural interpreter, and sometimes friend can make

vii

the relationship an emotionally charged one. From their side, brokers dream that someone who has come to fight AIDS will transform their lives. This mutual dependence, given the hopes and fantasies it arouses on both sides, creates a romance that often begins with a rush of infatuation but also can dissolve into disillusionment, disappointment, and even a sense of betrayal.

Coming from different worlds heightens both the excitement of discovery and the dangers of misunderstanding. Altruists who come from afar, however, rarely recognize the brokers' fantasies. This book, if it succeeds, should deepen readers' understanding of what the romance of AIDS altruism is like from the perspectives of the brokers, who are critical but often ignored actors in the AIDS drama.

We refer to altruists and donors almost interchangeably, although some altruists are volunteers who primarily give their time and effort, and others are institutions that just give money. The individuals who come in person to help and the institutional altruists—the giant bureaucracies such as USAID or Save the Children—all depend on publics that are moved to help distant villagers. We use the term "villagers" to refer to the objects of the donor's affections although they may be fishermen or small traders or live in urban slums. "Villagers" connotes to altruists and brokers poor communities in need of their help. Although villagers draw altruists, large and small, to Africa, most altruists have their deepest direct involvement with a broker. Few villagers ever meet either a donor or a broker, but they too dream that somehow, some day, they will be helped by an altruist from afar.

The intense emotions that draw altruists to Africa are displayed in Western accounts. In 2003, a British newspaper, *The Guardian*, published "Saving Grace," a special supplement about the devastating effects of AIDS in Malawi, focused on Grace Matnanga, a young, HIV-positive (HIV+) woman.

Once she had a husband. Once she had a child. Both are dead.

"I was married for eight years," she says. "My husband passed away in 1998. He collapsed and was taken to the Central Hospital and put on oxygen." Like most of the young people who die, he had not been tested for HIV, but there's little doubt that Aids killed him.

He survived longer than their little daughter. Tiyajane was born in 1993, the longed-for fulfilment of marriage in Malawian society, where almost every young woman has a baby strapped to her back. Tiyajane appeared to be healthy at first, but then the weight gain slowed. She stopped thriving. She began to get sick. She picked up infections. When she died, aged three, she was a pitiful, wasted scrap, the ulcers in her throat and mouth making the pain of swallowing more vicious than the pangs of hunger.

At the time that Grace's daughter was desperately ill, antiretroviral drug treatment (ARVs) had been developed in the West, but was neither widely available nor free in Malawi. The story concludes with the painful unfairness of Grace's situation:

"If ARVs were available and they were here, I would take them," she says. She is no more indifferent to her life than her contemporary in an up-market shoe shop in Durham or Leeds. She's just living on the wrong side of the global divide.[1]

The story drew such a response that the newspaper created the Saving Grace Foundation to buy antiretroviral treatment for poor Malawians. Later, as treatment became more widely available, the foundation provided nutritional foods and home based care for HIV+ Malawians, and beginning in 2007, "facilitators to work in schools and communities to raise awareness of HIV prevention through active and participatory theatre workshops."[2]

In May 2000, a member of the US Congress, Sheila Jackson-Lee, described the gripping personal experience that inspired her to propose a government trust fund to "combat the AIDS epidemic":

When I traveled to Africa, I went in to visit some of the locales and villages where HIV-infected persons were living in desolation, alone, and without family support....

When I visited these bedridden individuals, I saw so many of them suffering, not only from the devastation of AIDS but they were suffering from tuberculosis. Sometimes they were left to be cared for by children as young as 4 and 6 years old, because other families had already died.

One woman that I spoke to had already lost six members of her family, was HIV-infected herself along with her son. The reason is because she nurtured her husband who died of this disease, and none of the family members would explain what was occurring to him. It is a question whether they even knew. So, of course she contracted the disease subsequently as well.[3]

Such moving stories turned ordinary people in wealthy nations and their governments into altruists of the global AIDS enterprise.

Invisible in such stories are the brokers, the local Africans who led the American congresswoman to the bedsides of dying AIDS patients, introducing her to suffering at first hand, or the broker who guided the British reporter to Grace. But a broker was surely there.

Occasionally, a broker figures centrally in an altruist's account, as in this story from the charity Hope for Malawi:

> In autumn 2006, Elaine and Peter Zakreski—from Saskatoon, Canada— vacationed in Kenya, Uganda, Tanzania, Zimbabwe and South Africa. Elaine is an educator and author and Peter is a corporate executive. It was the trip of a lifetime, spectacular waterfalls and dramatic landscape. They also saw, and were deeply moved by, the sight of children without parents, without shelter and, in so many instances, without food. They encountered a population with limited resources, restricted access to health care and few educational opportunities. But they also saw boundless potential to become self-sufficient.
>
> The vacation would change Elaine and Peter forever. Returning to Canada, on a long flight from Nairobi to London, Elaine sat beside Jean Kalinga, an African woman. They were destined to meet. Jean was returning to Washington after visiting her family who still lived in their ancestral village in Malawi. Elaine and Jean talked through the entire flight. Jean shared her great disappointment. She felt that she had failed God because she had spent her personal savings building a safe house for the preschoolers in the village and ran out of money before the project was finished. Having just witnessed so many orphans and such extreme poverty, Elaine was praying and wondering what she should do.
>
> Jean and Elaine were the answer to each other's prayers.
>
> On May 16, 2009, what began as a dream became reality. The Malawi community got its medical clinic, and much more. Elaine and Peter travelled to Malawi and saw with their own eyes the power of HOPE—hope, opportunity, protection and education. They attended the opening ceremony of a fully completed preschool safe house, a porch for the community's grandmothers to come together and socialize and 13-room health clinic which will serve in excess of 3,000 people from the surrounding region of Malawi.[4]

Such face-to-face altruism can create a powerful emotional connection between individual donors and those whom they want to help.

The encounters of donors with brokers are as much matters of fantasy and longing as of fulfilling relationships. Nonetheless, the entangled partners need one another and, despite many awkward missteps, they find ways to get along. "Working misunderstandings"—pragmatic accommodations among donors and brokers who inhabit very different universes but nonetheless share in a joint endeavor—create real limitations.[5] Brokers and donors find that on the ground their efforts to prevent HIV by changing African behavior come down to a few routines: writing reports and tracking expenditures; training volunteers to deliver global AIDS prevention messages in their villages; and creating colorful billboards, songs, and dramas to be performed on the radio and at village gatherings. These shared rituals allow the partners to move, however haltingly, together. As in many real-life romances, the day-to-day reality turns out to be much less than the fulfilling union the partners imagined.

Seeing AIDS altruism as a romance will, we hope, allow readers to appreciate that good works in the developing world often entail a clash between noble dreams and everyday reality. Both individual and large-scale altruists can "do good better" if they gain insight into the fantasies that underlie their efforts as well as the aspirations they stimulate among those whom they want to help. Very often the programs designed in foreign capitals, like the efforts of individual altruists, reflect moral commitment to ideals, such as empowerment and self-reliance, participatory democracy, and gender equality, that deeply move citizens of advanced industrial societies. These ideals lie behind many AIDS-prevention interventions as well as other efforts to promote development around the world. Before attempting to transform the lives of others, however, it is important to understand the experience of those one is trying to help—especially, we show, the lives of the brokers upon whom altruists are so dependent.

* * *

Much of the research for this book was conducted in rural areas in Malawi, a small and exceptionally poor African country with a severe AIDS epidemic. Malawi has attracted many dedicated altruists. We explore the fraught relationship of donors and brokers in Malawi—and its consequences for both—largely from the perspective of the brokers. We also describe the experience of altruism from the perspective of villagers, who have their own ways of imagining their relationship with visiting donors, even if the hopes they imagine are rarely fulfilled.

Altruists often misunderstand the realities of both brokers' and villagers' lives in places like Malawi. They, of course, expect to encounter poverty and suffering; that is why they come. But altruists often fail to grasp the basic social and moral realities of African societies. The first and most important misunderstanding is imagining that, with just a bit of help, Africans will adopt Western values of individual autonomy that will make them self-sufficient rather than dependent on altruists. In reality, at all levels of African societies, life is defined by complex relations of reciprocal dependence best summarized as "patron-client ties." Each person, poor or rich, needs a relationship with a patron, someone from whom she or he can expect material help, advice, and support in emergencies. Each client is also a patron or potential patron to others.

Patrick Chabal, a leading student of Africa, writes that obligation is central to selfhood across African societies: "the question is not whether to be party to a system of obligations or not but how to manage one's place within such a system. To have no obligations is not to belong; it is not to be fully and socially human."[6] Others' obligations can be lifesaving for the poor; ties of dependence provide a safety net in countries with no institutional social security. Thus the village grandmother who may be feeding a dozen orphans, the broker an altruist meets on an airplane by happenstance, or the professional broker working for a nongovernmental organization (NGO, a nonprofit donor organization), all hope to recruit the donor as a patron whose assistance will allow them, in turn, to fulfill their own moral obligations to their many dependents. Recognizing that obligations to others are the fabric of everyday life and that these obligations often lie behind the hopes Africans bring to encounters with outsiders is key to understanding the attraction—the romance—of AIDS altruism from the African side.

The failure of those from wealthy countries to appreciate the contexts in which most Africans live virtually guarantees that the romance between donors and brokers and that between visiting altruists and poor villagers will lead to heartbreak on both sides. The insecurities of life in Africa and the reliance on ties of personal dependence define African lives—for African staff of large NGOs and poor subsistence farmers alike. Corruption is also a pervasive reality of Malawian life. The papers are full of stories of government malfeasance, and donors repeatedly suspend aid when funds go missing. Malawians themselves condemn these practices as well as the petty corruption of police officers demanding bribes or the treasurer of a local organization stealing its money. Nonetheless, one cannot understand the accounts we give here without unblinkingly seeing commonplace, often petty, corruption.[7]

For donors, understanding the African landscape is not about elephants and zebras, or even the challenges of mosquitoes, drought, and monsoon downpours. It is about appreciating the differing social realities of Africa and the West—in particular, the pressure on Africans at all social levels to share whatever resources come their way, including the resources belonging to a donor's project, with kin and other dependents. How Africans manage these pressures can create mistrust and misunderstanding. We urge the altruist who comes to Africa in order to visit malnourished orphans and major donors who care about vulnerable women to notice the broker who may be standing by their side as guide and interpreter and who may be key to implementing a project. Altruists should also consider the likelihood that they will become patrons to employees, guides, and friends. This book can serve as something of a guide to those experiences.

* * *

Writing this book has been both exhilarating and painful. We hope that despite the stark realities of AIDS, readers will find it an exciting book to read. But we also want to acknowledge that in an emotional sense, or perhaps a moral sense, it has been a difficult book to write.

During our time in Malawi, death was all around us. A 1998 survey conducted in rural villages in Malawi found that 96 percent of respondents knew someone who had died of AIDS and that villagers attended an average of three funerals a month.[8] We ourselves were spared the worst of this pain. In the days before antiretroviral treatment, we worried about those who told us they were infected, but none of our close friends or those with whom we worked died of AIDS, and those who became ill recovered with the help of antiretroviral drugs. Several of the brokers we know or have interviewed are HIV+, but even when this fact is widely known among their friends and acquaintances, it appears to play almost no role in their day-to-day lives. When we and other visitors are in Africa, even for extended periods, we do not see dying people, mainly because the dying are cared for at home.[9]

Friends and acquaintances did sometimes tell us wrenching stories about siblings, uncles, aunts, or spouses who died of AIDS. Many also told us of the burdens of caring for orphaned nieces and nephews. These conversations often had a matter-of-fact rather than an anguished tone, even when someone told us of a nephew who threw away the antiretroviral drugs his desperate family bought for him or when a man explained that he and his first wife had both tested HIV+ in the years before antiretroviral drugs were available, but his wife had died, while he had inexplicably survived. Thanks to the global AIDS enterprise that eventually made antiretroviral therapy accessible in rural Malawi, those with AIDS can survive for decades. But the pervasiveness of early death—both from AIDS and from more routine maladies like lower respiratory disease, diarrhea, and malaria—still hovers over all Malawians.

This book has also been painful to write because of our commitment to and respect for those whom we have come to know during our years of research in Malawi and elsewhere in Africa. We met many who fit the abstract category of "donor" as we use it in this book: a brother and sister from Scotland who collect used textbooks and donate them to a school in Malawi; a representative of the World Bank who has come to Malawi to discuss plans for a new project with a government minister. We also met long-term employees of international aid agencies. Many of these development professionals are immensely dedicated, generous, respectful of their African employees and co-workers, and devoted to the goal of assisting Africans. But we have come to see many of the donor projects they dedicate their work to as wrongheaded, pointless, or even perverse in their effects.

In the simple hotels and motels where we stayed, we also met many remarkable individuals who had left the comfort of their own lives back home to come to Malawi to try to help others. We describe the compassion and the sometimes-heroic efforts of these courageous altruists in the pages that follow. Some are naïve, and the assistance they imagine will help village orphans actually goes to enrich a local pastor or to build a house for a broker's family. Others, after setbacks and disappointments, have persisted, raising money back home and returning repeatedly to Malawi to provide real, if modest, material help.[10]

We also have made close Malawian friends. Many are brokers for us. We rely on them for guidance and help and we have, as is expected, become their patrons. Of course, our friends in Malawi are no doubt sometimes frustrated with and skeptical about us, as when they assume that we could easily have a child of theirs admitted to an American university and we reply that we do not have that power. In their world, such a favor would be expected. Thus, there are misunderstandings even with highly educated Malawians who are our professional peers.

Our difficulty is even greater when the distance between us and the Malawians we meet in wealth, education, and knowledge of the outside

world is greater. Twaina, a young woman in her twenties and a former interviewer for our project, walked many kilometers to ask whether the flyer
she clutched in her hand, promising access to scholarships at Canadian
universities in return for a $50 payment, was genuine. It pained us to tell
her that this was certainly a scam. When we hired Gift, a down-on-his-luck
trader in a local market, whom we discovered had a high school education
and superb English skills, as an interviewer, we assumed we were changing
his life dramatically for the better. But his newfound wealth was squan-
dered on alcohol and on a mercenary girlfriend who prevailed on him to
pay her school fees. He ended up back in his mother's village worse off than
before. Even happier stories such as that of another former interviewer,
Robert, who, after volunteering for years in one NGO after another finally,
in his early thirties, came to tell us with pride about his first paying job are
sometimes disappointing. We had to stifle our impatient sense that the
NGO that hired him to promote adult literacy in the villages was not addressing the real priorities of the villagers.

We are most sympathetic to the young people we met who were struggling to get enough education to qualify for a job with a regular salary in
an NGO—a job that would permit them to leave the life of subsistence agriculture behind. It has been hard to confront their urgent desire to continue their education and not be able to help them. Even when they do
manage with extraordinary effort to succeed, we find what we should have
expected: they do not want to remain in their impoverished villages, and
they look down on the villagers they have left behind.

For altruists, the villagers are the most sympathetic characters in our
story. We, too, sympathize with villagers' efforts to survive the AIDS epidemic and respect their hopes, however unrealistic, that altruists will transform their lives. But ours is a nuanced sympathy. Malawian villagers, far
from the abject, helpless souls many altruists imagine, can be shrewd, in-
dustrious, and highly entrepreneurial. Most altruists, whether paid staff or
individual visitors, first encounter villagers through dramatic stories in the
media. These stories, like that of Grace, are a genre, a performance of desolation and then uplift through a donor's help.[11] The villagers whom most
altruists encounter in person act out that same romance, whether describing their "needs" for a donor's benefit or dancing in gratitude for visitors.

Villagers are no more mercenary than anyone else; some are extraordinarily kindhearted and public spirited. But in a world of dire scarcity, of
urgent struggles simply to live, villagers rationally adapt themselves to
virtually any program, however nonsensical, that holds out even a hope
of material gain. A team from a donor organization that has come to tell

A Fraught Embrace

INTRODUCTION

Altruism from Afar

ALTRUISM FROM AFAR—THE FLOWS OF money and help from wealthy countries to poor ones—has become an enormous and enormously significant enterprise.[1] We describe the efforts of altruists to turn the tide of new HIV infections in Malawi, to alleviate the suffering of the already infected, and to assist the orphans of those who have died. We focus on AIDS prevention rather than treatment, since preventing HIV transmission has been the ultimate goal of the AIDS enterprise. Some altruists are vast international organizations, such as USAID, Save the Children, and Britain's DFID, with offices in many countries. At the other end of the spectrum are freelance altruists who hope to mitigate the effects of the epidemic, such as church groups and compassionate individuals. These alight briefly in Malawi and then fly home.

Malawi is a small landlocked nation in southeast Africa that shares borders with Zambia, Zimbabwe, and Mozambique. The two largest cities are Lilongwe, the capital, and Blantyre, the commercial center. In 2016, it had an estimated population of almost 18 million of which approximately 85 percent live in rural areas[2] and rely primarily on subsistence farming and small-scale trading. Formerly a protectorate of Great Britain, Malawi gained independence in 1964 and was then ruled for thirty years by President Hastings Banda. Although Banda made English the official language, he resisted Western influences. Male tourists with long hair were turned away, as were women wearing trousers; the Peace Corps was expelled for promoting family planning. Banda's reign was followed by a succession of democratically elected presidents who were eager for Western development aid and the arrival of streams of altruists.

Not all have come to respond to AIDS: Malawi is one of the poorest countries in Africa, which has perhaps brought disproportionate attention from altruists, including the pop star Madonna, who adopted two Malawian children. Malawi also has other, more practical features that make it attractive to altruists. Banda's legacy of reasonably good roads, built to control his population, permits altruists to travel with relative ease to the most distant rural districts. Unlike countries in the region that have been consumed by war, Malawi has historically been and remains very peaceful. It is not surprising then that altruists would come to Malawi rather than, say, the Congo.

In this book, we seek to explore the imaginations as well as the practical concerns of the actors in the drama of AIDS as it has played out in Malawi: altruists' visions of transforming the lives of those at risk of infection, brokers' visions of upward mobility through new careers in a multitude of AIDS organizations, and villagers' visions of what altruists from afar could do for them.

We undertook research unusual in its breadth and depth. Over more than fifteen years, we observed the organizations that sprang up in response to the epidemic, the altruists who arrived in Malawi, the brokers, and their struggles and successes. We also learned much about the lives of the villagers. We wanted not only to understand what altruists actually do, but also to understand the many other actors whose own aspirations inevitably shape—or frustrate—the altruistic projects imagined by those trying to do good at long distance.

A STORY OF COMPASSION

To explore what motivates altruists great and small, we turn to the testimony of a very successful one, Bill Rankin, who founded GAIA, the Global AIDS Interfaith Alliance, which works in Malawian villages:

Two years ago, when Bill Rankin visited Tiyamike School he had come away greatly disturbed by the 27 three- and four-year old orphans. Their nutritional status rendered them virtually inert and mute. All Mrs. Mpesi could afford was a half cup of maize porridge (*nsima*) for each child every other day, and sugared water or tea in between. But in May 2004 GAIA trustees Nancy Murray, Dr. Don Thomas, and International Programs Director Ellen Schell visited the little village in which the nursery school is operated, near Zomba, Malawi. They recorded a remarkable change that had taken place, owing to the generosity of many of you.

This year 75 orphans receive two meals each day: a breakfast of porridge, and a lunch of corn meal, vegetables, and sometimes dried fish. There is a new outdoor house in which the children gather and play. Though the number of orphans continues to grow, the kids are full of life, bouncing around the yard and eager to have their pictures taken.

Everywhere we went, we saw powerful evidence of hope in the face of HIV's ravages. For three days we visited our women's empowerment project funded by the Bill and Melinda Gates Foundation. Working in 25 villages in Malawi's famine-stricken south, the 125 community caregivers provide HIV prevention education, care for orphans, and care for people who are ill. All have energized their communities to mount a response to the epidemic. All caregivers have undergone voluntary counseling and HIV testing as a way of setting a personal example to others. The door-to-door strategy of encouraging testing has produced results to a degree for which none had dared to hope.[3]

Such descriptions of the suffering wrought by AIDS in Africa and of the remarkable transformations that are possible inspire broad publics in far-off lands to believe that they too can make a difference. During our stays in rural Malawi, we saw the institutionalized altruism of citizens of rich countries made evident in the many 4x4s with NGO logos on local roads and in the wistful eagerness of those we met who asked whether we had a "project" to assist them. We were impressed by just how many freelance altruists came in person to do good; we chatted with them on our flights to Malawi, in visa lines at the airport, in the motels where we stayed, and at hotel breakfasts in Lilongwe, Malawi's capital.

Day-to-day, of course, most of the help poor Malawians get is from each other. In a very insecure world with no formal social safety net, support networks are largely comprised of family members.[4] Malawians also draw on friends and the patron-client ties we described in the preface. Small loans go back and forth in local social networks, larger ones when someone has a medical emergency; relatives cook food for a funeral and help with farming when someone is too sick to work. Malawians have a long tradition of mutual help and a deep appreciation of the moral obligations of redistribution and reciprocity that are the bedrock of everyday life. Almost everyone is helping—and receiving help from—others.[5] Members of the many religious congregations cook, clean, bathe, and pray for the bedridden, and wealthier relatives in the city take responsibility for the AIDS orphans of their extended families in the villages.

In this book, we distinguish between Malawian networks of mutual aid and the altruists from afar.[6] Those within local networks know each other well. In contrast, the foreign altruists vividly and sympathetically imagine afflicted Malawians, but they do not—and usually cannot—know much about their daily lives. On the other hand, the foreign altruists have vastly greater resources than do members of local networks. The foreign altruists also differ from Malawians in that, while they redistribute resources, they do not expect reciprocity, except perhaps thanks.

The roots of contemporary AIDS altruism are deep, going back to the eighteenth- and nineteenth-century humanitarian movements that sought to end slavery and bring enlightenment to the African continent, Christian missionary work, and, more recently, efforts of Western governments, foundations, and other organizations to spread the modern gospels of family planning, gender equality, and universal human rights.[7] In the era of AIDS, the goals of altruistic organizations are equally broad: to transform women and men into rational, self-reliant citizens of the modern world capable of preventing HIV infection, and for those infected, capable of adhering to strict regimens of medication.[8] In this century, the preaching occurs not from the pulpit but through messages disseminated by the media and through ubiquitous trainings—a noun referring to small group sessions led by brokers.

It is inherent in the nature of altruism that the objects of the altruist's concern can neither get what they need on their own (otherwise they would not need the altruist's beneficence) nor choose what they are given. An important consequence is that hopeful beneficiaries must watch and wait to see what the altruist might feel moved to offer. Even—or especially—when the altruist wants to create not dependence but self-reliance, the potential recipients—as well as the brokers—must anticipate and interpret altruist wishes.[9]

FRUSTRATED EMBRACES

While we are interested in what altruists imagine they are doing and in the aspirations they arouse, we pay special attention to brokers, whose lives have been transformed by the AIDS enterprise, often in ways the altruists did not expect. Many brokers work for NGOs on projects for HIV prevention and on orphan care (antiretroviral treatment is provided primarily by the Ministry of Health). NGO brokers range in status from cosmopolitan elites with graduate and post-graduate education who staff NGO offices in the cities, to district elites based in smaller towns, to young men and women with a secondary school education who desperately want a way out of the village through a job with an NGO. Malawians at all levels sometimes serve as impromptu brokers, such as a teacher or civil servant who comes across a foreigner and asks about the possibility of accessing funds to form his or her own NGO, or a taxi driver who offers to take a visitor to his village to see the orphans his mother is feeding.

All altruists, both institutional and freelance, are profoundly dependent on brokers to reach down into the grassroots. NGOs sell their proposals to potential donors by emphasizing that they have contacts with beneficiaries in the villages or urban slums: in this sense, knowing beneficiaries is part of the pitch.[10] Freelance altruists need to find a broker who will guide them to a village where there is a grandmother who needs resources to care for orphans or a pastor who needs money for a new church roof. For all their importance, little attention is given to the brokers who provide the crucial channel—or, as it sometimes turns out, form the critical bottleneck— between the good deeds envisioned by the altruists and the village huts or slum dwellings where imagined recipients reside.[11]

Freelance altruists eventually encounter hopeful and often enthusiastically grateful beneficiaries. Visiting staff of donor organizations usually deal with elite brokers, not villagers. The main exceptions are when brokers mount end-of-project celebrations in a village, treating visitors to songs, dances, and testimonials to the transformations that the organization has wrought. Mostly, institutional altruists make do with documents reporting statistics (the number of posters distributed, the number of dramas presented by youth groups to entertain and educate villagers) and the more compelling before-and-after testimonials, such as those of suffering widows and their return to health. Such stories then feature in the brochures of NGOs or in media stories about the success of an NGO project.[12]

But the Malawians with whom the institutional donors *actually* interact— sometimes face to face, sometimes through directives and reports on paper— are the educated elites who staff the large urban NGOs that donors fund to implement their visions. Even an amateur altruist can reach the village and speak with villagers only through the help of a guide and translator. Like the biblical Jacob who worked for seven years to win Rachel but after his wedding night found that he had consummated the marriage with Leah instead, altruists large and small bond not with villagers but with brokers.

Behind the scenes, larger structures organize the relationships of donors, brokers, and villagers. In the specific case of AIDS, that structure is the global AIDS enterprise.

THE AIDS ENTERPRISE

The AIDS enterprise is in some ways like other development efforts—to contain malaria, boost crop yields, and so on—but in others it is distinct.

5

It is distinct in scale: defined as an unprecedented emergency, AIDS stimulated a massive global effort to combat a single disease.[13] Unlike earlier campaigns against smallpox and polio, and unlike the humanitarian relief organizations that rush into an area after an earthquake, for AIDS there is no short-term end in sight. Unlike development efforts focused on improving agriculture or building roads and bridges, preventing HIV transmission seems to require not only providing effective modern technologies, but also accomplishing diffuse and hard-to-achieve goals such as inducing millions of people to radically change their patterns of intimate behavior.

The AIDS enterprise is, however, structurally similar to other development projects in that it relies on a chain of intermediaries to reach its beneficiaries. Giant organizations with headquarters in Geneva, Washington, London, Tokyo, Oslo, and Seattle dominate the global AIDS enterprise. Precisely because of their global reach, the architecture of aid for AIDS—as well as that for development aid more generally—is similar in countries as different as Malawi, Nigeria, and Nepal. In Malawi, huge international NGOs (INGOs) like World Vision, CARE, PSI, and ActionAid have satellite offices in Lilongwe (the political capital) or Blantyre (the commercial capital) staffed by cosmopolitan brokers. The cities are a long journey from most of the 85 percent of Malawians who live in rural areas, however. Thus, national offices often subcontract the implementation of their projects to smaller organizations closer to the villages. Money and responsibilities pass down an aid chain.[14] Not surprisingly, the activities of subcontractors play a major role in our book.

The AIDS enterprise has shaped Malawian society. Institutional altruists and brokers have collaborated to produce a riot of cultural creativity as brokers work to satisfy their own aspirations and to interpret the imported themes and practices of the AIDS industry for their countrymen. The AIDS enterprise has also transformed the landscape of aspirations not only of the brokers, but also of villagers who long to benefit from the altruists' largesse.

PRODUCING CULTURE

A striking feature of the AIDS enterprise is its lavish use of cultural symbols, emblems, and messages. The red AIDS ribbon can be found from Los Angeles to Lilongwe, decorating a church tower near Sunset Boulevard, or worn by members of village AIDS committees in Botswana and Malawi. There are cultural artifacts such as T-shirts, caps, bumper stickers, or radio and TV programs. But brokers and donors also work together to produce other sorts of culture, such as these specialized activities Malawi's National AIDS Commission (NAC) listed in an accounting of its donor-supported AIDS-prevention efforts:[15]

320 HIV and AIDS corners established
5000 Copies of Life Skills manual printed and distributed
225 Community Dialogues (10 sessions/district)

In studying AIDS altruism, we sometimes felt like anthropologists exploring the exotic culture of some unknown tribe. We had to learn what "life skills" are and why they require manuals (for teaching youth about "gender roles" and "empowerment," with separate versions for primary and secondary students). But what is an "HIV and AIDS corner"? What would one expect to find happening at a "Community Dialogue"? Only insiders in the culture of the AIDS industry know.

Throughout the AIDS world, two cultural rituals are as ubiquitous as the mandatory cake at a child's birthday party. The brokers and donors who collectively create these rituals probably don't see them as culture at all, but they are works of art nonetheless. One is workshops and trainings, the other monitoring and evaluation.

Workshops and trainings work for everyone—donors, brokers, and village participants alike. Workshops are for brokers and trainings are for villagers. For example, the head of World Vision in Malawi might organize a workshop for selected members of the staff to discuss ways of implementing a new donor directive on financial tracking systems or a new approach to food security.[16] Brokers like workshops; they are often held in fancy hotels with mid-morning and mid-afternoon rituals of tea and sandwiches, and brokers receive allowances for attending.

Trainings are for those who are considered to need education and enlightenment through exposure to donor messages. The aim is that after the training, participants from the village will serve as volunteers, educating and enlightening their neighbors. The rituals of a training are less costly and simpler than those at a workshop. Trainings take place in inexpensive motels or guest houses, the mid-morning snacks are a Fanta and a sweet bun rather than tea and sandwiches, and the teaching aids are usually flip charts rather than the PowerPoint presentations used in workshops. The allowances are much smaller, but they are still enough to attract participants.

The cultural rituals of workshops and trainings instill in the brokers as well as the donors the belief that they are doing something important by

7

transmitting information that can, in itself, eventually transform the villagers who receive it. The allowances participants and trainees receive and the salaries of those brokers who are trainers sweeten the deal.

Brokers dislike the rituals of monitoring and evaluation as much as they enjoy—or at least believe in—the transformative effect of trainings. Many NGO brokers spoke of the donors' constant demands for paperwork. Brokers spend much of their time creating the paper trail that sends numbers and reports up the aid chain. But these rituals of monitoring and evaluation bind the brokers to the donors, and vice versa. Elaborate record keeping reinforces the donors' belief that they can monitor and control activities in distant, often unfamiliar places. The comforting stream of numbers provides reassurance that their money is being spent on measurable outputs, such as numbers of posters printed, or the Life Skills manuals and Community Dialogues mentioned above—whether or not these actually reduce HIV infections or improve the lives of those infected. Moreover, when donors require project evaluations, the brokers can shape the results in ways that virtually guarantee that projects will be deemed successful, allowing donors to feel good about what they have done and allowing brokers to justify continued funding.

Brokers try to align the disparate perspectives of the altruists and the villagers, as when the donors want resources to go to AIDS orphans and the village chief wants resources for all of the children in his village. The alignment in this example is an acronym created abroad, OVC (orphans and vulnerable children), which more or less satisfies each side. It is more difficult to construct a shared understanding when "vulnerable women"—a primary target of many HIV prevention interventions—are the imagined beneficiaries. For the donors, Malawian women are vulnerable to HIV infection because they are poor and have to sell sex to provide for their children, whereas for Malawian brokers at all levels, women are mercenary and so seductive that they endanger the good husbands who cannot resist. The tacit solution that papers over this discrepancy is for both parties to refer to AIDS as a "disease of poverty," even though in Malawi, as well as in some other African countries, the wealthy are more likely than the poor to be infected with HIV.[17]

THE LANDSCAPE OF ASPIRATIONS

Just as the AIDS enterprise stimulated cultural creativity, it also stimulated new aspirations. Most important, it offered subsistence farmers—and their children who aspired to leave the village—a new pathway out of poverty.

NGOs poured into the country to assist those at risk of dying of AIDS. This expanded what had previously been a very small formal economy: the AIDS NGOs needed brokers, so suddenly there was a new source of white-collar livelihoods. Between 1985 and 2005, the number of advertisements for positions in an NGO increased by a factor of twelve. AIDS NGOs constituted the vast majority of the increase.[18] As a Malawian NGO broker said, "NGOs want to be seen as doing something ... if you do not engage in AIDS you're looked upon as if you're not doing anything by communities and other NGOs."[19] Since NGOs typically paid well, brokers—at least those near the top of the aid-chain—could aspire to, and perhaps even achieve, a comfortable middle-class life with private schools for their children, private health care, and an SUV. And the expanded demand for brokers trickled down to those lower on the aid chain, encouraging village youth to seek higher education so that they could qualify for these new jobs.

The flood of NGOs also stimulated commercial aspirations. Entrepreneurs built or expanded restaurants and motels that could host workshops and trainings. Since brokers who led trainings had to travel to the small towns and trading centers to conduct the trainings, they created a demand for petrol stations—many with mini-marts—which in turn provided opportunities for jobs for rural youth who otherwise would have little alternative but subsistence agriculture and small-scale retail trade. New streams of income, in turn, led to aspirations for consumer goods such as bicycles, radios, cell phones, and shoes, even if only flip-flops.[20]

As elsewhere in Africa, the enormous gap in resources between Western altruists and local brokers, and the even greater gulf between Western altruists and villagers, means that everywhere they go, whatever their intentions, altruists by their very presence reshape local hopes and dreams.

HOW TYPICAL IS MALAWI AS A DESTINATION FOR ALTRUISM?

Altruism in Malawi is in most ways similar to altruism elsewhere in Africa. We have read widely and visited AIDS projects in other African countries, and much of what we have learned resonates with reports from other parts of Africa, such as Daniel Jordan Smith's observation of the centrality of "workshops" and "training" in donor projects in Nigeria.[21] But Malawi is in some ways less typical of other African countries than it is archetypal: it embodies the altruists' image of a poor, desperately needy African country. Malawi is very poor, very rural, and very dependent on donor aid.[22] The high proportion of its adult population that is HIV+ (currently about 10 percent for those age 15–49), the high proportion that lives in rural villages and the low proportion in urban slums, its small size, and its peacefulness have made Malawi a donor darling.[23] Malawi is lightly governed: the central government does not have the capacity and perhaps not the interest in strictly controlling its population.[24] Thus, as in other "lame leviathan" states,[25] altruists have considerable freedom. Formally, NGOs should register and get permission from the District Social Welfare Officer to work in a particular area, but in practice, NGOs may bypass this requirement and go unnoticed by the government.

Malawi has two parallel systems of government: a hierarchy of traditional leaders (chiefs) and a national government represented by a District Commissioner and other officials in each of the country's twenty-eight districts. But in the villages, chiefs are the ones who really matter. While Malawi's government employs Health Surveillance Assistants—the lowest level of the hierarchy of health providers—and agricultural extension agents in rural areas, Malawian villagers are mostly on their own, dependent on mutual assistance and their own energies, mobilized more or less effectively by a hierarchy of traditional leaders. It is the village chiefs (sometimes called "headmen") who are responsible for organizing such public works as maintaining roads and paths, repairing wells, and providing basic security in their villages, as well as resolving disputes and enforcing claims to land, spouses, and possessions.[26]

Virtually all benefits, whether the valuable fertilizer subsidies that the government provides to the poorest villagers or the blankets or food a donor gives for orphans, flow through the village headman, in part because villagers have no mailing addresses to which a package could be sent—no post boxes or bank accounts—and in part because of the chief's status as "the owner" of the village. When government officials want to announce a new program or when an NGO offers village-level trainings on AIDS prevention or on how to care for the sick, the chief calls villagers to a meeting where the potential benefit is announced. This system, of course, provides the chief with a valuable opportunity for patronage, since he or she typically selects those who will go for the training.

Malawi's rural poor live much the sort of lives altruists imagine. As in many documentaries on Africa, the houses are mud brick with thatched roofs, the women may have to walk miles to get water and firewood, paraffin lamps provide light, health is poor, and children attend schools where class size may be over one hundred per teacher. This seemingly simple life belies the great uncertainty with which villagers as well as brokers live. Villagers are uncertain about whether they and their children will survive; brokers are uncertain about whether their jobs will continue or not.

FIGURE 1.1. Women chatting as they draw water. Many Malawian villages do not have a source of clean water, like this borehole. *Photo: Gerald Cotts.*

Malawi's per capita yearly income in 2015, the most recent year for which there are data, was estimated at $350, placing it among a handful of the poorest countries on earth.[27] In the rural areas, households depend primarily on subsistence agriculture, which for a substantial proportion of the rural population does not provide sufficient food for the last months before the next harvest, creating a several-month "hunger season." When there is too little or too much rain, the hunger season is longer and more severe. Since cash is necessary for buying food in the hunger season, as well as for salt, soap, sugar, and tea, and for buses and for school uniforms in ordinary times, household agricultural production is often supplemented by small-scale trade, such as selling tomatoes in a market, or by small-scale retail, such as weaving and selling palm mats, or by temporary agricultural labor for neighbors. But these strategies provide a very uncertain income. When someone needs to go to the hospital or buy medicine, the fortunate families are those with a relative or a patron who has a steady source of income, such as selling tobacco or cotton, the primary cash crops, or has had a windfall. It is not surprising that villagers hope that altruists from afar will provide them with money, or at least a well to supply clean water, and that brokers and aspiring brokers prize a regular salary.[28]

FIGURE 1.2. Bicycle taxis waiting in Balaka. One of the few ways that men without education can earn money is transporting people by bike taxi. But as we see here, customers are few. *Photo: Ann Swidler.*

As in many African countries, insecurity is a pervasive feature of life not only for villagers, but also for the urban poor and elite groups, especially those dependent on foreign donors.[29] The formal job sector is small and dominated by government and NGOs, with business providing a relatively small, albeit growing, share. Although NGOs pay more than the government, brokers' jobs are more insecure. A civil service position is for life (though nurses or teachers may not receive their salaries for months on end), whereas a donor organization may decide to turn its attention to another country or withdraw funding because of corruption or mismanagement of funds. Jobs in a particular sector may become vulnerable as donors turn from agricultural development and relief, the largest job sectors at the beginning of the epidemic, to AIDS, by far the largest job sector in the early 2000s, and yet more recently, to maternal and child health, human rights, and climate change.[30]

Finding a new job can be very difficult. We heard many stories of brokers whose careers depended not only on merit but also on miracles, such as being alerted by a friend to an unadvertised job opening with an NGO, and malice, as when an envious boss or colleague refuses to sign a document required to take up a fellowship abroad. If one job ends, elite brokers may not be able to find another that provides enough to satisfy their aspirations for adequate health care and private education for their children. Mid-level brokers may not be able to find a job at all. Trying to defend against such uncertainties is a continuing preoccupation for many of the brokers upon whom donors depend. To manage uncertainty, brokers may run side businesses or engage in farming to supplement their NGO jobs. They also turn to their networks to learn about new job openings. Our interviews show, unsurprisingly, that brokers are almost always more concerned about maintaining their local networks than satisfying their NGO employers.

Donors aspire to mitigate the insecurity of village life, but they are reluctant to provide direct monetary or material benefits over extended periods. Instead, they mount short-term projects in scattered locations, with varying goals: creating AIDS clubs for village youth one year, training village women to negotiate condom use the next, and educating villagers about the risks of HIV infection from "harmful cultural practices" the year after that. Projects appear according to no logic that the locals can discern and then just as quickly disappear. NGOs thus often amplify rather than moderate the unpredictability of village life. Capricious NGOs, like capricious rains, leave villagers unable to predict or control the forces that shape their fates.

The unpredictability of altruists' help does not reduce the urgent longing of villagers for that help. Indeed, their unpredictability gives altruists, both large and small, an outsized role in local imaginations, precisely because no one can ever be sure when or where an alluring opportunity to find a patron who will help might suddenly materialize.

HOW IDIOSYNCRATIC IS MALAWI'S RESPONSE TO THE AIDS EPIDEMIC?

Malawians would, and do, say that their country is different—a different history, different languages, and different cultural practices. With respect to AIDS policies and practices, however, it is not so different: the AIDS enterprise is a global enterprise. As Evan Lieberman has cogently written,

> In the area of AIDS policy, we have witnessed one of the most extensive, steadfast, and concurrent set of international pressures on domestic policy-making across countries in human history. I label the

13

associated set of best practice recommendations the "Geneva Consensus," in reference to the headquarters of the UN agencies taking lead roles on AIDS policy, but ... the "authors" or "architects" of this consensus reside in governments, institutions, and networks around the globe. Because efforts to extend the global governance of AIDS, including offers of foreign aid, have been so far-reaching, national governments have not been as budget-constrained as they have tended to be for other types of policies, and they have shared a common menu of options for facing the pandemic.[31]

In the rural areas, where we spent most of our time in Malawi, prevention is by far the most visible activity of the large-scale AIDS enterprise. Despite the many differences from other African countries in social structure and culture, the prevention messages disseminated by NGOs and NAC echo those disseminated by UNAIDS and the large donors. Not only is one size meant to fit all, our reading of the academic literature on HIV prevention in other African countries leads us to conclude that the venues through which the messages are disseminated are the same: they appear on billboards, posters, and in feature stories in the newspapers that announce the success of an NGO project; they are heard in educational dramas on the radio and TV and at meetings called by the chief; they appear in dramas enacted for villagers by youth clubs.

WHAT DIFFERENCE DID AIDS PREVENTION EFFORTS MAKE?

Readers are likely to wonder whether these HIV prevention activities have been successful. There is no doubt that there has been a decline in both HIV prevalence (the proportion of people at a specified time point who are infected) and incidence (the ratio of new infections over a time period, usually a year, to the population at risk of infection over that time period). The preferred measure of the growth or decline of an epidemic is incidence. In 1992 and 1993, incidence in Malawi among people 15–49 peaked at 2.59 percent per year. By 2001, incidence was 1.58, a decline of nearly 40 percent. By 2015, the last date for which UNAIDS has incidence data for Malawi, incidence was estimated as only 0.38.[32]

There are two common hypotheses to explain the dramatic decline in HIV incidence. One is population heterogeneity, which posits that at the early stages of an epidemic those with the riskiest behavior (or the greatest physiological vulnerability) become infected most easily, while those with less risky behavior are less likely to become infected, thus reducing later transmissions. This may account for some of the rapid decline in incidence in Malawi after its peak in 1992–93. The second is behavior change due to new information disseminated by international and national organizations. The information that HIV is sexually transmitted was crucial: once Malawians had this information, they knew that eschewing promiscuity would reduce their risk. A 1993 survey of villagers in southern Malawi showed that 99 percent knew that AIDS was sexually transmitted and about two-thirds knew that healthy-looking people could have HIV.[33] It is thus likely that Malawians began changing their behavior once they understood how HIV is transmitted, but it is very unlikely that the massive influx of NGOs and their behavior-change projects were the cause.[34] Since the decline in HIV incidence began in the early 1990s, well before the AIDS enterprise ramped up in the early 2000s, the increase in NGOs specializing in AIDS is unlikely to have been a major factor.

A third possibility for explaining more recent declines in incidence is the growing availability of antiretroviral treatment after 2006, since HIV treatment is highly effective in reducing HIV transmission.[35] Since those on antiretroviral drugs are much less likely to transmit HIV to their sexual partners, this may account for much of the recent continuing decline.[36] The evidence is far less clear for HIV prevention programs. The only systematic review of experimental studies found that behavioral interventions had no effect on HIV acquisition.[37] Thus, the early efforts to educate Malawi's population about the basic nature of AIDS may have helped people change their own behavior, but the avalanche of later NGO projects explicitly designed to change behavior—to teach abstinence, fidelity, and condom use—appear to have had little or no effect.[38] The very structure of donor projects makes it difficult to know what the consequences of donor funding on behavior change have been. It is rare that donors provide funds for a rigorous evaluation. There is no incentive to report failure. We return to this topic in chapter 10.[39]

The explanation for the decline in incidence from its peak in 1992–93 that we find most compelling features Malawians themselves: that when they saw friends and neighbors, people like themselves, dying miserable deaths, they changed their behavior.[40] Malawians began reducing their numbers of sexual partners and employing additional strategies of HIV prevention, such as relying on local knowledge to choose sexual partners more carefully and divorcing unfaithful spouses.[41] The effect of seeing relatives, friends, and neighbors die is evident in this excerpt from a journal written by one of our Malawian ethnographers, describing the reactions of a young man to such deaths at a time when antiretrovirals were not available:

> Only because I have seen for myself, some of my friends have died because of this disease AIDS, and I do care for my life. AIDS troubles a lot! ... there was a certain army pensioner who was living up there in my village.... He was very sick indeed, going to the hospital, no treatment, private hospitals—just wasting money and then he came home and was sick until he became like a very little young child. I was going to see him during the whole course of his suffering. You could liken him to a two-year-old child when he lay down sick.... And the way I had seen him suffering, that's when I came to my senses that indeed AIDS troubles a great deal before one dies.[42]

HOW WE KNOW WHAT WE KNOW

Much of our analysis takes the form of vivid stories, personal histories, or examples from the interviews that we, our students, and our colleagues conducted over the roughly twenty years that we have annually visited rural Malawi (for a month or more), and where we saw the everyday reality of the AIDS-prevention enterprise up close.

We practiced what we jokingly call "motel ethnography." In simple, sometimes grubby rural motels, we met freelance altruists and many brokers conducting trainings in "AIDS awareness," "decision-making," and other themes of the global AIDS enterprise. The large-scale donors, whose money energizes the AIDS enterprise, also fascinated us. We sometimes met them in the cities when they were visiting their partner organizations in the capital, or in the case of some medium-sized NGOs, we met the donors when they came to a district capital or, rarely, to a village for an end-of-project celebration. We were repeatedly struck by the emotional experience that an encounter with Malawi's poverty seemed to offer visitors. As one member of a group raising money for village schools told us in 2015, she came to Malawi once and "got hooked." When we asked what had hooked her, she said, half incredulous and half awestruck, "Have you been to the villages?"

We interviewed many brokers in their offices, but we also met many as they passed through rural motels, sometimes conducting trainings, sometimes stopping for lunch on their way to a workshop or to visit their organization's projects. Many were delighted to chat about their work over lunch or dinner.

FIGURE 1.3. Men socializing in a trading center. Settings like these are where the conversations captured by our local ethnographers take place. *Photo: Gerald Cotts.*

We also have a trove of additional materials collected by us, students, and colleagues, including systematic survey data collected between 1998 and 2010 by the University of Pennsylvania-based Longitudinal Study of Families and Health; 147 formal interviews with donors and brokers, civil servants in government ministries and NAC, and expatriate staff of international organizations; "gray literature"—bureaucratic documents, proposals, consultants' reports, budgets, and requests for funding; the websites of NGOs and church groups working in Malawi; and stories and advertisements from Malawi's newspapers. We also visited local churches and markets and attended public events, such as concerts to raise AIDS awareness.[43]

Our most unusual data are more than twelve hundred vivid diaries written between 1998 and the present by local ethnographers—villagers whom we asked to be our eyes and ears in their community to observe and listen to what people said about AIDS in public and to write what they learned in field journals.[44] These journals provide insight into the experience of villagers, those "beneficiaries" most donor programs are meant to reach, but who, as we shall see, find their perspectives largely ignored by the donors and brokers who directly shape the AIDS enterprise.

We focus on the encounter of donors with brokers and on the fantasies that both harbor about the poor villagers who are the ultimate objects of their efforts. As in a love story, there are heady dreams, and sometimes dashed hopes, emotional highs and lows, followed by the mundane work of getting along.

We begin by introducing the potential partners, describing the fantasies that lure them into a first embrace (chapter 2), followed by a description of the structure of the AIDS enterprise—the money and organization that bring donors and brokers together (chapter 3). We contrast this weighty enterprise with its products, the often-frivolous cultural productions meant to make AIDS prevention appealing (chapter 4). In the second part of the book, we focus on brokers. We describe the array of brokers on whom donors depend in their efforts to reach the villagers whose lives they seek to alter (chapter 5). We then follow the careers of some brokers and the effects of merit, miracles, and malice on their lives (chapter 6). Finally, in the third and last part of the book, we describe the progeny of the union of donors and brokers: the discourses, practices, and programs through which, despite their differences, the donors and brokers become reconciled and sometimes even get along quite happily (chapters 7, 8, 9, and 10).

CHAPTER 2

FEVERED IMAGINATIONS

DONORS, LIKE THE BROKERS UPON whom the success or failure of donor projects depends, are moved by powerful fantasies. The term "fantasy," of course, can carry a negative connotation, implying wishes totally divorced from reality, or a positive one, an image of a desired future state. Fantasy can impair effective action, but ambitious plans often begin as fantasies. Here we wish to retain precisely this ambiguity: "fantasy" and "imagination" are critical elements of all human endeavors, and they can also get us into trouble. Exploring the fantasies that both motivate and entangle the altruistic enterprise is a crucial step in trying to understand it.[1]

It might seem that AIDS has little to do with fantasy. It is a devastating disease that has caused immense suffering and millions of deaths. The World Health Organization (WHO) reports that globally there were 36.7 million adults and children living with HIV at the end of 2015;[2] UNAIDS estimates that globally from the beginning of the epidemic to the end of 2014 there have been 35,621,000 AIDS deaths, of which the vast majority— 25,525,000—were in sub-Saharan Africa.[3] The epidemic is not yet over: more are at risk in coming decades. As we shall see in chapter 3, the scale of the response to the emergency reflects the scale of the epidemic: since the mid-1980s, tens of billions of dollars have been spent on HIV prevention, treatment, and mitigation.

This chapter explores the intersecting fantasies that lock donors, brokers, and villagers together in a fraught embrace. Donors imagine the poverty and powerlessness of their potential beneficiaries—poor villagers or desperate slum dwellers—and the empowering, transformative help they can offer. Brokers and villagers imagine that the NGOs have a lot of money and that anyone from a wealthy country is rich, and thus that the altruists have the potential to improve their country and, particularly, their own lives. They draw on images of rich countries in the media, but they also see the visitors and their material possessions, the clothes they wear, their computers and iPhones, and the 4x4s that take them around the country. Their embrace of altruists, like the altruists' of them, rests on powerful fantasies. The frustrations arise as those with differing and often-conflicting imaginations attempt to collaborate in transforming the lives of the poor who are living through the tsunami of AIDS in Malawi.

SMALL-SCALE ALTRUISTS AND THEIR BROKERS

In 2009, we spent a month at the Catholic Women's Association guest house in Balaka *boma*, the capital of Balaka District in southern Malawi, a perfect vantage point for observing some of the things that Malawian brokers—and those aspiring to be brokers—do. We ourselves were there because we knew American researchers staying there. They had been led to the guest house by a trusted Malawian colleague who grew up in the district.

The place is by no means fancy—although the reception room and the dining hall were imposing, large and with high ceilings, the bedrooms were small, there was limited hot water, and there were cockroaches in the kitchen. But because the prices were low and there were few other options in the town, as many as fifty people stayed there at one time. Not counting our group of fourteen Americans (faculty, faculty family, and students), the visitors—both Malawians and expatriates—who passed through would not have been there without altruists from the West who aspired to "do good" in Balaka. Indeed, without a grant from the US National Institute of Child Health and Human Development for a study of rural Malawians' responses to the AIDS epidemic, it is likely that none of the faculty and their students would have been there either.

During our stay, most of the Malawians at the guest house were small-scale, freelance altruists and brokers: low-level staff of one or another NGO who were there to conduct a training and the trainees, many of whom were unemployed secondary school graduates who were hoping that after the training they might be able to get a job with an NGO. Generally, the trainer came from the city to teach the trainees, who had come from the local area for a few days or a week to be trained. The trainees were being taught lessons, which they were to disseminate to their neighbors and friends. The trainings could be on any topic; most frequent were trainings to teach participants that "AIDS is here" and to provide injunctions on how people should behave to avoid HIV infection. But we also saw trainings on early childhood education, on caring for orphans and those with AIDS, and occasionally on something technical, such as a training for nurses on infant resuscitation. For the trainees, there were highly welcome benefits of attending a training: donors, such as USAID or World Vision, paid for sleeping quarters and transportation, a breakfast of white bread and chips in the morning, an ample meal of chicken and *nsima* at lunch, and per diems for all. Participants also enjoyed other more intangible benefits as they got to know people from elsewhere in the district, sang hymns together, participated in games and exercises, and expanded their sense of connection to the world beyond Malawi.

The guest house also hosted other Westerners who appeared at the dinner table eager to tell us all about what they were doing to help poor Malawians. An American, Jim Humble, came shortly after we arrived and was still there when we left: he had come to test a cure for AIDS that he claimed to have developed.[4] There was a group of Canadian Christians who spent a week helping a woman who cared for orphans in one of the villages. They bought bags of the maize flour used to make *nsima*, pots and pans to cook it in, and cups and bowls for the children; after dinner, a teenager strummed a guitar while the group sang hymns. An American was there, bringing money to support a small NGO that was providing adult literacy classes. An American evangelist who had come to Balaka to preach to pastors and to distribute inexpensive computers to them enthusiastically demonstrated a "zapper" that he insisted cured diseases by delivering an electric charge to kill "pathogens."[5]

So how did all these would-be altruists find the Catholic Women's Association, or Balaka *boma*, the capital of Balaka District and a four-hour trip in a crowded minibus from Malawi's capital? It is not so surprising that someone who wants to help the poor would think of Africa as full of suffering people who need help: bad news is more compelling for journalists than good news, especially bad news about Africa.[6] Nor is it surprising that some of these altruists would end up in Malawi, one of the poorest countries in Africa, known to the West primarily through media descriptions of famines and the ravages of AIDS.

It is one thing to arrive in the airport in Lilongwe, another to find the way to Balaka *boma*, and quite another to find a village with needy Malawians. For this, it is necessary to know a Malawian who can lead you to a village, tell you what is needed, interpret from the local languages, and for the altruists who aspire to an ongoing project, run the project after the altruist goes home—in short, a broker. The giant institutional altruists also need a way to locate poor villagers to help, but they solve the problem organizationally by subcontracting the search for villagers through a chain of ever-smaller NGOs and their salaried brokers.

FINDING ONE'S TRUE BROKER

There is something haphazard in the stories of how our companions at the Catholic Women's Association found the broker who guided them to Balaka—accidental meetings, false starts, and surprising connections.

21

"Hopes and Prayers for Africa," a small Canadian-American group, were led to Malawi, and to Balaka, by their ties to Halleluya, a Minnesota mega church, and a Canadian Evangelical group, EDUCATE Malawi, that already had a presence in Malawi. Hopes and Prayers had come to Malawi to do good, but weren't quite sure just what or where. At a feast celebrating a new school that EDUCATE Malawi had built in a nearby village, they were introduced to Pastor Daniel, who quickly offered to take them to a village where a parishioner, Esnart, was struggling to feed a group of orphans. This, it turned out, was the answer to their prayers. They returned the next year, with Pastor Daniel as their friend and guide, staying at the Catholic Women's Association while they made forays to the village to visit orphans or to church or dinner at Pastor Daniel's home.

Jim Humble came to Malawi in hopes of demonstrating that his Miracle Mineral Solution could cure malaria and AIDS. We learned from others that after spending time in the capital, he was befriended by a man who worked in a fast-food restaurant he frequented, who offered to take him to Balaka, where the man's relatives lived. On arrival in Balaka, Jim was introduced to Father Torino, the head of the Catholic Mission in Balaka, who offered him a place to stay for a few days and introduced him to the director of a local herbal clinic, who became his guide in seeking patients who might try his cure. After a few days, Father Torino encouraged Jim to move to the nearby Catholic Women's Organization. We also heard the story of Dominique (no one knew his last name), who had come from Paris to Malawi to promote the growing of spirulina, as a nutritional supplement for those with AIDS and a potential cash crop. At the airport, Dominique met a man who suggested he seek out Father Torino in Balaka; Father Torino gave him permission to grow spirulina in the church's clinic, and he then received permission from two nearby prisons to have prisoners grow spirulina.

Even the more ordinary visitors, like church mission groups, often rely on "accidental" contacts, as this US church group's blog suggests:

MALAWI JOURNAL
APRIL 2

We flew arrived in the late morning and drove to the center of Blantyre for a lunch meeting with Mr. Kapanga, the gentleman with the Malawi High Court that we met on the flight to Johannesburg when returning home last November. After a conversation that built a strong, open, sharing relationship with Mr. Kapanga, he asked if he could join us for a visit to sites along mission road on April 4, "because I can't sit in my nice offices in Blantyre knowing that white people are out under the blazing sun helping my people. I must join you!" (He did!)

We got to Mvuu river in the dark and as we boated to the camp, a huge, full, silvery moon lit the way. It was with us the whole time. Clearly our arrival was anticipated and staff welcomed us back.[7]

The task of finding a broker is made easier by pre-established connections among organizations, such as Hopes and Prayers' relation with EDUCATE Malawi, but the fortuitous meetings are really not so accidental: there are so many Malawians seeking to be guides and interpreters that any foreigner is likely to be approached multiple times. Many would love to find a visitor who would become their patron. Some may already have a proposal to start an NGO and are only waiting for a willing altruist to appear; some are simply eager to learn about America or England or to practice their English, like the young people who approached our students at church, saying simply, "What is your name? I would like to be your friend." And sometimes eager guides and interpreters may hope that an altruist, impressed by their energy and commitment, can be persuaded to help with school fees or even bring a project to their own village.

Our account of the roles of brokers is part of the narrative of seduction— and sometimes heartache and betrayal—that characterizes the fraught embrace between foreign altruists and locals. Of course, the very term "locals" is inadequate for the enormous variety of brokers and translators, from the much-sought-after Malawian consultant hired by an NGO to collaborate on a study or smooth relations with a crucial government ministry, to a village youth who has the good fortune to impress a foreign volunteer with his intelligence and public-spiritedness. But the term "local" expresses exactly what the donor/altruist, newly arrived on the scene, is desperate to find: someone who is authentically "local," who knows and can interpret the local language and the local customs, who legitimates the need for the donor's efforts, and who can navigate the many practical obstacles—from transportation, to contacts, to getting around regulations or restrictions— that the aspiring altruist might face. However inadequate the term "locals" is to describe Malawians as they see themselves, a connection to the "locals" is precisely what a would-be altruist needs and what many eager intermediaries are ready to provide.

The task of finding a trusted broker is more institutionalized for the large altruists—such as the US and British foreign aid organizations (USAID and DFID respectively)—than just happening to meet someone at a fast-food joint in Lilongwe, but it is similar in several respects. The organizations that subcontract the task of reaching the villagers to a chain of smaller organizations depend on finding an organization that they can imagine will fulfill their aspirations, which they can embrace. They search for an organization that can, above all, both provide contact with authentic villagers and can be trusted to account for money properly. Such is the premium for the large donor organizations on finding smaller partner organizations that help them reach poor villagers that they sometimes continue to give grants or collaborate even with organizations they suspect of mishandling funds.[8] We begin with stories of how amateur altruists find a broker to embrace, and then with the efforts of the institutional altruists to find a suitable partner.

Trusted Intermediaries: Small, Medium, and Large

Just as a tourist shopping in an African market, surrounded by swarming vendors waving curios and shouting "cheap, cheap" and "look only" wishes for a guide to help her select a particular vendor, to recognize more authentic local crafts, and to know whether—or at least by how much—she is being overcharged, so also altruists who want to identify orphans to support, or researchers like ourselves who want to hire interviewers for a survey of rural Malawians, need a guide. Watkins, then a faculty member at the University of Pennsylvania, first visited Malawi in 1997 to plan a survey on the responses of rural Malawians to the AIDS epidemic. She selected Malawi as the site of the study because she had a Malawian graduate student, Eliya Zulu, who had just finished his PhD dissertation and was ready to return to his position as a lecturer at Chancellor College, University of Malawi. He would be a full research partner as well as a trusted guide: he identified potential research sites, took Watkins to visit them, and figured out the rules and logistics of getting the project money to the research site (not easy at the beginning of the study because of government restrictions on foreign exchange). Eventually he moved on, but by that time the study had identified Davie Chitenje, an interviewer in the first round of the study, whom Watkins came to trust to withdraw millions of kwacha from the project bank account in Blantyre and come by minibus with a backpack stuffed with money to pay the interviewers, supervisors, and data clerks. The research project came to serve as an informal broker organization for generations of graduate student researchers with their own projects.

In altruists' reports of how they came to Africa or how they developed their projects, the role of these intermediaries, and a sense of the multi-faceted roles they play, emerges again and again. These accounts often have the awestruck tone of gratitude for one's good fortune that recalling the first meeting with one's true love might have. A sense of the altruist's longing for connection, of anxious anticipation and then relief at having "found someone" to trust, pervades these accounts.

The example below is taken from the website of Good Futures, a small NGO established by an American couple who came to Malawi to volunteer and ended up founding the NGO with the help of Teresa, their trusted broker.[9]

> Teresa is surely the sincerest, kindest, most caring, and most cheerful woman you will ever meet. She is "The Boss," and she is also a loving mother and grandmother. She is active in local politics and in her church. She is known as "Mother" by the young people who come to learn from her and just be with her at Good Futures' youth centre. In many ways, she is the glue holding her family and her community together. Her role at Good Futures is no different.... In Balaka, Good Futures' programs provide models of how outstanding community and youth leadership development can be done—and Teresa has been central to this process.

From the moment they met her, the founders were smitten by Teresa:

> In 2006 Good Futures' founders met Teresa when they held community meetings in Balaka to learn how Good Futures could best help to meet the community's many unique needs. Teresa from the start showed herself to be a strong woman who was greatly respected in the community. During the community meeting, she stood out because she kept raising her hand, offering amazing ideas, excellent advice, and even an occasional rebuke of people who were too comfortable with the status quo.

In the history of GAIA, the Global AIDS Interfaith Alliance mentioned earlier, one could again see the role of seemingly accidental contacts and the need for trustworthy intermediaries. GAIA's founder met Joseph, the Malawian who became his trusted broker, at a conference in Malawi, when a mutual friend introduced them. As the two talked, the founder came to see that Joseph

> seemed very knowledgeable about how to make interventions work in Malawi villages, and he had a side to him that I thought was very honest (which also, as you know, is not a quality to be taken for granted), and I could tell in our conversations that he cared genuinely about poor people and about women as much as men.[10]

The founder asked Joseph to organize a training; he did a superb job and accounted precisely for all the funds given to him.

> In the months that ensued, I had a chance to see how he did with more requests from me and more sums of money. At every moment everything he touched had a quality of excellence to it, as it seemed to me. When we needed to name someone later as our Malawi Country Director … it seemed obvious that he would be the person we should ask to do this job. I am certain that he has both done a lot that is very good, and for all I know, he has saved us from a lot that could have gone bad but for his experience and wise judgment.

This story is less ardent and impulsive than the story on Good Futures' website, but in both cases, there seemed to be an immediate sense of trust, of finding just the right person.

The large institutional donors rely on broker organizations rather than individuals to reach the actual orphans or the poor, but they too need to work with a trustworthy organization that can ultimately connect them to the needy. For the largest donors—aid agencies in Washington or Oslo, the World Bank, UN agencies based in New York or Geneva—the aid chain to reach the potential beneficiaries is long.[11] The large donors first determine a global strategy to be implemented over the course of three, five, or even ten years. They then put the project out to bid with parameters, overall goals, specific objectives, and deliverables (the activities subcontractors will be paid for completing). Those bidding, typically large INGOs or for-profit firms, then respond with a proposal highlighting their particular angle on achieving those goals and objectives. The winning bidder then subcontracts to an in-country implementing organization, which in turn may subcontract to successively smaller organizations to do the job of actually reaching the orphans and the poor.

FIGURE 2.1. Sign for AIDS Youth Club in rural Malawi. This youth club, in a village, may have hoped its sign would attract visiting altruists. *Photo: Gerald Cotts.*

The budget may be enormous—in the tens or hundreds of millions of dollars. As with the small mom-and-pop altruists and the medium-sized altruists such as GAIA, there are two key requirements. The broker organizations must be able to claim that they can reach orphans, or poor women, or people living with AIDS, and they must have a reputation as being trustworthy. This applies particularly to financial reporting. With so much money passing down the chain of organizations, it is understandable that a broker, knowing that there is a lot of aid money and facing an inability to pay school fees for his children, or a broker organization that is short of funds, might not be able to resist the temptation to borrow a bit and fudge the financial report. The larger organizations also have to worry about another danger: if the broker organizations to which they subcontract perform badly, the reputation of the higher-level organization will be at risk.[12] This risk resembles that of large manufacturers with international brands whose reputations can be damaged if their subcontractors abuse workers or ignore their safety.

This search for an organization with direct contacts with villagers can lead to manipulative practices when established NGOs try to take credit for the work of small community organizations. When one of our interviewers established a youth club at her home, the Salvation Army invited her to be trained by them as a volunteer to tell her neighbors about the problems of AIDS, promised her soccer balls (which never arrived), and then listed her youth club as one of theirs, thus increasing the number of youth groups that the Salvation Army could claim.

A striking story reported by the journalist Helen Epstein describes an INGO trying to highjack a small orphanage in South Africa. A giant INGO, Project Hope, contacted a small and struggling orphanage, Sizanani, led by Elizabeth, who had worked for Project Hope.

> Eventually, Elizabeth quit her job at Hope to run Sizanani full time. She received occasional donations of food or other items from Hope, but otherwise did not hear from them. Then in 2004 officials from Hope contacted her again. They wished to offer Sizanani a "Memorandum of Understanding," or MOU. According to this document, Hope would promise to help Sizanani by "reviewing its current HIV/AIDS-related needs and responses"; by "developing/strengthening a local working group on HIV/AIDS"; by "developing HIV/OVC strategies"; by "developing community competency"; and by performing other, similarly vague activities. Meanwhile, Sizanani would continue to pay its own staff, purchase all supplies of food and other commodities for the children, and provide "space and resources" for its own programs. In addition, Sizanani would be required to fill out three sets of forms each month listing the number of children helped, the "kids clubs" set up, and other data, and send these forms to Hope. Hope would provide no money.
>
> Elizabeth declined the offer. "I'd been running this program for three years," she said. "Why do I need advice from them?" The offer did seem odd. Project Hope's South African budget is several million dollars a year; Sizanani's is $60,000. Sizanani has offices in a shipping container; Hope has offices in one of the most exclusive neighborhoods in South Africa.[13]

For the NGOs in the AIDS industry, beneficiaries are valuable commodities in their efforts to attain funding, and brokers who can reach those beneficiaries are invaluable.[14]

INTERPRETING LOCAL SOCIETY TO OUTSIDERS

Donors, like the general public, imagine the landscape of AIDS in Africa as one in which everyone is suffering; the media focus on pictures of skeletal

Africans and orphans in tattered clothes. We ourselves imagined this before we first went to Malawi. But journalists, freelance altruists, and other
visitors arriving in Malawi or any other AIDS-afflicted African country see
not people suffering and dying (again, those who are severely ill are at
home, being cared for by relatives), but lively, sociable people, laughing
and talking as they work, gossiping as they wait for water at the well, sitting together at the market chatting, or enthusiastically praising God at
church. To see suffering up close, visitors need to be guided to the home
of someone dying of AIDS.

The most valuable gift that local intermediaries can give altruists is to
take them to the orphans, elderly, or impoverished villagers they have come
to help. The intermediary both interprets Malawian society to the donor—
usually emphasizing its poverty and its many "needs"—and helps the altruist navigate the cultural differences that threaten the sense of connection
the altruist hopes for.

Intermediaries up and down the broker hierarchy, from educated cosmopolitan to local villager, play the role of "authentic African" for foreign
visitors to embrace. For altruists, these stories of personal experiences
often shape beliefs about the real nature of Africans and their problems.
Shortly after antiretroviral medications had become available in Africa,
one of us attending an international meeting was told by an African colleague she had just met about the terrible choice his family had to make
about which AIDS-affected brother to help: the bad character whose illicit
business might pay school fees for some of the children in the family, or
the "good" brother who had no job. Such a revelation made the epidemic
and its suffering suddenly real.

The Ritual Dance of "The Visit"

At more local levels (and sometimes among urban elites as well), Africans
are very eager to have a foreigner "visit" them, see their village, and learn
what their "challenges" or "needs" are. Such visits are an organized element of donor programs, as when churches organize "mission trips," when
World Vision or Save the Children arranges for those who have contributed to sponsoring an orphan to visit the orphans they have supported, or
when representatives of powerful donors are welcomed with dances, ceremonies, and testimonials to show the donors that their support has indeed
transformed lives.

The ritual practice of "visiting" has powerful local meanings as well,
meanings that often integrate altruists' aspirations with those of local

people. When a Malawian says that she should "visit" her relatives in her home village, she means specifically that she should bring them supplies of such costly staples as cooking oil, sugar, salt, and tea—the commodities they could not provide for themselves. A pastor in a small town Assemblies of God church we attended exhorted his congregants to "visit your relatives" on the grounds that if congregants had failed to do so, their kin might not feel an obligation to take in their children if they themselves were to die. Indeed, in societies where obligations of generalized reciprocity are strong, simply to know of another's misfortune or need is to acquire some obligation to meet it if one is able.[15] Elizabeth Colson, studying Zambian villagers, has pointed out that the pervasiveness of such obligations leads people to try to arrange their lives to "creat[e] claims on others that they can be shamed into acknowledging while at the same time avoiding claims upon oneself."[16]

Foreigners' visits are a great opportunity to display needs that, at least in Malawians' view, may create claims on the foreigner, and indeed the foreigner may find it hard to resist helping when he sees the "challenges" (the NGO euphemism for "problems") and "needs" of the locals. A visit to the office of an elite broker may lead to discussion of what university in the United States would be a good place for her child to study or what international meeting the broker could attend. A visit to a national NGO from the head of SIDA, the Swedish foreign aid organization, does not arouse expectations of receiving an immediate individual benefit, but the NGO will certainly display the urgent needs that SIDA funds have permitted it to address in the hope that SIDA will continue to fund the NGO's projects.

The structuring power of such expectations is especially evident when they are disappointed. A graduate student, eager to learn more about NGO projects in Balaka villages but naïve about the implicit agenda of a "visit," spent an entire day being toured around a village NGO project by his urban host, Madalitso, the project's director. The student's field notes make clear his repeated failure to pick up on his designated role as a patron. First, his host showed him the "resource center" for youth, explaining that the solar panel that used to power a video player to keep the young people out of trouble no longer worked because it needed a new battery, which they couldn't afford. They next visited the village nursery school where the student learned that the

> nursery school is specifically for orphaned children and they all seemed to be around three or four years. Madalitso told me that there are 60 to 80 children "registered" but that "today the turnout

is low because of the weather." (It was unusually cold today—I was wearing a sweater, Madalitso was wearing four layers of clothes.) Madalitso said by this he meant that some children don't have warm clothes, don't have sweaters and so if it is cold, like today, they'll just stay at home.[17]

The children recited the alphabet and their numbers, and then the visitor was offered a taste of the nutritious porridge a donor provides. He was then taken to visit the homes of several elderly people for whom the organization was providing "home based care." His host emphasized more than once

> that it's important just for me to see these people "first hand" and see "first hand what conditions they live in." He said that not all the elderly people live in the same level of condition, some living better than others, but that their problems are all "the same" in that they have trouble "meeting their basic needs" on some level.

The student found the visit "very awkward":

> I felt a little like they were being paraded in front of me, and I couldn't really chat to them since they would speak Chichewa. Additionally, I was always given the first or only chair to sit on whilst others would sit on the floor nearby, or I was given the most central seated position, nearby the elderly person, even though I couldn't talk with them and I didn't know what I should be talking to Madalitso about. So I would just get seated near an old person and told something sad about them or their health problems or their history by Madalitso, then sit there awkwardly whilst some people had a conversation in Chichewa, then we'd leave.

After lunch in his host's mother's comfortable house, they continued their tour of the organization's programs, visiting the committee in charge of the Youth Club where the youth blithely went off script:

> Madalitso then asked the committee if they could talk a little bit about the problems they face as youths in these villages. I suppose he was wanting them to say they face the "challenges" of avoiding sex and beer drinking and so on, but they didn't speak up, then one joked (in Chichewa—Madalitso translated for me) that he really liked the jacket one of the other committee members was wearing, so one

31

problem was that there weren't enough nice clothes to go around for everyone. They all laughed. Then Madalitso said can you try again, think of other problems and challenges you face. There was silence from the committee, until the president said that the [organization] t-shirt that one committee member was wearing was nice but that there was only one, and even he the president didn't have one, so it would be good if the whole committee could each get a [organization] t-shirt, then everyone would know they were [the organization]. We laughed. I don't think this was the kind of problem that Madalitso was wanting them to talk about! After this, Madalitso didn't push them further to talk about problems they face.

The host must have realized that since his repeated hints weren't working, it would require a direct appeal. He made explicit what the choreographed dance of "visiting" is supposed to produce by way of sympathy and altruistic desire. After watching a last performance by the children, the visitor was asked to give

a short inspirational speech ("just give a few words of encouragement to the committee") and he'd said this is normal when a visitor comes and they look forward to the speech because it encourages them and makes them know their work is valuable and valued by others. One of the committee members first gave a short speech addressed to me (but in Chichewa—Madalitso translated it to me) where he said the usual stuff like we're very pleased to have you come and visit and "we don't take for granted your visit" and asked that when I go home I tell friends and colleagues about [the organization] and that they could do with some more funding etc.

I asked Madalitso afterwards if my speech was okay, if my visit was okay and so on, and he told me that it's just really good that I even just came to visit, even if just for one day, and came to see what they do. And, he said, in Malawi we have a saying that "once the white man has touched the earth, it's changed—one way or the other ..." (after this he gave a small laugh, and a smile) and then suggested that perhaps I'll help them somehow get a little more funding in the future too.

The "visit" is thus one of those cultural constructions—an intersection of altruists' needs with those of local brokers (such as the host of this visit, who was not himself a villager, but a town dweller who brought visitors to his mother's village to see the work of the NGO he had built)—that spur the reciprocal fantasies of locals and donors, as locals imagine the possible assistance donors might bring, and potential altruists are aroused by images of suffering and need.

Aside from giving a face to altruists' understandings of Malawi's poverty, local intermediaries play a critical role in portraying how other less educated Malawians think and feel. This can range from describing exotic cultural practices to reassuring the donors that Malawians really do not want to be dependent, they want to be the kind of independent, self-reliant individuals that donors would like them to be.

BROKERS' PRESENTATION OF THEIR COUNTRY AND THEMSELVES

The colorful details of brokers' stories vary, but we have found that they present their country and themselves skillfully, and in predictable ways. There are, however, evident class differences in their presentations, reflecting their location on the ladder of educational and employment status.

Brokers with university and post-university degrees and employment in offices in the cities signal that that they are familiar with the latest international AIDS initiatives. They understand that AIDS is what brings foreigners to Malawi, and they can easily talk the language of donor programs, from long-term strategic plans to more specialized buzzwords and acronyms. Inevitably, these brokers change their interests as the global donors change their priorities. A broker with expertise in vulnerable children may segue into concern for early childhood education; climate change replaces AIDS in another broker's portfolio.

Brokers also frequently tell donors what they believe the donors want to hear. In the following excerpt from a description of an NGO project, a Malawian intermediary stresses Malawians' desire for self-reliance in a society that is enormously donor-dependent and where "ties of dependence" are the social norm:

Do Not Do For Us. The words were spoken in one of the earliest planning meetings, and it became one of the foundation principles for the project. It was spoken by a Malawian, Napoleon Dzombe, and was given in the [con]text of asking that we help them learn to fish, not give them the fish. "Do not make us a nation of beggars," he pleaded. "Help us to get on our feet. Do not do for us what we can do for ourselves."[18]

33

The broker both reflects back to the donors the ideal local partner the donors would like to imagine, and shows that he himself shares the donor's values: he is cosmopolitan. The brokers simultaneously empathize with and seek to distinguish themselves from the rural poor who are the typical beneficiaries of Western projects by telling "foolish villager" stories that accentuate their own role as valuable cultural insiders while emphasizing the differences between themselves and backward villagers. Such "foolish villager" stories (not unlike stories urbanized Europeans told about their backward country cousins)[19] may then become the basis for the donor imaginary and ultimately for donor policy.

AIDS money has clearly altered the landscape of aspirations for villagers, but also for both local and cosmopolitan brokers. The following excerpt comes from a conversational diary written by one of our journalists in 2006 when antiretroviral therapy was becoming available in rural areas and the sense of the epidemic as a death knell for the whole population was fading. It illustrates how the AIDS enterprise had entered local imaginations, even in an out-of-the-way rural trading center.

It was in the afternoon of the 6th of October 2006 that I was chatting with one of the radio repairs at Metemera Trading centre, near the veranda where we sat there was a group of people mostly youth who sat at the barber shop chatting.... [One said] But I think AIDS is good you see it has given people what to do, it has created jobs, what could this people being doing without this disease, what will these organisations being doing without AIDS, as of now a lot of people are rich in the name of AIDS, in the name of orphans. The first speaker continued. And even our government too it is depending on AIDS money too, that's why when some people said that they have found a cure for the disease they are not taken seriously and they are not recognised, why? Government does not want to lose AIDS money from the donors and you can just imagine if the government said openly that AIDS medicine has been found what can be happened to these organisation who claim that they are helping to stop the spread of AIDS, all of them will end and these people will have nothing to do.[20]

THE ROMANCE OF AIDS ALTRUISM

We do not take AIDS or those who struggle to combat it lightly. We have described the "romance" of the relationship among donors, brokers, and villagers not to make light of their motives, but to underline that the com-

34

ponents of a romance—anxious anticipation, the unexpected chemistry of a first meeting, sometimes an exhilarated infatuation, and then the struggle to come to terms with conflicts and disagreements—are also crucial components of the altruistic enterprise. In the next chapter we turn to the enormous scale and organizational complexity of the global AIDS enterprise. Remembering that this herculean effort was driven by an outpouring of altruistic concern, and that its day-to-day operation is colored by the intersecting fantasies of donors, brokers, and villagers, is crucial for understanding what shapes the effort to combat AIDS, as well as the larger visions of global health and human rights, of development and empowerment. In exploring the fantasies that lie behind the romance of AIDS altruism, we are exploring the motivating tensions that structure its world.

CHAPTER 3

LUMBERING BEHEMOTHS AND FLUTTERING BUTTERFLIES

Altruists in the Global AIDS Enterprise

IN THE PREVIOUS CHAPTER, WE described the alluring promise that the AIDS effort has created. Here we describe the innards, the messy and convoluted routes by which money and programs move through the global AIDS system.

What does it take to create the encounters between altruists and brokers that we described in the previous chapter? The short answer is "a lot of money for AIDS." This chapter is a longer answer: it takes the huge, chaotic, and frenetic organization of the global AIDS enterprise and, for those who come in person to help, a commitment of significant time and money.

The institutional altruists with deep pockets dominate the enterprise. They are behemoths, not just because they are gigantic, but also because they are ungainly, churning the ground as they lumber along. And they move slowly. It took two years after receiving the needed funding for the US Government to organize a meeting in Washington to get advice on instituting an initiative on a new theme, "multiple and concurrent partners" as a risk factor for HIV.[1] In contrast, altruists who come on their own can just book a flight and go. Like butterflies, they alight and then fly away.

It is extraordinarily difficult to develop satisfactory estimates for AIDS funding; figures 3.1 and 3.2 represent our best estimates.[2] Figure 3.1 shows funding sources before the global financial crisis of 2008. Figure 3.2 presents the post-crisis distribution.

As figures 3.1 and 3.2 show, the United States is clearly the predominant funder, providing considerably more than the Global Fund, to which many countries contribute. Taken together, bilateral donors—governments that give aid directly to a recipient country—provide about three-quarters of total funding. Initially, funders focused on HIV prevention. The President's Emergency Plan for AIDS Relief (PEPFAR), launched by President George W. Bush in 2003, provided for prevention, treatment with antiretroviral drugs, and mitigation of the effects of AIDS.[3]

Pre-Crisis Average

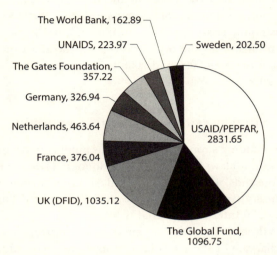

The World Bank, 162.89

UNAIDS, 223.97

Sweden, 202.50

The Gates Foundation, 357.22

Germany, 326.94

Netherlands, 463.64

USAID/PEPFAR, 2831.65

France, 376.04

UK (DFID), 1035.12

The Global Fund, 1096.75

FIGURE 3.1. Pre-crisis average yearly global spending on HIV/AIDS, 2006–2008 (in inflation-adjusted millions of 2014 USD).

Post-Crisis Average

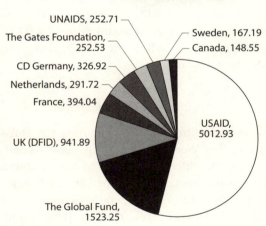

UNAIDS, 252.71

The Gates Foundation, 252.53

Sweden, 167.19

Canada, 148.55

CD Germany, 326.92

Netherlands, 291.72

France, 394.04

USAID, 5012.93

UK (DFID), 941.89

The Global Fund, 1523.25

FIGURE 3.2. Post-crisis average yearly global spending on HIV/AIDS, 2009–2014 (in inflation-adjusted millions of 2014 USD).

37

Figure 3.2 shows annual average global spending on HIV/AIDS for 2009 through 2014, after the global financial crisis. The role of PEPFAR, the largest donor, grew even more dominant during this period. Notably, the global economic crisis did not reduce overall AIDS funding. Annual total contributions of all the organizations on the chart increased from US$7.08 billion between 2006 and 2008 to an average of US$9.06 billion from 2009 to 2014.[4]

THE BEHEMOTHS AND THEIR PROGENY

Overall, AIDS funding supports an enormous number and variety of AIDS organizations. In Malawi from 2000–2014, donor aid stimulated the development of thousands of new or repurposed AIDS organizations, including 2,309 Community Based Organizations, 337 Faith Based Organizations, 180 NGOs, and 20 International NGOs.[5]

We begin a description of this organizational landscape with figure 3.3, a schematic diagram of the kinds of organizations involved in the global AIDS enterprise. At the top of the Institutional Actors diagram in figure 3.3 are the large multilateral and bilateral organizations that together provide global governance and coordination for combatting AIDS. The multilateral organizations set (and change) global policy and decide on themes for HIV prevention strategies, as when UN Secretary General Kofi Annan pronounced that "AIDS has the face of a woman" or when USAID decides on priorities for a new multi-year strategy (e.g., Prevention of Mother to Child Transmission, Multiple and Concurrent Partners, or Voluntary Medical Male Circumcision). The bilateral organizations, like USAID and DFID (discussed below) provide the bulk of the money, giving them clout in influencing policy, themes, and practices.

Multilateral Organizations

The multilateral organizations lead in structuring the global response to the AIDS epidemic. The World Bank and the Global Fund collect funds from wealthy countries, which they funnel to poorer countries, but with conditions. These two organizations shaped the early organizational response to the epidemic. Even as the epidemic changed, this structure remains as a legacy. As James Putzel explains, "[t]he two most important instruments of multilateral assistance, the World Bank's Multi-Country AIDS Programme (MAP), launched in September 2000, and the Global Fund to fight AIDS, [Tuberculosis and Malaria (GFATM)], launched in

2002, . . . [required] countries to demonstrate a commitment to mainstreaming and to a multisectoral approach as conditions for gaining new resources to fight the epidemic."[6] The aim was to ensure that HIV prevention efforts would not be solely the responsibility of ministries of health. Rather, other government sectors, such as the Ministry of Agriculture and the Ministry of Defense, and a variety of civil society actors, such as NGOs, churches, and community groups, would be involved in the AIDS response; there would be an AIDS component in programs from poverty reduction to gender equality campaigns. To coordinate AIDS prevention activities, the Bank and the Fund also required countries receiving money to establish free-standing AIDS organizations. Both the imposed conformity and allowance for national differences in the details can be seen in the national level governance of the epidemic. Malawi has a National AIDS Commission (NAC), Botswana has a National AIDS Coordinating Agency (NACA), and Swaziland has the National Emergency Response Council on HIV and AIDS (NERCHA). All of them, however, have a similar structure.

Conformity is also promoted by two other global organizations: UNAIDS through its announcement of new themes and WHO through informing countries of preferred biomedical approaches to prevention (e.g., recommendations about breastfeeding and HIV) and treatment (e.g., particular treatment regimens).[7] The WHO specializes in the technical aspects of AIDS, such as determining the appropriate drugs for treatment and certifying male circumcision as a highly effective method of HIV prevention.[8]

The Global Fund requires another level of administrative conformity. To win a grant, a country's proposal requires a Country Coordinating Mechanism (CCM) that includes a range of stakeholders and actors.[9] The Fund considers the CCMs to be central to a country's "local ownership and participatory decision-making," two mantras of the global development industry.[10] CCMs are supposed to develop and submit grant proposals to the Global Fund and to oversee their implementation. As with many aspects of foreign aid, however, global policy and national practice may diverge on the ground.

Malawi's CCM is composed of representatives of groups of ordinary people considered to have a stake in AIDS, such as support groups of people living with AIDS and sex workers. The NAC, however, appears to have considered genuine participation by the CCM members in decisions regarding money to be as foolish as giving students control of a classroom; NAC remained in charge. A pastor from a rural church who represented both religious leaders and people living with AIDS (he himself was HIV+) said in an interview that at the meetings, the CCM members deferred to

CATEGORIES OF INSTITUTIONAL ACTORS IN THE GLOBAL AIDS ENTERPRISE

MULTILATERAL ORGANIZATIONS

World Bank	UNAIDS	WHO	Global Fund (GFATM)

BILATERAL ORGANIZATIONS

JICA [Japan]	USAID [United States]	GIZ [Germany]
Irish Aid	EuropeAid Development and Cooperation [EU]	CIDA [Canada]
DANIDA [Denmark]	Ministry of Development Cooperation [Netherlands]	DFID [UK]
NORAD [Norway]	SIDA [Sweden]	AusAID [Australia]

FOUNDATIONS

Firelight Foundation	Gates Foundation
GOAL Ireland	Pangea Global AIDS Foundation
Global Fund for Women	Elizabeth Glaser Pediatric AIDS Foundation
Rockefeller Foundation	Ford Foundation

UNIVERSITIES AND SCHOOLS OF PUBLIC HEALTH

University of North Carolina	Baylor College of Medicine
Johns Hopkins Bloomberg School of Public Health	Columbia University Mailman School of Public Health
London School of Hygiene & Tropical Medicine	Harvard School of Public Health

INTERNATIONAL NGOs

Save the Children	World Vision International	Engender Health
PSI [Population Services International]	DanChurchAid (DCA)	CARE
FHI 360	Catholic Relief Services	PATH
Pact International	Pathfinder International	ActionAid

FIGURE 3.3. Categories of institutional actors in the global AIDS enterprise.

NAC, which was fine with him—"NAC is the one that knows what happens on the ground."[11]

Invisible on our diagram is a form of global coordination that sometimes governs responses to crises like the AIDS epidemic. This is the creation and legitimation in a global forum of aspirational "targets," goals that countries are expected to accomplish within a certain period of time. International organizations monitor countries' progress and thereby pressure them to achieve their goals. The United Nations included an AIDS

INTERNATIONAL DEVELOPMENT CONTRACTORS

Chemonics	John Snow Inc. (JSI)	Abt Associates	Management Sciences for Health

NATIONAL GOVERNMENT STRUCTURES (MALAWI)

Ministry of Health	Office of President and Cabinet Department of Nutrition, HIV and AIDS
National AIDS Commission	Other government ministries, e.g. Gender, Child Welfare and Community Services, Rural Development

REGIONAL/NATIONAL UMBRELLA NGOs (MALAWI)

African Council of AIDS Service Organizations	Council for NGOs in Malawi (CONGOMA)	Southern Africa Network of AIDS Service Organizations	Malawi Network of AIDS Service Organizations (MANASO)

NATIONAL-LEVEL NGOs (MALAWI)

Catholic Development Commission in Malawi (CADECOM)	Salama Shield Foundation	National Association of People Living with HIV and AIDS (NAPHAM)
Youth Network and Counseling (YONECO)	World Vision Malawi	Society for Women and AIDS in Malawi (SWAM)

LOCAL GOVERNMENT STRUCTURES (THE SAME FORMAL STRUCTURES IN EACH OF 28 DISTRICTS, MALAWI)

Zomba District Health Office	Mchinji District Youth Officer	Nkhatabay District Social Welfare Office
Mangochi District Assembly	Chiradzulu District AIDS Coordinating Committee	Rumphi District Agriculture Office

COMMUNITY-BASED ORGANIZATIONS (MALAWI)

Bondo Youth Club	Limbikani Orphan AIDS Support Group	Phinda Community Home Based Care Organisation
Chimteka Village AIDS & Orphan Care Support	Noor Women Group	Mponela AIDS Information and Counseling Centre

target in its Millennium Development Goals (MDGs), to which 189 nations committed themselves in 2000.[12]

While these goals are at one level cotton-candy wishes rather than policy commitments backed by power or money, monitoring appears to have had real influence.[13] Countries were obligated biannually to report data that permitted tracking their progress toward the goals, and most did so on at least some issues.[14] Global monitoring both focuses the efforts of donors on global targets and embarrasses—or is intended to embarrass—

countries into making progress toward the goals. As Thomas Weiss, an expert on the United Nations and global governance, notes, "The MDGs illustrate a quintessential UN shortcoming: besides trying to shame a country that fails to provide education to girls or increase development assistance, little else can be done."[15] Similarly aspirational are the goals set by UNAIDS to eliminate new infections by 2030. "That is our goal—zero new infections, zero stigma and zero AIDS-related deaths."[16]

Bilateral Agencies, International Non-Governmental Organizations, and Contractors

Bilateral government agencies such as USAID and DFID do not have the same responsibility for governance and coordination of the AIDS enterprise as do the multilateral organizations, but they are as, or more, powerful because of their financial muscle. The bilateral donor agencies are accountable to their national taxpayers and influenced by domestic politics. Their reach is not global to the same degree as that of the multilaterals, but the largest of them work in multiple countries in multiple regions of the world. On AIDS, they have been particularly active in sub-Saharan Africa where the epidemic has been most intense.

The bilateral organizations determine themes for new multi-year and multi-country programs and targets, such as "Prevention of Mother to Child Transmission" to protect children and "Multiple and Concurrent Partners" to encourage faithfulness. They usually determine whether the approach will be through capacity-building (training), communication through the media (billboards and radio), or service delivery. They manage their massive responses to the epidemic through subcontracting.

Donors implement programs through an array of big international non-governmental organizations (INGOs) and for-profit international development contractors. Reliance on for-profit development contractors has grown dramatically. In the 2012 fiscal year, 61 percent of the contracts awarded by USAID went to for-profit firms.[17] These organizations, staffed by development professionals, have become a major channel for development assistance. In response to requests for proposals announced by a bilateral donor, they submit bids to design and implement programs through which the aid flows.[18] The bidders typically have to make the case to the donor that they will implement the donor's chosen theme by providing innovative approaches and original activities to transform individuals and communities.

The INGOs and the for-profit organizations compete with each other for huge contracts, often in the tens or hundreds of millions of dollars. For example, the Academy for Educational Development (AED), won a $175 million contract from USAID for a multi-year and multi-country program called "C-Change: Communication for Change," which aimed "to improve the effectiveness and sustainability of communications as an integral part of development efforts." The successful bidders then create an aid chain by subcontracting to one or more large in-country organizations charged with actually reaching the targeted beneficiaries. These large NGOs in turn often subcontract to yet smaller organizations, providing each organization with funds to rent an office, pay broker salaries, buy vehicles and supplies, and the like.

INGOs and for-profit contractors thus stand at the head of the tributary of funding that flows from donors to subcontracting organizations, to brokers, and on occasion, to villagers. They are large. PSI (formerly Population Services International) is one of the largest INGOs to receive US government funding. It has an enormous array of health projects, including substantial programming for HIV/AIDS, which it implements in many countries. Among its AIDS programs are condom distribution, counseling and testing for HIV, male circumcision, and communication projects meant to mobilize communities to change their behavior. But PSI is only one, albeit among the largest, of many large INGOs, such as Save the Children, World Vision International, and ActionAid. On our diagram, we showed ten or so, but a full list would include hundreds.

The global AIDS enterprise is more chaotic than our diagram suggests. Many of the INGOs are globe-spanning non-profits that both receive funding from a variety of donors and send funding to a variety of subcontracting organizations to implement donor programs. Some also raise money from individuals, for example through World Vision's child-sponsorship programs. The for-profit international development contractors (e.g., Abt Associates, Chemonics) live almost entirely on government contracts. In the United States, for-profit contractors for USAID circle Washington and are often referred to as the "beltway bandits" of international development. Finally, some INGOs are mixed: John Snow, Inc. is a for-profit INGO with a non-profit research arm.

The INGOs on our diagram have progeny: satellite or affiliate offices abroad. For example, PSI-Washington has an affiliate office in every country in which it works, some of which are PSI country offices and others more independent affiliates with long-standing collaborative relationships with PSI. Generally, the large donors require that activities be implemented in specific countries; INGOs with a presence in those countries bid on these projects through their affiliate offices. In other instances, INGOs receive

centrally funded grants and then send funding, accompanied by directives, to their country affiliates such as PSI-Malawi in Lilongwe. In either
case, the PSI-Malawi office will use some of this money to directly implement projects, such as the "One Love" TV series on HIV prevention and
trainings for local health workers. PSI-Malawi may use other funding to
establish a daughter office in a district or to collaborate with a local NGO
in the capital—a "partner organization"—to carry out specific program activities (such as peer education sessions). PSI Malawi or its partners may
in turn send funds and directives even further downstream to smaller national NGOs, which either deal directly with would-be beneficiaries, subcontract with another even smaller organization, or give grants to community groups. Eventually, the rushing tributary that began with a bilateral
or multilateral donor becomes many tiny rivulets, some of which actually
make it to the rural villages where beneficiaries live.

Academic Institutions

Large universities and schools of public health also play an important
role in the donor response to AIDS in Africa. US and European medical
schools or schools of public health form alliances with health providers in
an African country, providing services such as HIV testing and antiretroviral treatment as part of a research project. University research projects
are not, of course, purely or even primarily altruistic, since the researchers
are pursuing their own goals. Donor money often goes not directly to assisting Africans, but to university research projects investigating what are
hoped might become replicable models for how to treat or mitigate the
effects of the epidemic. Indeed, many large-scale altruists, including the
Gates Foundation and the World Bank, conceive some of the assistance
that they provide as research designed to test models that, if successful,
can be "scaled up" and implemented by national governments or other
donors.

   In some ways, these academic institutions are similar to the giant INGOs
and the for-profit beltway bandits: they compete for the same funds and
may do research or implement health interventions overseas, or both. The
University of North Carolina's School of Medicine has a long-running
project in Malawi that has produced path-breaking research on AIDS; it
also provides free clinical care in its research sites. An affiliate of Johns
Hopkins University, Jhpiego, a non-profit health organization, has received
funding from USAID, from DFID, and from the Bill & Melinda Gates
Foundation to collaborate with the Ministry of Health, Save the Children,

and PSI to implement a maternal and child health program. While not usually considered part of the aid chain, universities are important players in AIDS prevention and treatment.

Non-Governmental Organizations

We distinguish between the globe-spanning INGOs and the in-country NGOs. NGOs occupy a special place in the imagination of donors large and small. Because they are designated as independent, non-profit organizations, they are thought to avoid the bureaucracy and potential corruption of governments and the mercenary motives of the marketplace. For us, the national-level NGOs are the most interesting actors in the AIDS enterprise. Their brokers are tasked by donors with bridging the distance from the INGO satellite offices or their own national offices—usually located in the capital city—to the imagined beneficiaries, usually in a village or slum. These brokers scour the landscape for smaller NGOs or indigenous community based organizations to be subcontractors. When one is located, the larger NGO checks to see if it is actually functioning, which in practice means that it has found a way to write successful proposals to donors and demonstrated that it has managed its money appropriately.[19]

As elsewhere in the developing world, Malawi's NGO sector has grown dramatically.[20] Initially, the goals of the institutional altruists who flocked to the country were to assist in economic development by improving agriculture, health, and education. Some continue to do so. But increasingly, attention turned to AIDS. This is not surprising given the magnitude of the epidemic in Malawi. In the mid-1990s, an estimated 12 percent of the adult population (age 15–49) was HIV+, and by 2000–2002 that figure had risen to 14 percent, making Malawi the eighth most affected country in the world.[21]

In 2003, NAC attempted to list all the non-profit organizations engaged in AIDS-related activities. It found slightly over three hundred, some large and registered in a foreign country, others so small that they appeared to be aspirational, having neither a phone number nor a post office address.[22] The larger organizations are an important source of jobs for Malawians fortunate enough to find formal employment. There is no official listing of how many brokers were employed in AIDS NGOs, but Simon Morfit used a clever proxy to estimate trends—the advertisements for NGO positions in Malawi's newspaper. As we see in figure 3.4, as AIDS became a global cause célèbre, the number of NGO jobs advertised mushroomed and AIDS came to dominate the NGO scene.

NGO Job Sector Advertisements, 1985-2005

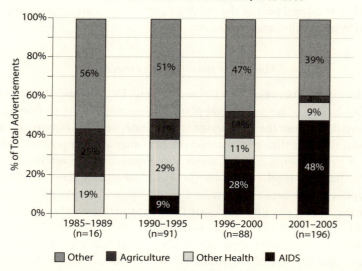

FIGURE 3.4. NGO job sector advertisements, 1985–2005. Figure is based on sampling NGO job advertisements for one full week, every other month, every year. *Adapted from N. Simon Morfit, "AIDS is Money,"* World Development *39 (2011), figure 3, p. 68.*

Community Based Organizations

One of UNAIDS' key goals is mobilizing local people to respond to the epidemic, which requires a final layer of AIDS organizations. In practice, this entails that NGO brokers train villagers in the donor's current theme (such as empowering vulnerable women by teaching them to negotiate condom use). The trainees are then expected, as volunteers, to spread the message to their neighbors. The trained volunteers may be members of existing community based organizations (CBOs) or faith based organizations (FBOs), or they may be individuals selected by NGOs for specific training. The CBOs may be indigenous, formed by villagers to help members of their community, but most are created by a higher-level organization, typically either a national AIDS commission or an NGO.[23]

CBOs proliferated in Malawi after NAC received grants from the Global Fund in 2004 and 2005. The funders stipulated that a certain percentage of the grants had to be spent on mobilizing citizens to address the epidemic.[24] NAC then called for proposals from existing community groups. Not sur-

FIGURE 3.5. Mkanda churches, HIV/AIDS, aged, youth, and orphans care. This community-based organization, in a trading center rather than a village, was founded by the Assemblies of God church. It had enough resources to rent a small office. *Photo: Ralph Chikadza.*

prisingly, many new groups formed in response. In 2006, NAC listed grants to 582 CBOs. It appears that the villagers who benefitted most from NAC's largesse in that era were the dozen or so members of each CBO executive committee and village elites (chiefs, pastors, schoolteachers) who received small allowances for training sessions.[25] We do not have similar data for other countries in the high-prevalence AIDS region, but given that both the structure of the AIDS enterprise and its goals are not unique to Malawi, we can assume that community mobilization elsewhere also relies on CBOs[26] and has similar outcomes.

Despite a trickle of unpredictable funding to village-level CBOs, community mobilization and the dissemination of HIV-prevention messages primarily depend on internationally funded NGO projects rather than on NAC. NGO brokers find local volunteers in several ways. One is through the remnants of the NAC structure. After NAC's money for village CBOs was largely exhausted, it simplified its operations by decreeing that there should be a single CBO for a set of villages.[27] These new CBOs are an important source of volunteers for NGOs. The CBO can still apply for funding from NAC—or, if its members have the skills, submit proposals to small foundations or other NGOs they find on the web—but the more usual path is that its members wait for an NGO to arrive looking for volunteers to train.

When a trickle of AIDS-prevention funding finally arrives in the villages, it often pays for activities like an annual AIDS Candlelight Vigil or an AIDS Day celebration conducted by local district AIDS coordinators. It is the smaller-scale altruists, many of them church groups or simply individual idealists like those we described in the previous chapter, who make the strongest connections with local Malawians. The behemoth altruists have to go through a chain of subcontractors; the butterfly altruists can form personal ties.

FLUTTERING BUTTERFLIES

The global AIDS enterprise is not simply a landscape of organizations with streams or rivulets of money flowing among them. More importantly, it is a landscape of meanings and aspirations best expressed by the "butterfly altruists": Arkansas Baptists staying in a fleabag hotel in the capital, whom we met as they were heading off to dig wells in Malawian villages; Irish town officials who send funds to their Malawian sister city; and medical students, former Peace Corps volunteers, and freelance individuals who are moved to help poor Malawians in any way they can. Many of these people are religious, like some of those we met in chapter 2,[28] but many others simply feel the urge to do something about AIDS, to help orphans, or to assist impoverished Malawians. Butterfly altruists matter greatly even though they make no appearance on our diagram of the "Global AIDS Enterprise." We believe that on the ground, amateur altruists make more of a difference than do the professionals, both symbolically and practically.[29]

Amateur altruists are neither controlled by nor responsible to the global AIDS enterprise. Their initiatives are too small, too erratic, and often too transitory to come to the attention of the state, the behemoths, or indeed the lower-level NGOs. They often come and go. Many of their projects quickly die, and even the ones that succeed are scattered capriciously across the landscape. But unlike most projects funded by the large donors, those of the amateurs usually provide material help. Several foreigners bring bags of grain and pails for water to a grandmother caring for orphans. A church group from a small town in Delaware that we stumbled across collects funds to dig a village borehole to provide clean water.

For most villagers, however, altruists large and small are both everywhere and nowhere—pervasive, yet for the many who have not thus far benefited, a kind of mirage, always just out of reach.

THE AIDS ENTERPRISE IS INCOHERENT

The orderly levels of our Categories of Institutional Actors diagram mask considerable incoherence in practice. Indeed, the multifarious, overlapping, sometimes dizzyingly circular ties among organizations involved in global AIDS make evident the mind-boggling complexity of the AIDS effort.

No one has yet succeeded in mapping the complexity of the global AIDS enterprise. There is, however, a fantastical diagram—almost an insider's joke—that has been floating around the AIDS world since at least 2005.

Labeled "AIDS stakeholders and donors in one African country" and shown here as figure 3.6, it appeared in a 2005 UNAIDS report and as a slide at the 2006 AIDS conference in Toronto. The absence of a key to the acronyms underlines the chaos.[30] Schematic as it is, leaving out almost all the detail of the myriad foundations, NGOs, and implementing partners that work on any given project, this diagram nonetheless nicely captures the convoluted structure of what are supposed to be the major coordinating mechanisms among the big players in the AIDS enterprise. That no one has even attempted this mapping for the full set of major organizations involved in AIDS projects, in even one country let alone for the global enterprise, indicates just how daunting this structure is even for insiders.

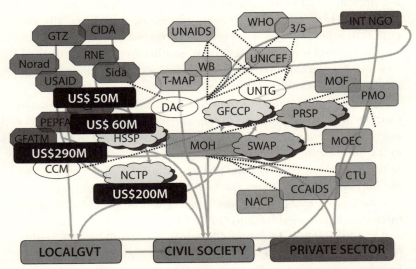

FIGURE 3.6. AIDS stakeholders and donors in one African country. This figure captures the chaotic flows of aid for AIDS. *Modified from "The 'Three Ones' in Action: Where We Are and Where We Go from Here." UNAIDS, May 2005, figure 1, p. 19.*

A sense of this complexity also emerges from an extended description, taken from the website of Family Health International (now FHI 360) in 2005, of a program to reduce mother-to-child transmission of HIV in Namibia. "Namibia President's International Mother and Child HIV Prevention Initiative" begins with a list of the "Implementing Partners":

Catholic Health Services
Lutheran Medical Services
Catholic AIDS Action
Evangelical Lutheran Church AIDS Program (ELCAP)
Evangelical Lutheran Church AIDS Action Program (ELCIN)
Lifeline/Childline

After recounting the epidemic's devastating consequences, the website describes the project:

Under the USAID Initiative, FHI together with Johns Hopkins University/Health Communication Partnership (JHU-HCP), Population Services International/Social Marketing Association (PSI/SMA) and Rational Pharmaceutical Management (RMP) will be implementing a comprehensive community mobilization program for the prevention of mother to child transmission through support to faith-based hospitals and their faith- and community-based affiliates (FBO) to provide access to prevention programs as well as voluntary counseling and testing, prevention of mother to child transmission, treatment, maternal and child health services in predominantly rural areas for women and their families.

Specifically, FHI will improve the infrastructure, and build human capacity and provide support to implement quality PMTCT services at five ministry-supported faith-based hospitals, located in Rehoboth in the South, and in Oshikuku, Nyangana, Andara and Onandjokwe in the North, respectively managed by Catholic Health Services and the Lutheran Medical Services.

Community mobilization and support will be provided through three faith-based organizations (FBOs): Catholic AIDS Action (CAA) and the Evangelical Lutheran Church in the Republic of Namibia (ELCRN) through its church and community based Evangelical Lutheran Church AIDS Program (ELCAP) and the Evangelical Lutheran Church in Namibia (ELCIN) AIDS Action (ELCIN-EASA). This support will enable the FBOs to build and expand on their current community-based activities, to include community-mobilization activities promoting VCT and PMTCT, capacity-building, advocacy and establishment of effective referral systems between health facilities and the community using their over 2,000 trained volunteers to ensure that women and their children infected and affected by HIV will receive care and support they deserve. To ensure quality training in counseling and supervision, LifeLine/Childline has been selected to develop standard training curricula to ensure that a pool of well-trained and qualified counselors will be available both at the community and health facility level.[31]

Here we see the complex cascade of a USAID-funded project, mobilizing the big INGOs, FHI and PSI, and a pharmaceutical-management organization, but working through Johns Hopkins University, several hospitals run by religious denominations, and a welter of faith-based local organizations to provide the "community mobilization" understood to be necessary for bringing women into the program.

This extended example points to the tangle of relationships hidden behind our "Categories of Institutional Actors" diagram. Moreover, the international donors and the INGOs have to deal with governments, and many of their projects for prevention are coordinated with government ministries, such as those for gender, youth, or rural development. Indeed, the ideologies of "mainstreaming" and "multisectoral" activities were, as we noted, core requirements of the World Bank and the Global Fund in their approaches to the governance of the epidemic.[32] These mandates, however, virtually insure the administrative inefficiency of the AIDS industry.

The behemoth NGOs deploy a variety of techniques to acquire the funding that will permit them to reach the intended beneficiaries. World Vision and Save the Children, for example, raise funds through "child sponsorship" efforts, appealing to sympathetic individuals to donate to help orphans like the ones pictured in ads. Those same organizations' Malawian branches may also apply to NAC for funding. As an example of just how convoluted the funding process can be, in 2010, Malawi's NAC gave large grants of 119 million Malawi kwacha and 163 million Malawi kwacha respectively to Population Services International (PSI) and Malawi Counseling and Resource Organization (MACRO), both of which are largely supported by USAID, which had itself contributed a substantial share of the Global Fund budget that funded NAC.[33] Some of those same INGOs played a central role in administering NAC's program of small grants to CBOs in towns and villages by serving as "umbrella organizations" to review applications. From 2004 to mid-2008, Save the Children US, World Vision International Malawi, ActionAid Malawi, Canadian Physicians for Aid and Relief Malawi, and PLAN Malawi received large grants from NAC for their administrative services while they also were recipients of NAC funding for their own AIDS projects.[34]

The AIDS industry's funding structure promotes incoherence. In scale and complexity, it is like a large for-profit company such as General Motors. But commercial organizations have a central headquarters that sets goals, develops an administrative structure, pays staff, and hires and fires to get its work done. The AIDS industry operates largely through a complex structure of subcontracting (now common in for-profit companies) and grants, followed up later with monitoring reports, and then, sometimes and much later, with evaluations. Organizations higher up in the structure put out calls for proposals to implementing organizations, which in turn seek out partners on spec. The implementers might, if the proposal is funded, help them fulfill the promises they made to the funding organizations.

Other large donors, such as the Global Fund or the World Bank, wait for countries to apply for funding. Even if those applications are in reality negotiated beforehand, with the funding organization making known what sort of proposal it wants and sometimes helping draft the proposal, the AIDS funding structure is not straightforward. There is no clear hierarchy with a central management defining objectives, assigning responsibilities, and measuring results. The funding process can go wrong. In 2010, two proposals by Malawi to the Global Fund, an important source of the country's resources for AIDS treatment, were rejected, leaving a large hole in its AIDS budget. Further down the aid chain, NGOs often lose their funding, either because someone somewhere in the aid chain mismanaged money or simply because the donor lost interest in the topic.

The AIDS enterprise actually runs more like Hollywood studios than like General Motors, with creative enterprises "pitching" proposals to potential funders. Just as a producer might claim that Brad Pitt is committed to his film, an NGO might claim that the Ministry of Gender is committed to its project to empower vulnerable girls to "Say No to AIDS." The largest organizations, like PSI or World Vision, strive to have enough different areas of expertise, enough different proposals in the pipeline, and enough different upstream funders that they can maintain a stable organization even as donor priorities come and go. Nonetheless, the whole structure is capricious, uncertain, and often based more on promises and self-promotion than on performance.[35]

Why would the global actors responsible for combating AIDS—or those dedicated to other global health or development priorities—organize themselves in such an anarchic way? Over the years, many policy documents have urged coordination among donors, consistency in funding, elimination of duplication and competition, and the like.[36] But donors and their myriad subcontracting partners have many incentives to maintain the central features of the current non-system. The most important is that, unlike governments, which are at least in principle obligated to provide consistent and reliable services to all citizens, donor agencies neither wish to nor are able to provide long-term, comprehensive services to entire populations. That is, they cannot take on the responsibilities that in effect would make them governments for people in far-away places. Their interventions are necessarily patchwork and temporary.

Furthermore, major donors seek to keep their options open. They want the freedom to try an approach in one place and a different approach a year later in another, to provide "transformative" aid without having to maintain it for the long term, and to alter their funding strategies as their own priorities change. As in all systems, one actor's freedom to do as he wishes inevitably means uncertainty and insecurity for those who depend on him. But since funding recipients, from the behemoth NGOs to small CBOs, depend on donor largesse, in the end, they have no real power to compel comprehensive, predictable, or desired services.

Such a system inevitably creates a competitive scramble among grant-seeking organizations, whether governments or behemoth NGOs.[37] Even grassroots NGOs that begin as indigenous community groups must become highly entrepreneurial, constantly writing proposals if they are to survive and grow. The larger ones propose ambitious projects in order to try to bring major contracts their way while smaller organizations scramble for crumbs from the table. Both to spread risk and to build up allies in this contest, organizations often form multiple partnerships, becoming each other's subcontractors as well as competitors. This arrangement is more like the patron-client system we described in the preface than like a smoothly-rationalized hierarchical system. Players seek as many potential patrons as possible, because they cannot predict which one may win a grant or contract, and because even winning one contract means little for the next. At the same time, large donors prefer having many potential subcontractors vying for their favors, both to keep these potential partners on their toes and to have a choice of projects, innovative-sounding programs, and new initiatives to fund.

Any structure this complex inevitably requires intense activity by brokers to manage the linkages among very disparate actors. Because the AIDS enterprise is a jumble of entrepreneurial organizations that both compete and cooperate, looking for opportunities wherever they can find them, it needs brokers to mediate relations at every level. While it involves many actors motivated by money, the AIDS enterprise is nonetheless an altruistic enterprise. Rather than producing goods or services for a market, it produces "projects,"[38] which in turn produce images of success—and sometimes real success—for donors. Brokers link donors to those whom they would help and are thus critical to the entire enterprise.[39]

THE AIDS ENTERPRISE IS FRENETIC

Early in the epidemic, AIDS was defined as a humanitarian emergency. Just as the global community is expected to respond quickly and urgently to natural disasters such as tsunamis, so it was expected to respond to AIDS. Convening as a special session in 2001, the UN General Assembly declared that the epidemic,

> through its devastating scale and impact, constitutes a global emergency and one of the most formidable challenges to human life and dignity, as well as to the effective enjoyment of human rights, which undermines social and economic development throughout the world and affects all levels of society—national, community, family and individual.[40]

Secretary General Kofi Annan called on the global community to make unprecedented efforts.

> The global AIDS epidemic is one of the greatest challenges facing our generation. AIDS is a new type of global emergency—an unprecedented threat to human development requiring sustained action and commitment over the long term.[41]

The implicit alternative was to "do nothing," which was intolerable: the global community was morally obliged to do something, but what? Global actors rushed in with only the vaguest of ideas, many of them recycled from earlier family planning campaigns. The director of a large NGO in Malawi, a person with years of experience in foreign aid organizations, explained that family planning activities were incorporated and redefined as AIDS

54

activities in order to set up PEPFAR.[42] Organizations dedicated to family planning became dedicated to AIDS; individuals who had worked for family planning organizations now worked on AIDS.[43] And new organizations, such as the Global Fund, UNAIDS, and amfAR (the Foundation for AIDS Research) were created *de novo*, both to address the epidemic and in an effort to coordinate the ever-shifting scrum of organizations eager to enter the fray.

As early as 1996, UNAIDS claimed to know what worked,[44] as did USAID in 1998:

> The interventions developed, in part, by USAID-supported efforts, have become the basic tools for HIV/AIDS prevention. They are:
>
> * information, education, and counseling to raise awareness of the threat of HIV/AIDS in an effort to promote behavior changes, such as abstinence, that will reduce risk;
> * treatment of sexually transmitted diseases which, if untreated, can facilitate transmission of the HIV virus; and
> * promotion of increased condom use through condom "social marketing," or advertising the availability and appeal of using condoms.
>
> These interventions have been proven to have an impact on HIV/AIDS because they result in behavior changes that reduce the risk of disease transmission.[45]

Despite this air of certainty, preventing AIDS was not—and still is not—a discrete problem with a known solution (like distributing drugs for river blindness or vaccinating children to eradicate polio), but a crisis that seemed to require remaking whole societies and transforming even people's intimate lives. The frenzied rush to do something meant that interventions were implemented on a large scale before there was any possibility of rigorously evaluating them.[46] Moreover, most actors were not interested in rigorous evaluation. Driven by a sense of urgency, they wanted to assure donors and the global public that they knew what worked, so that they could keep money and resources flowing.[47] Many seemed convinced that because the problem was urgent, at least some of what they were doing had to work. The response to specific studies showing that particular interventions did nothing to reduce HIV transmission was simply to insist on doing more of the same—or even, for advocates of "combination prevention," which bubbled to the surface in 2008, to propose that biomedical, behavioral, and structural approaches that had been each shown to be ineffective would work if implemented simultaneously.[48]

For both donors and those working in HIV prevention organizations (as opposed to researchers), rigorous evaluation of their programs is not a priority. As one head of an INGO office in Malawi said to us of his PEPFAR funders, for them neither research nor evaluation was important in such an emergency; what was important was to get stuff out there.[49] The NGOs feel that research is not really their job—"it's not what we do." Participants at a PEPFAR meeting in Washington, when asked why organizations did not want to figure out what works, replied, "There isn't time." Another said "it's too expensive."[50]

The mysterious, frightening nature of the disease and its explosive growth around the world certainly drove a sense of emergency. But there was another reason as well for urgency. Anything on which the donor world focuses—climate change, maternal mortality, poverty, or hunger—must be defined as an emergency, even if it is among the oldest scourges of humankind, in order to spur action. Only by describing a problem as urgent can NGOs and other altruists raise the sense of alarm and desperate need that can motivate donors to focus resources on a problem. Such problems suddenly become "emergencies," which justifies the "NGO scramble" and the frenzied urgency that is the normal mode of operation of the INGO world.[51] Of course, often the urgency is quite real.

The need to do *something* and the uncertainty about what precisely needs to be done leads to multiple paradoxes. The very organizations that aspire to transform Africans whom they see as vulnerable to infection into what they consider to be modern, rational, and forward-looking decision-makers often create a funding environment that is chaotic and unpredictable, leading villagers, as well as brokers, to see program benefits as windfalls created by a capricious, sometimes benign, sometimes indifferent, but always inexplicable patron. That is, the organizations reinforce beneficiaries' views of the world as irrational. Also, the organizations that attempt to change people half a world away do not have the sorts of measures of success that are available in the medical field.[52] They thus find themselves focusing on creating the rich profusion of cultural materials we discuss in the next chapter: materials meant to turn Africans into people who inhabit the same mental and moral universe as the donors.

CHAPTER 4

CULTURAL PRODUCTION

A Riot of Color

ONCE THE PREMISE WAS ACCEPTED that AIDS was an emergency and that prevention was central, there was the question of just what the organizations described in the previous chapters could do.[1] Institutional altruists supported technical approaches, such as screening the blood supply for the HIV virus, providing antiretroviral drugs to HIV+ pregnant women so as to prevent transmission to their babies, and voluntary counseling and testing. Donors also spent heavily on information, education, and communication about the ABCs—abstain, be faithful, and condomize—since it seemed impossible that Africans would persist in their sexual practices if they really understood how dangerous AIDS was and how to prevent it. It was not clear, however, and still is not clear, just what programs can effectively change longstanding practices of intimate sexual behavior. But something had to be done. Thus, the welter of organizations described in the previous chapter created a profusion of cultural objects and activities: posters and billboards, T-shirts and ribbons, messages disseminated through the media, and trainings. As this chapter illustrates, some of the cultural creations delighted the villagers while others offered stern admonitions with internationally sanctioned advice that villagers already knew.

THE DRAMAS OF AIDS

From the beginning, AIDS was a dramatic disease, and the global AIDS enterprise has been a cultural blockbuster.[2] It is no accident that the global rock star Bono has been a major player in international AIDS policy nor that AIDS in Africa has been the focus not only of celebrity endorsements, but of large commercial promotions like the Product (Red)™ campaign that combines the romance of altruism on behalf of distant others with the pleasures of consumption.[3] Like tuberculosis in the nineteenth century and cancer in the mid-twentieth century,[4] AIDS became a focus of fantasy, melodrama, horror, and mystery.

AIDS as a global cultural phenomenon emerged from the convergence of several forces. First, when the disease was diagnosed in the West, it was frighteningly mysterious biologically and medically, generating both panic and an enormous political mobilization by gay communities in Europe and North America, as well as in Brazil, Australia, and South Africa. The gay community's response to AIDS raised issues of identity and stigma, and responses to the epidemic in Africa also engaged those concerns.[5] Second, the same template for celebrity attention to Third World suffering that had already been set by the Live Aid concerts for famine relief could be adopted for AIDS.[6] Third, AIDS also coincided with, and partly stimulated, an eruption of globalized altruism, not only in giant development bureaucracies, but among citizens of rich countries who could afford to send money or go themselves to poor countries with an AIDS epidemic.[7] Fourth, the growing recognition by Evangelical Christian churches that their future lies in the Global South brought them to the AIDS enterprise.[8] Their support was symbolized by the strange-bedfellows alliance between the rock star Bono and the socially conservative US Senator Jesse Helms in the global AIDS crusade, and importantly, by the passage of PEPFAR in 2003.[9] Both glamorous and frightening, AIDS generated a sometimes riotously colorful cultural enterprise.[10]

Much of what the behemoth organizations we described in chapter 3 do is create cultural objects. Some fit everyday conceptions of culture: *products* such as songs, radio soap operas, T-shirts with logos and *performances* such as concerts and dramas. Others are cultural in the sense that they are an elaborately constituted set of symbols with a ritual significance that goes beyond their practical application: *themes* indexed by buzzwords, such as "empower women"; *categories* referred to by acronyms, such as OVC (translation: Orphans and Vulnerable Children); and *practices* such as testimonials to "positive living," training for volunteers, and paperwork (writing training manuals, national strategies, frameworks, and action plans). We analyze the themes and practices—what we think of as the "deep culture" of the AIDS industry, so taken for granted as not to seem like "culture" at all—in chapters 7 through 10. Here we take seriously the "froth," asking why donors and brokers produce so much of it, what it is supposed to accomplish, and how the conflicting pressures for innovation and conformity that shape other culture industries work themselves out in this one.[11]

PREVENTING AIDS WITH ENTERTAINMENT

The myriad concerts, dramas, and sports competitions promoted in the name of preventing AIDS are an odd commingling of instruction with enjoyment. A 2013 story from Kenya describes a concert for HIV prevention; it is easy to imagine the safe-sex message getting lost in the fun:[12]

Last week Durex sponsored a party at Galileo to inspire young people around the world to take charge of their sexual life. The event which was attended by the who-is-who in the showbiz arena in Nairobi is part of the world's largest youth-focused HIV and AIDS awareness and prevention campaign. [A representative of the sponsor] said, "We want to empower young people to adopt positive sexual attitudes and behavior—the project's aim is to work towards achieving an HIV-free generation while revolutionising sex education." On the decks during the fully attended event were DJ Nruff and DJ KYM who brought the house down with a mix of both old club hits and local hits. The gig dubbed the Durex Easy Connect party is part of the initiatives driven by aspiring young leaders to promote HIV awareness in high schools and universities. They also empower the youth to make informed decisions about sexual health and contraception through street theatre and train DJs as peer educators, relaying safe sex messages through their music.

Another example: a story in the Zimbabwe *Herald* announced the launch of "The SportAIDS Project, which seeks to contribute to the reduction of new HIV cases among youths through sport."[13] The SportAIDS spokesperson promised that

In the next two weeks we are going to unveil SportAIDS ambassadors and SportAIDS coaches who are sports personalities of repute who have either retired or are still active to spearhead the dissemination of basic information on HIV/AIDS to the youths in schools and communities.... These SportAIDS ambassadors and coaches will undergo HIV/AIDS awareness training so that they impart this knowledge together with their skills to talented young people in football, netball, volleyball, rugby, cricket, athletics, handball, basketball, tennis and swimming.

On a smaller scale, Malawian girls at a UNICEF-sponsored three-day camp combined soccer with HIV-prevention education. An American volunteer reported on her blog the camp's "GREAT SUCCESS!" concluding, "I think that the moment for me that made all of the planning and work worth it was one afternoon following the male and female condom demonstrations when I walked into the courtyard of the school only to find all of the girls at the tap filling the condoms with water and having a condom balloon fight ... sex education at its finest!"[14]

Another burst of cultural creativity led to condoms that promised "extra sexual pleasure." In 2004, a large Malawian NGO, Banja la Mtsogolo, launched the "studded, chocolate flavoured" Manyuchi condom. A reporter covering the launch wrote that even the packaging provided pleasure: "Whether a marketing strategy or not, on the pack's cover there is an attractive, strikingly beautiful, and sensually arousing picture of a young woman with the creamy, silky cleavage of her breasts in evidence—a picture that is likely to hook condomisers."[15] And condoms can be re-purposed as a fashion accessory. A wonderful example comes from Ghana, where news of "High Demand for Female Condoms" turned out to mean that enterprising women were making and selling colorful bangle bracelets by cutting out and dyeing the plastic rings meant to hold the female condom in place.[16] A newspaper article scolded the women:

When the demand for female condoms went up recently, health workers were expressing hope that finally its use was becoming popular with Ghanaian women.

They were wrong. The *Mirror* has learnt that there is a developing trend in the Odododiodoo area in Accra, particularly James Town and Bukom, where many patrons of female condoms have been using them for wrong purposes.[17]

Condoms are not the only material objects that sweeten the often bitter dictates of HIV prevention. The three-day soccer camp ended with games and "goodie bags of t-shirts and certificates." T-shirts with AIDS logos or prevention messages are everywhere. In Malawi, even bottled water carries HIV prevention messages—each bottle of Aqua Pure features a tiny red AIDS ribbon and the message: "Aqua Pure Cares. Love Life. Avoid HIV/Aids."

There are many reasons why HIV prevention takes such exuberant forms. Donors believe that their messages will go down more easily when conveyed in drama, music, or song, and they may be right. But there is another benefit to the profusion of cultural objects: donors, volunteers, and even more important, the donors' representatives on the ground—the brokers—need the conviction that their programs are successful, that they are reaching the youth, the villagers, or the at-risk girls the donors want to help. From talking with donors and brokers about their projects, we realized that events such as girls delightedly playing with condom-balloons, or enthusiastic youth participating in a netball tournament, make brokers and donors feel that their event has been a success, that they have really reached the people they hope to engage.

AIDS programming, whether it originates in Washington, Copenhagen, Geneva, or Lilongwe, is validated through the gut experience of the brokers and donors. When we interviewed brokers about their projects, they would first run through their program's official talking points. Then they would describe with evident pleasure villagers' delight in playing an AIDS-prevention game or students' enthusiasm about an AIDS drama. Those in charge of an annual AIDS Day event knew that it was successful when people laughed at the comedians, clapped and shouted to the music, ululated after an engaging drama.[18] In the visceral experience of the brokers, the entertainment that produces delight, engagement, joyous fun affirms the success of their efforts.

When it comes to creating major media campaigns, donors typically provide the theme and the target beneficiaries; an INGO is then selected to draw the blueprint. When the donor project is to be implemented by national NGOs in multiple countries, the INGO may design the cultural products centrally, using a photograph of Ghanaians for a poster portraying an ideal Malawian family, for example, or creating a media campaign with identical scripts for actors to deliver in multiple countries. What actually reaches villagers on the ground, however, may deviate from the script, often reflecting the local brokers' ingenuity in adapting to the context.

The scope of the cultural enterprise goes far beyond T-shirts, sports events, and chocolate-scented condoms. We show below the cultural products that NAC, charged with coordinating the AIDS enterprise in Malawi, listed in the column "Targets for the Year" in its 2006 Technical Progress Report, to show the Global Fund and the other major AIDS donors how Malawi had spent their money (items mentioned in chapter 1 are omitted).[19] Here is a sample of what "HIV prevention" largely consisted of:

PRIORITY AREA 1: PREVENTION AND BEHAVIOR CHANGE.

Goal: To Reduce the Spread of HIV in the General Population and in High Risk Sub-Groups

Objective 1: To Expand the Scope and Depth of HIV Communication for Effective Behaviour Change

1.1.1

80,000 copies of 5 types posters produced and distributed in 32
district and city assemblies
525,000 copies of 6 types leaflets produced and distributed in 32
district and city assemblies
200,000 copies of 6 types booklets produced and distributed in 32
district and city assemblies
930,000 copies of newsletters (including Youth Link newsletter)
produced and distributed in 32 district and city assemblies
45,000 copies of 5 types stickers, cards etc. produced and
distributed
52 TV programmes produced
104 hours of TV programmes aired on TVM
120 Radio programmes produced
300 hours of radio programmes/diaries aired on 6 radio stations
4,000 copies of 6 types of video programmes
300 Quarterly video shows in communities in all traditional authorities (Community outreach)
138 Concrete and steel billboards
26,250 T/shirts, caps of 10 different designs produced
30,000 of other communication materials (flipcharts, red ribbons,
wristbands, bandanas, pens, neck ties, placards)
225 Community Dialogues (10 sessions/district)
300 District Drama sessions (30 sessions/district) (including
PMTCT)
32 district based competitions (Quiz, drama, songs, best newspaper
articles, debate) held
4 Tours for media and performing artists conducted
2 Message Development workshops conducted

1.1.2

320 HIV and AIDS corners established
2,500 copies of books of 20 different titles procured and distributed
5 titles of books published and distributed
3 Book fairs organized and participated

Objective 2: To Promote and Support HIV Interventions Specifically
Designed for Youth

1.2.1. Action Plan Developed and disseminated

5,000 copies of action plan printed
Standard Lifeskills manual for out of school youths developed
5,000 Training packages for 5000 Youth Clubs printed
5,000 Copies of Lifeskills manual printed and distributed
32 District Youth Festivals conducted
3,000,000 Lifeskills learners guides for primary schools printed and
    distributed
20,060 lifeskills materials for secondary schools printed and
    distributed
43,000 primary school teachers trained in life skills by gender
9,000 Secondary school teachers trained by gender
600 Tertiary education teachers trained by gender
1,280 Lifeskills Master trainers and TOT [Trainers of Trainers] for
    schools and colleges trained by gender
3,200,000 Primary School pupils trained in lifeskills
180,000 Secondary School pupils trained in lifeskills
4,000 Tertiary School students trained in lifeskills

Objective 3: To reduce the Vulnerability of Malawians to HIV, Especially
Girls and Women

43,000 primary school teachers trained in life skills by gender
9,000 Secondary school teachers trained by gender
600 Tertiary education teachers trained by gender
1,280 Lifeskills Master trainers and TOT for schools and colleges
    trained by gender
3,200,000 Primary School pupils trained in lifeskills
180,000 Secondary School pupils trained in lifeskills
4,000 Tertiary School students trained in lifeskills

Many of the items on this list are manuals, learners guides, and other
materials for teaching "lifeskills" (more often written "life skills"), or they
are training for students in life skills, or training of teachers and others to
teach life skills. Life skills classes, which are supposed to teach decision-
making, self-esteem, and other skills for coping with life, are required in
Malawi's primary and secondary schools.

These objects and activities are scattered profusely across the landscape of AIDS altruism in Africa, raising two interrelated questions: Why
AIDS? And why has the response to AIDS relied so heavily on cultural
products to wage the fight? These two questions seem distinct, but the answers converge.

African AIDS became a global *cause célèbre* precisely because the initial culture assault was directed not at African villagers, but at Westerners. When AIDS was largely concentrated in Western countries' gay communities, advocates campaigned for recognition of the disease to generate sympathy and support for its victims (the creation and display of the AIDS quilt, for example, with its now more than 48,000 hand-made memorial panels), to fight stigma, and to galvanize support for treatment.[20] This campaign was the first identity-based social movement focused around a single disease.[21] Now that ribbons for everything from breast cancer to autism are everywhere, and walks, bicycle rides, and races testify to supporters' advocacy for varied diseases, it is hard to remember that AIDS advocates pioneered these forms of cultural mobilization.[22] Earlier celebrities had occasionally raised money for specific diseases—Jerry Lewis for Muscular Dystrophy, the March of Dimes for polio. But the cultural mobilization around AIDS in the West was unprecedented in its depth and breadth, and in linking disease to identity.[23]

The view of AIDS as requiring cultural struggle is rooted in the gay movement's focus on the assertion of identity.[24] For a movement whose central political act was "coming out," asserting an AIDS identity and fighting stigma made powerful sense. The fight against AIDS was, at its core, a cultural campaign directed outward to the wider public as well as toward mobilizing the gay community itself.

This model of a two-front cultural campaign provided the template for the battle against AIDS in Africa. Global publics had to be alarmed, moved, and inspired. Prominent figures like Stephen Lewis, the UN Special Representative for HIV/AIDS, and Kofi Annan, the UN Secretary General, gave speech after impassioned speech, produced press release after press release on the tragedy of AIDS, pleading for support.[25] Foundations funded authoritative reports detailing the dimensions of the crisis and the need for a response, and of course UNAIDS and its predecessor organization, the Global Program on AIDS, existed not only to coordinate the global response to the epidemic, but to mobilize financial and moral support for that response among governments and publics. Documentaries, celebrity supporters, and publicity from advocacy organizations highlighted the tragedy of AIDS orphans, the vulnerability of women to AIDS, and the suffering and death caused by the disease. Partly because of its protean image—a massive threat, poorly defined, seeming to touch on every area of life—AIDS also attracted diverse advocacy organizations, from human rights and feminist organizations, to those devoted to children, to those concerned with population, global security, peace and war. Each of these organizations found that it could join the AIDS fight, claiming its share of global attention and adding to the cultural construction of AIDS as a unique disease requiring urgent solutions.[26]

As in the gay communities of the West, transformation of African individuals and communities became central to HIV prevention. The behemoths did not have to start from scratch, however, but could draw on the past. First, as in the earlier campaigns in the West, people had to be taught, before it was too late, to name AIDS, to acknowledge its reality, and to see themselves as at risk for the disease.[27] Second, as in the international family planning movement of the 1960s, 1970s, and 1980s, which predicted and attempted to prevent a global catastrophe of overpopulation in poor countries, HIV prevention required a change in intimate practices, so reeducation was necessary. Indeed, many cultural objects on the landscape of HIV prevention (village dramas, condom songs, training volunteers) come directly from the repertoire of family planning programs.[28]

As the family planning movement discovered, transforming distant individuals and communities is extraordinarily difficult. For the case of HIV prevention, however, our argument is paradoxical. Precisely because a purely technical fix for HIV prevention remains elusive (condoms or vaginal microbicides, for example, don't work if people don't use them), the disease and the cultural transformations required to combat it appeal to donors and altruists who want not just to bring physical health, but to promote a more active, participatory, gender equal, autonomous modern selfhood.[29] At the same time, the absence of straightforward technical answers to the riddle of HIV prevention makes the creation of cultural objects, from children's games to song festivals to radio dramas and religious outreach, seem the best—or perhaps the only—way of combating HIV infection.

SOFT TECHNOLOGIES FOR HARD PROBLEMS

Getting people to change their behavior is hard: for some, experiencing the joys of sex with many partners, or, for many of us, eating ice cream or lounging on the sofa watching TV is an integral component of the good life. Changing the social norms of a community is even more difficult. So what is it that AIDS prevention organizations do? Outsiders to the AIDS enterprise may envision altruists cradling dying infants or emaciated women in their arms, but as the list of NAC's cultural products shows, much of what AIDS brokers actually do is produce posters, banners, dramas, songs, and billboards, organize the workshops and trainings that are central cultural practices of the AIDS enterprise, and write the myriad reports to be sent up the aid chain. Tragedy lurks backstage, inside huts or in clinic waiting rooms, but in public AIDS activities are often joyful, with laughter, clapping, and songs.

TECHNOLOGIES TO PREVENT HIV INFECTION IN YOUTH

As the efforts to prevent AIDS moved from targeting socially stigmatized "high risk groups" (such as sex workers and IV drug users) to the general population, "youth" became a popular target group. Perhaps youth seemed to the organizations that designed HIV prevention campaigns to be more malleable than adults, plus, they could be advised to abstain on moral as well as practical grounds, thus side-stepping the arguments we heard in Malawi that condoms were both illicit and ineffective. For youth, the NGOs' favored prevention technology was youth clubs. For youth clubs, the favorite activities were producing dramas to enlighten the villagers and organizing sports events, which were thought to keep youth too busy to have sex.

In the early 2000s, all sorts of organizations created youth clubs, often in secondary schools. We made a list of the diverse organizations that sent out brokers to create these groups in the areas where we stayed in rural Malawi: NAC, PSI, ADRA (Adventist Development and Relief Agency), UNICEF (United Nations Children's Emergency Fund), Save the Children, World Vision, the World Bank (through MASAF, the Malawi Social Action Fund), MACRO (Malawi AIDS Counseling and Resource Organization), Banja la Mtsogolo (a reproductive health organization), the Salvation Army, and DAPP (Development Aid People to People). A broker, or sometimes a government official, would visit the head of a school or a chief and ask him to call for youth volunteers to spread HIV prevention messages to villagers. The broker's stay was brief; on the second, and usually last, visit, the broker would conduct a training.[30]

Some AIDS clubs organized around sports, but we heard more about the dramas. In our descriptions of AIDS dramas, we rely mainly on the media and our local ethnographers. In addition, in 2006, we asked interviewers to visit some schools and find out whether their youth clubs were still active.[31]

In the accounts of the local ethnographers, the dramas delighted both audiences and the young actors. The description below has not been edited; the name of the ethnographer is a pseudonym:

We entered the class room and found many people laughing to what was happening. We found the group performing a drama concerning

AIDS. In the drama there were five people, father, mother, a son and a daughter and a doctor. The father and mother advised their children not to have sexual partners because it is through sex that one can get the disease of AIDS but the daughter did not follow her parents' advice and used to have sex with elders. She used to tell her brother that if she listens to the advice then she will not enjoy with life. She used to give her brother money to use for his break at school and tell him not to tell her mother that on that day she did not enter into the class. For she liked money and got a lot of money. She told her parents that she has left school and want to start a job in town, but instead of searching for job she went to live with a certain man who was a doctor who told her that he had much money to support her but she was unfaithful to the man and used to have sex with other men and later she started suffering seriously and then she went back to her parents but she was rejected and told that she did not listen to their advice and what did she want now.[32]

The drama also illustrates what we believe is quite common: the initial words of rejection are followed by forgiveness and care rather than stigma.

She apologised to her parents. Her father told her that he cannot help her because she is sick but that she must go [for help] to the one who have gave her the disease. Her brother and mother were caring for her in the kitchen where they had prepared a place for her but her father said that he will help her if she will be fine again but he is not sure that the daughter will be fine again.

Then there is a break for didactic interpretation and instruction lest some villagers miss the points.

Then the drama ended there and one of the actors come in front and said that we have seen what had happened to the daughter and that we should take an example, we should try to listen to elder's advice, AIDS is very dangerous and it has no cure so it is better for us to abstain from sex before marriage. He also said that when one wants to get married she must firstly have her blood tested for HIV together with her partner so that they should have a good plan for their future.

A second drama presented that day had an elaborate plot featuring a "sugar dad" (an older, wealthy man with many sexual partners) and the man's attempts to cure himself of AIDS by burying traditional medicines given him by an herbalist. When this fails, tragedy ensues: one of the sugar dad's partners takes poison and dies, and the man hangs himself (although he is rescued at the last minute by his watchman). The finale is again met with delighted laughter from the audience and another didactic scolding from a broker-in-charge, probably a teacher or a nurse charged with instructing the audience. In the excerpt below, it is clear that the speaker thinks that the audience of villagers is not sufficiently serious: AIDS is not a laughing matter.

> All the people who were watching the drama laughed and laughed because the actors were serious with their job. Then a certain lady came in front and said that we should not just laugh for nothing but we should learn something and she advised that if one tries to follow the advice that are given through many ways from different people such ways include through News papers, on the Radio, Posters, Magazines, Dramas and so many other ways one can be able to prevent the disease of AIDS and other sexually transmitted diseases such as gonorrhea and syphilis. She said that if one finds that she/he is HIV positive she/he must not worry because she/he is not going to die to-day and that if she/he can follow the advice given she/he must live longer before she/he started suffering.[33]

Just as there is little variation in the themes of country music (love, faithlessness, and heartbreak), there was little artistic innovation within the genre of youth dramas. The first part of the drama focuses on how HIV is spread and its deadly consequences, the second part on encouraging behavior change, testing for HIV, and compassion.

One of the reasons both donors and brokers consider youth AIDS clubs an ideal technology for HIV prevention is that they appear to be a way of changing youth behavior at little additional cost to the NGOs doing the implementation. The actors themselves are volunteers and thus do not need to be paid, and no money is provided for scenery or costumes. The dramas are clearly fun for the actors as well as the audience. Another reason may be that they are titillating; they depict people with loose, immoral sexual behavior. Apart from the fun of seeing friends and acquaintances dress up or play roles, there is the fun of depicting the very sexual licentiousness being criticized.[34] Seeing peers dress up as leering "sugar dads," mercenary strumpets, or staggering drunks is hilarious entertainment.

The actors in the drama are usually secondary school students, who in the context of the village are elites. Nationally, at the time, only 18 percent of students of an appropriate age to be in secondary school were enrolled (the percent is likely to be even lower in the rural areas than in the cities).[35] For these young men and women, delivering messages to villagers offers them an opportunity to confirm to themselves and others their identity as educated elites with an obligation to enlighten those less educated than they are.

Although the donors and brokers consider the dramas to be ways of "informing" or "sensitizing" the villagers, they often do not actually convey new information. Even those with only primary school or no schooling at all knew well before the country-wide formation of youth groups that HIV is sexually transmitted and that multiple partners put one at risk.[36] And they already knew the moral truths that AIDS leads to death and that this tragedy arises from succumbing to the temptations of wealth.[37] Nor do the dramas lead either actors or the audience to see themselves as at risk: stock characters who are flamboyantly immoral are used to make the moral points.

There is nothing new about using entertainment to deliver behavioral injunctions. Malawians and other Africans are used to having entertainment provided by those, from missionaries to NGOs, who are trying to enlighten them. Indeed, such efforts are very old, and post-independence African governments as well as outsiders have long used the media for their own purposes. During the years after independence in Malawi, Chancellor College had a drama group that went to the villages to show how to be a good farmer; later, dramas were used to promote population control through family planning.[38] And the practice of didactic interpretation would be familiar to the audiences for AIDS dramas, since it is also practiced in churches and classrooms.

AIDS dramas are sponsored—and their messages sometimes carefully massaged—by NGOs. A radio program, heard and summarized by an ethnographer, described how the dramas should be designed. At least as the adult educators envision it, the design should not be left up to the players. The instructions that the announcer, Chimwemwe, gives to listeners appear to be from a training manual:

Chimwemwe said it is very important that drama is not used to tell people what to do or not to do. When thinking of writing a play, the following things should be remembered. Firstly, there should be a brief introduction for each play before the performance. After the play, you should ask for comments about the play from the audience. The plays should try and create awareness about HIV/AIDS among young people and the general public.

The plays should help young people recognize HIV/AIDS as a problem that affects them too. The plays should help young people to face up to the risk of HIV/AIDS in their own lives and help to take preventative action. He also said that the plays should foster a caring attitude in communities for people living with AIDS. The play should try to avoid blaming anyone for the AIDS problems, like bar girls or truck drivers. Finally he said that the plays should have boy and girl characters. Boys and girls should not pretend to be adults and do adult things. The plays should be about relationships and problems faced by boys and girls. That was the end of the program and the announcer said that he will continue chatting with them next time.[39]

The youth dramas are repetitive, not only because the same messages appear over and over, but because they contain a few stock characters and stories (sugar dads, seductive school girls, family members who refuse to be advised or behave selfishly and learn to regret it) that the local audiences find engaging. But that entertainment value is costly for the implicit AIDS message: the people who are depicted as at risk are those who violate local cultural mores of cross-generational relationships, ignore the advice of elders, or refuse to share. If you do not fit that bill, you can be comforted that you are not really at risk.

Villagers and secondary school students had fun watching—or acting in—AIDS dramas. Those far from the villages, such as NAC or INGOs that developed AIDS communication strategies for broadcast media, tried hard to make sure that audiences were getting the proper messages (i.e., ones in which the idiom is that of the international injunctions rather than the local idiom of the youth dramas). Our information on media dramas suggests that the ratio of entertainment to stern advice is lower.[40] In a weekly program on AIDS broadcast on the Malawi Broadcasting Company, "We Are One," funded by NAC, the stock characters were more likely to be health officials delivering NAC-approved messages than sugar dads and seductive girls.[41] Programs typically began with a song or a drama followed by talking heads who interpreted the messages and advised listeners to heed them. The first episode began with a drama in which people were advised to get tested but refused, followed by a song. Then experts interpreted the entertainment: two doctors from Kamuzu Central Hospital (a government facility), a counselor from the National Association for People Living with HIV and AIDS in Malawi, and a journalist from the Media Institute of Southern Africa.

In 2005, NAC produced a compendium of 451 recommended AIDS messages organized by topic. The topics are those of the NAC strategy plans, which in turn reflect the priorities of the international AIDS community. Below are some of the sober injunctions:

Abstinence: "A wise girl doesn't engage in sexual activities in the name of love. A wise girl abstains." "Wise boys do not prove their manhood by having sex with girls."

Condom use: "If one of you has been found with HIV use condoms all the time to protect the other person." "Always use a condom even with your most trusted partner."

Gender-based violence: "Men respect yourself. Don't force your wife to have sex with you." "Leaders discuss with men the evils of violence against women."

The ABCs of prevention, added together, account for the largest proportion of NAC's recommended messages, 128. Abstinence, which we think is the least likely to be practiced, is clearly favored. Gender-based violence and giving care and support are preoccupations of donors, as is the emphasis on gender equality that infuses many of the messages.

NAC also hired the Media Council of Malawi to police whether media presentations of AIDS followed their guidelines.[42] For media presentations in January 2004, the monitors reported that, "Some plays and advertisements still do not send the intended HIV/AIDS awareness messages. TVM and MBC Radio 1 Tikuferanji play and Chishango Condom advertisement fall in this category of confusing messages." The monitoring report also objected to using Miss Malawi to deliver AIDS messages since, they wrote, some people think those in beauty pageants have loose morals. The report noted, however, that a beauty queen might deliver AIDS messages if she revealed her serostatus to support the claim that she does not change partners.

The barrage of cultural products assures the educated that the less educated cannot miss the point. Although our ethnographic data show that by the early 2000s it was widely known in rural villages that abstinence and fidelity would prevent HIV, the endless profusion of educational cultural activity reassured donors and brokers that they were doing something.

OTHER INTENTIONAL CULTURAL PRODUCTS

Like dramas and like much of AIDS cultural production, songs are produced locally by musicians who use their skills to educate. The brokers commission songs to accompany media presentations, and musicians sometimes write AIDS songs on their own, but in both cases they aspire to educate.

At many gatherings, we heard the participants sing a song referred to simply as the "AIDS song." Written by a Japanese volunteer working in a Malawian village, it was translated and recorded by a popular musician, Mlaka Malira, and became a number one hit on the radio. We heard it sung at HIV prevention trainings, as well as a training for early childhood educators. Although it seemed to us to have little to do with early childhood education, it appears that the AIDS song, like much of the AIDS culture, has become a taken-for-granted fixture of the local cultural scene.[43]

Malawi is not unusual in the popularity of AIDS songs, or in their use to deliver messages. A collection of articles on AIDS in music and the arts includes the music of Uganda, Zimbabwe, Kenya, Botswana, South Africa, and Ghana.[44] When AIDS arrived, the practices of promoting good behavior through culture had already been set: both donors and brokers knew what to do. They adapted cultural products, themes, performances, and practices—from advocacy for population control and family planning in the 1960s, Primary Health Care for All in the 1970s, Safe Motherhood in the 1980s, and Reproductive Health in the 1990s. The adaptations are minor: AIDS prevention campaigns now "sensitize" the public to the risk of AIDS instead of "raising awareness," the term of art in the population crisis era, and they produce curricula on "life skills," such as "decision-making," instead of curricula on "family life." As Paula Treichler has written, "Despite local adaptations, it sometimes seems as though public health campaigns draw ideas and images from some secret central vault, so similarly are they structured over time and space."[45]

Each of the national affiliates of PSI, a major contractor for USAID for decades, designs its own logo, but the social marketing strategies are standard. As one example, PSI produced a set of videos for multiple countries showing glamorous young people in a nightclub-like setting with the tag line: "One of these people is HIV positive. Can you tell which one? If you think it's hard to tell, you're wrong. It's impossible." The actors are local, and local brokers select their dress and the party venue. But the videos' visuals, theme, and wording are identical across countries, from Côte d'Ivoire, to Kenya, to Mali.[46]

Mixing entertainment and edification (sometimes called by their producers "infotainment" or "edutainment") can of course lead to trouble. A report on the failure of condom marketing to slow the AIDS epidemic includes visuals from a Kenyan condom commercial showing a stranger—an attractive boy—coming to the rescue when a pretty girl finds her water bottle is leaking. He unrolls a condom over the leaking water bottle (demonstrating that condoms are strong and don't leak) and then the boy and girl—strangers at the beginning of the episode—walk off together, sending a complexly mixed message.[47]

Whether or not deluging Malawians with cultural activities and cultural objects about AIDS actually adds to people's knowledge or influences their behavior, all this activity gives people something to do—the brokers as they produce and disseminate AIDS messages and the youth as they attend AIDS-themed concerts or participate in AIDS clubs which, their elders hope, will at least keep them out of trouble.

UNINTENTIONAL CULTURAL PRODUCTS

Many cultural products are "unintentional" in the sense that those who create them don't think of them as cultural products. But cultural products they surely are. Like the international rock concerts, the youth dramas, the banners, posters, and candlelight vigils, these are meant to instruct; unlike the dramas and songs, they are rarely intentionally humorous. We discuss these unintentional cultural products in more detail in chapters 7–10: here we introduce them briefly.

Unintentional cultural products include both themes and practices. By *themes,* we mean, for example, injunctions of global actors such as "end stigma and discrimination" or "empower vulnerable women." Announcing such themes can be used to focus attention and funding, as in the themes that UNAIDS makes central to its annual policy documents, with sections on "rights-based approaches to HIV" or "gender inequality and harmful gender norms" and calls for "programmes to empower those vulnerable to or living with HIV."[48] Malawian brokers then translate these themes into policy documents, and an AIDS NGO may introduce the new theme at an official "launch" by announcing a campaign to promote the female condom or to address the psychosocial needs of orphans. The messages are

73

then simplified for further dissemination through slogans (e.g., UNICEF banners on front pages of the newspapers in Malawi, saying "Stop Child Trafficking," the ubiquitous training manuals used to teach volunteers how to avoid "gender based violence," or the thousands of life skills manuals for teachers to instruct students in decision-making).

We distinguish *practices*—taken-for-granted categories of people and activities—from more concrete cultural products because they are so embedded in the normal routines of the AIDS enterprise. By categories, we mean the basic concepts and terminology NGOs and policy makers use to define officially designated recipients of programs and officially recognized activities. These are often established by donor policy and are useful for imposing order on the unruly confusion of actual AIDS activities through a standardizing rhetoric.[49] The categories become reified: HBC (Home Based Care), PMTCT (Prevention of Mother to Child Transmission); CSW (Commercial Sex Workers), MSM (Men who have Sex with Men), and OVC (Orphans and Vulnerable Children)—are, almost literally, terms of art with elaborately encoded meanings.[50] The early programs, for example, referred to those with AIDS as "victims," or those suffering from AIDS or dying of AIDS. But to make the point that people with AIDS were "living," not "dying," activists eventually settled on the term PLWA (People Living with AIDS), or sometimes PLWHA (People Living with HIV or AIDS), which rapidly became universal in programs, planning, funding, and administration.

Some of the terms have practical meanings, signaling consequential changes in policy. So VCT (Voluntary Counseling and Testing) became HTC (HIV Testing and Counseling) as it became less "voluntary," when health care providers sent their patients for testing before putting them on antiretroviral treatment.[51] Prostitutes became "commercial sex workers" in order to eliminate the derogatory implications of the term "prostitute" (even as African sex workers protested that what they did wasn't commercial, wasn't work, and wasn't about sex!).[52] The switch from programming for "gay men" to "MSM" signaled programs directed to all men who have sex with men and not just men who consider themselves homosexual. Acronyms then become reified: thus, caring for sick relatives is one thing, home based care is another; a traditional village activity of caring for the sick has become an institutionalized category for which community committees can receive HBC training and an HBC kit with aspirin and bandages.

Although it may sound strange to describe the themes donors promote, the categories they codify, and the performances they sponsor as "cultural products," this is precisely what they are. AIDS organizations "produce" symbolic elements like acronyms and slogans, performances like candlelight vigils, workshops, village meetings, and media campaigns, and objects such as T-shirts and condoms. The AIDS enterprise has also created a "market for testimonials" as HIV+ Africans are rewarded for testifying openly about their HIV status.[53] Thinking of these unintentional cultural products as "culture" fits John Meyer and Brian Rowan's argument that the apparently solid furnishings of the organizational world—offices, rules, programs—are all "myth and ceremony."[54] But thinking of themes and programs—and their many acronyms—as "cultural products" also emphasizes that policy makers are constantly reinventing the categories of AIDS policy in a dynamic, creative process.

INNOVATIONS AND ADAPTATIONS

The institutional altruists who are engaged in the production of AIDS culture are often deeply committed and frenetically busy. They have a lot to do. Institutional altruists specialize in designing and funding the products, paying the salaries of the brokers, monitoring the flows of funding to ensure that the money is spent and spent properly by the end of the fiscal year, and counting the numbers and types of products. Each of these activities requires standardized forms and reports, and requires the donors to train those who will have to fill them out.

The AIDS enterprise, however, also depends heavily on the brokers to reach the villagers. Sometimes they disseminate the cultural objects unchanged. At other times, the producers depart from the script—with results that can be very different from what the funders intended. Below is an excerpt from Watkins' field notes describing a trip to a village where her project was conducting a survey in the summer of 2006:

We get to the village and as usual a lot of standing around waiting for respondents. An old man comes to sit on a veranda, so I ask [an interviewer] to go with me to talk with him. Sitting near the old man is what looks like a couple—the woman is nursing a baby, the man is holding an older baby (not yet walking) and after a few minutes an energetic woman holding a notebook arrives. I ask about NGOs that do dramas in the village, the man says yes, a group called CRC does them, the man said he had watched it 3 times, the last time in March. I asked him and the others whether they went to the dramas because they were fun, entertainment, or whether it was to learn anything about AIDS, they said both. I asked what they learned that was new, lots of giggling, I heard *chimwerewere* [promiscuity], so I asked [the interviewer] to say they must have already known about stopping *chimwerewere*. The energetic woman said yes, but they also learned new things. I asked what? The woman giggled and said she couldn't talk about it, so I sent her and the interviewer behind the house. He came back and told me that the old man is her father-in-law so she can't talk freely, but that what they learned new was masturbation, "that was very new to her."

And another, even more creative adaptation, emerges in an ethnographer's description of a health talk at a local clinic:

Today I went to the under-five clinic where I wanted to weigh my baby. Before everything started the health surveillance Assistant (HSA) came with advise [*sic*] concerning Aids. He started with a question which states "what do you understand by the word AIDS" he repeated the question several times but nobody responded. Then he told us that if we are going to answer then we will go home early but if we will not answer he will leave us there up to twelve noon.[55]

The women finally offered that "AIDS is uncured disease" and that "AIDS is a disease that a person suffers from different diseases." The HSA then quizzed them on what those diseases are.

Before continuing with the advice the HSA started [a call-and-response song] which was going like this in Chichewa:

START: Dolo, dolo, dolo

ALL: Eeeeeeeeeee

START: Dolo, dolo, dolo

ALL: *Samala mayendedwe*

ALL: *Kuli Edzi, Edzi Adzi Eeeeee kuli Edzi samala payendedwe.* [Translated by the ethnographer as "one should take care when walking because there is AIDS."]

We all laughed because of how the HSA was singing and dancing while pointing where he said you can find AIDS (his secret part).

Even though Malawians did not need to be informed that AIDS was in their communities, they clearly enjoyed the performances produced by the AIDS enterprise—the youth dramas, the songs, and the occasional public celebrations such as AIDS Day. From the point of view of donors, these and the other activities described in this chapter counted as "doing something" to persuade people to prevent HIV. It is difficult, however, for us to believe that any of these were more effective than the experience of seeing relatives, neighbors, and friends die. Nonetheless, for donors, brokers, and villagers, the profusion of AIDS culture was a major way—often *the* major way—of fighting the epidemic.

CHAPTER 5

GETTING TO KNOW BROKERS

IN THE ROMANCE OF AIDS altruism, brokers must bridge the distance between the imaginations and aspirations of the altruists and those of the people they aim to help. For some brokers, this is simply a job that puts food on the table and pays children's school fees; for others, it is also a mission to bring development to their countrymen; and for still others, it is an occasional gig—when an opportunity arises, they offer their services.

Brokers do not get much attention from the altruists; it is the beneficiaries who captivate the altruists' imagination. But it is the brokers who ultimately have the power to fulfill or waylay donor dreams. We begin getting to know them better by showing how the AIDS money that flooded into Malawi stimulated aspirations for social and economic mobility. We then introduce brokers along the aid chain—first formally, in their offices, and then informally, in their homes, as they try to juggle their professional and personal obligations and as they attempt to buffer the insecurity produced by the frenetic AIDS enterprise.

We start with the brokers nearest the top of the aid chain, those whom we call the Cosmopolitan and the National Elites. But we pay most attention to the two sets of brokers who are most critical for turning donor dreams into realities: the District Elites, NGO brokers in offices in dusty district capitals whom donors charge with reaching the beneficiaries in the villages; and the Interstitial Elites, young men and women from the villages who have no offices but volunteer to deliver global messages to villagers in the hope that one day they too will find a job with an NGO.

THE LANDSCAPE OF MONEY

The headline of a 2007 article in a Malawi newspaper, *The Nation,* was succinct: "So AIDS is money?"[1] Money poured into the country to mitigate the consequences of AIDS. Newspapers announced the amounts: "Canada Grants K700 Million for HIV/Aids"; "UNFPA, BLM Launch K437.5m Youth Project"; "MSF Assists Orphans with Items Worth K130,000"; "Bush Pledges $500m ... to Help Fight HIV/Aids"; "GAIA Launches K42.6m Project for Orphans, Aids Projects."[2] From the perspective of villagers, these were huge sums; from the perspective of brokers, AIDS offered new opportunities.

Donors dedicated much of the AIDS money that flooded into Malawi to paying the rent of NGO offices, funding the salaries of the brokers, and expanding the number of NGOs working on HIV prevention or orphans. Some NGOs emerged *de novo* as existing community groups caring for relatives and neighbors transformed themselves into NGOs to qualify for foreign funding. Some NGOs that had focused on agriculture or education became AIDS NGOs. Many NGOs took an easier route, simply adding AIDS to their portfolios. With the surge in NGOs, brokers and those who aspired to be brokers did particularly well.

Civil servants also benefited, not only from the money donors spent for cultural productions that might discourage HIV transmission and encourage care for the infected, but also from Global Fund money NAC wisely distributed to government ministries as a form of patronage and justified as a "cross-cutting" AIDS intervention. Whatever the ministry's task, from "Gender, Children, Disability and Social Welfare" to "National Defense" to "Transport and Public Works," it also needed to do AIDS.

Poor villagers benefitted from programs that offered HIV testing, and later, from antiretroviral drugs. But villagers who got material resources were usually village elites: those related to the chief and those able to speak English. They were the ones who received invitations to attend a training with allowances. Villagers might also benefit if they were fortunate enough to have a relative in the city who held an NGO job and could be tapped in emergencies. Mostly, however, the brokers with offices in the cities or in district capitals were the ones who benefitted materially from the torrent of AIDS money.

BROKERS IN THEIR OFFICES

Where brokers are in the aid chain is determined almost entirely by differences in their educational credentials. Educated elites, unlike the vast majority of Malawians, have a credential that qualifies them for a white-collar job. Their credentials also largely determine where their office is and thus both their social and geographic proximity to donors and their social and geographic distance from the would-be beneficiaries.[3] We describe Malawian brokers here. The specifics are likely to vary across African countries, depending on factors such as the country's size, colonial past, and economic status, but the general patterns are common throughout sub-Saharan Africa.

Chapter 5

Cosmopolitan Elites

These Malawians perch at the top of the aid chain, farthest from the imagined beneficiaries and closest to the donors to whom they are directly accountable. They gain legitimacy with an internationally prestigious credential such as a PhD or MD from a foreign university. They may personally meet with donors, and they have contacts outside the country forged through attendance at international meetings. They work in the country office of an international organization, such as World Vision or Save the Children, or in a UN agency, with offices in Lilongwe, the capital city, where they—and visiting donors—have convenient access to the larger of the country's two international airports. Their primary responsibilities are to translate the policies of the behemoth aid organizations into national policy strategies and to monitor the expenses and outputs of the subcontracting organizations that implement the donors' projects. Cosmopolitan brokers can afford private hospitals and private schools for their families, and they can patronize the new supermarkets selling goods imported from South Africa.

High-level brokers are more likely than others in the aid chain to interact with international development professionals such as the director of the London office of ActionAid or a consultant who has come from the World Bank to provide technical expertise. These are the brokers who are most likely to brief donors about Malawi. But we have found that the highly educated brokers often know less than we do about rural life. Most of those we interviewed were the children of teachers or civil servants, grew up in a city, and were educated in English. If they go to their father's or mother's home village, it is for a brief holiday. When they describe the villagers to visitors, they emphasize their backwardness and what they call the villagers' "harmful cultural practices" (see chapter 8).

Interactions with visiting dignitaries may result in invitations for travel to international conferences, which in turn provide opportunities to learn the latest "best practices" that the brokers bring back to their organizations or to hear about the next new thing on donor agendas, permitting their organizations to get ahead of the curve.[4] Meetings abroad also provide allowances at international rates, so that by sleeping on an American friend's floor for a few nights, brokers can net enough cash to buy land or build a house back home.

Cosmopolitan brokers help shape donor images of local customs and culture. Anthropologist Sally Engle Merry notes "a whiff of the notion of the primitive" when human rights activists at international meetings discuss "culture" in their native countries: "As I observed UN meetings, I found that transnational elites often located culture 'out there' in villages and rural areas rather than 'in here' in their offices and conference rooms."[5] Merry describes a Nigerian human rights activist, speaking in an "elegant conference room" in Geneva:

> She described the plight of widows in Nigeria and the humiliations widowhood rituals inflicted on women. Widows were forced to marry their dead husband's brother, blamed for their husband's death, and forced to undergo ordeals to determine their responsibility, such as drinking the water used to wash the corpse. They were forced to stay in a room alone and sit on ashes, expected to wear tattered clothes, fed on a broken plate, and sometimes prohibited from looking at the person who brings their food. Widows were expected to cry so loudly that their wails were audible to people outside the compound and were taunted by their in-laws if they failed.

This picture of devastation changed, however, when she later explained to the anthropologist that widowhood rituals

> were particularly difficult for urban educated women like her. She is a lawyer, fluent in English, and living in a major urban center. She is employed by a US-based human rights NGO. When women in her class are widowed, they find themselves journeying to the village of their husbands where they are subjected to rituals by relatives who may not have liked the woman or the way she treated the family while her husband was alive. Village women, she told me, do not really mind these rituals.[6]

Cosmopolitan elites thus participate as peers with international donors and other global elites, even while they are expected to represent the experiences of local people—poor village women, for example—of whose lives they know very little.

National Elites

Many well-educated Malawians have found jobs staffing the offices of the international and national NGOs in Malawi. They may occasionally have direct contact with foreigners, but they are more likely to broker by processing crucial documents, such as proposals for funding and monitoring and evaluation reports that travel from their offices to donor offices abroad.

Although similar in many ways to the cosmopolitan elites, the national elites differ in ways that matter. They are less likely to have a PhD and their MA or diploma is likely to be from a university in Malawi or in another African country. They are also less likely to know expatriates and to travel to international conferences; they do attend well-funded workshops in their own or in nearby African countries. Most work and live in Lilongwe, but some work in one of Malawi's three other cities: Blantyre, the sprawling commercial capital; Mzuzu, the third largest city, far in the north of the country; and Zomba, the cool and leafy pre-independence capital.

District Elites

The district elites may work in a local office of an INGO, or they may be individual altruists' personal brokers, like Teresa whom we described in chapter 2, providing guidance and running projects when the altruists go home. These brokers work and live in one of the twenty-eight district capitals. For most of them, it is a long drive to the airports in Lilongwe and Blantyre. But they are much closer to the beneficiaries than are the cosmopolitan or national elites. The district capitals are surrounded by villages. The task of NGO brokers in the districts is to implement donor dreams on the ground—to reach and transform the beneficiaries. Although donors are unlikely to know their district brokers, the success or failure of donor projects depends far more on them than on the cosmopolitan or national elites.

Balaka District in southern Malawi is a good setting for observing district elites. Balaka is popular with both institutional and freelance altruists. It ranks second among all districts (excluding the cities) in the amount of foreign aid per capita allocated between 1999 and 2011: approximately $4.50 per person.[7] This does not mean that many, or even any, beneficiaries ever see the amount of kwacha that $4.50 represents; rather, it is the best estimate of money spent for aid projects of all sorts—from agricultural subsidies to antiretroviral therapy provision—in Balaka. The density of altruists in this district made it an attractive setting for our research.

Readers will have an idea from television of what a third-world city and a third-world village look like but are unlikely to have an image of a district capital. Below is a description, taken from the field notes of a graduate student, Tom Hannan, who was studying the activities of district brokers and staying with us in the Catholic Women's guest house in Balaka.[8]

Access to the town is via one of two paved roads, usually by sharing an aging minibus with people making up perhaps double its nominal seating capacity, and most likely either the comforting aroma of huge bags of sundried fish, or bags of maize.

As one wanders through the town, the two paved roads surround the town's bustling center of activity, a large open market where women sit next to the displays of fruit and vegetables they are selling—tomatoes neatly stacked in pyramid formation—and men and women stand and sit by coolers packed with freezer bags of fruit juices for sale.... [T]hree small supermarkets in a row sit adjacent to this central market. Other shops and several bars surround this marketplace.... Surrounding this small town, and throughout Balaka district, are hundreds of villages of subsistence farmers.

At the market, there were walls dedicated to large painted, often faded, advertisements, including one for the CARE female condom, one for Population Services International, instructing people to wash their hands before cooking, and one for the Balaka Debate Club ("For civic and sensitisation development: Knowledge is power") featuring a group of nine men and women sitting on a rug under a tree, arms by their sides or on their laps, all facing and listening to one man with arms raised, gesticulating as if making an important point.[9]

It was not difficult for Hannan to locate the district offices of international and national NGOs, but harder to find the small NGOs, some of which were established by Malawians and others by butterfly altruists. The subcontractor NGOs were on NGO row, not far from the market. At the time of Hannan's research, these included Concern Universal, World Vision, the Women's Legal Resources Centre, the USAID-supported Basic Support for Institutionalizing Child Survival (BASICS), the USAID-supported Management Sciences for Health (MSH), and two microcredit organizations, the Foundation for International Community Assistance (FINCA) and the Finance Trust for the Self-Employed (FITSE). A few small one- or two-room local NGOs were scattered around the town. Some were functioning, some had hand-lettered signs but were shuttered, and others appeared to be largely aspirational, with plans but no funds.

To find the independent NGOs, Hannan walked around the town, looking for signs on buildings. He then interviewed a staff member, usually the director (who was sometimes the only staff member), and asked about the location of other small NGOs. Like the subcontractor NGOs described in chapter 3, many claimed multiple aims in order to attract multiple donors. Among those that Hannan found was one that the director said was addressing AIDS, human rights, "civic education," agriculture, improving

FIGURE 5.1. NGO signs on road leading into Balaka, capital of Balaka district in southern Malawi. Most district capitals, and even small trading centers, have a cluster of NGO signs, like these near NGO Row in Balaka. *Photo: Donald J. Treiman.*

school education, youth and child development, and life skills. Others claimed to conduct disaster relief, to "sensitize people on how to develop themselves," and to pay some children's school fees. Two foreign-funded NGOs, with assistance from church groups and a wealthy donor, had built a health center and a primary school.

The district elites include not only NGO brokers but also government officials and town fathers such as prominent businessmen, local politicians, religious leaders, traditional leaders such as important chiefs, and directors of small NGOs. NGO brokers and government officials are likely to have a degree, or at least a one-or-two year diploma, from a Malawian university. The duties of the district government officials intersect with those of the brokers: they assign intervention areas for NGOs wishing to work in the district, and when funds for transportation and allowances are available, they attend meetings with NGO brokers to keep track of project activities in their areas. Some of the brokers and government officials whom we, our graduate students, or colleagues interviewed were eager to enter the national elite and advance to an office in Lilongwe or Blantyre; others have made a life for themselves in the district and intend to stay.

The town fathers have more diverse educational credentials, or perhaps none beyond primary school, and they are more closely tied to the local community than the more transient NGO staff. Earlier, we described the eager brokers who welcome and guide the small-scale altruists arriving in backwaters such as Balaka town. Like Pastor Daniel and the director of the local NGO our graduate student visited (see chapter 2), they may have their own group of orphans for whom they seek donor support or they may, like the district officials and the local staff of national or international NGOs, help direct potential altruists to the projects of their friends or clients. They are often eager for whatever contacts a foreigner might provide and talk wistfully about the possibility of going abroad for a credential or moving to the city. But many town fathers are locally oriented and seek to use whatever resources outsiders provide to reinforce their own relationships and their standing in the community. Their local networks of mutual support and patronage are a priority, and they often see themselves as guardians of moral order in their community.

District brokers encounter villagers daily. Many back-country people, for example, sell produce at an open-air market in the center of town, not far from the offices of the district government and NGO row. District brokers also often encounter each other. They, district civil servants, and town fathers meet and mingle at lunch or outside the office of the district commissioner where they gossip, share newspapers, and check to see if the sole district government vehicle might be making a trip to Lilongwe or Blantyre so that they, or a relative, can hitch a ride.

District brokers are, however, unlikely to meet a visiting representative of a behemoth donor. A Crisis Corps volunteer (a specialized position in the Peace Corps) at the office of a District AIDS Coordinator told us that in the months she had been there, only once did anyone from NAC, which at the time had Global Fund money to support dozens of tiny CBOs, come to the coordinator's office. The lone visitor came in a NAC vehicle, called a meeting, explained a new mode of reporting, and left in time to be home for dinner.[10] Unless district brokers are fortunate enough to be invited to a workshop in the capital, making the trip by minibus is a hassle, and if they go, they are unlikely to be home for dinner.

Geography in a poor country like Malawi—and in much of Africa and the developing world—has implications that donors and other outsiders can scarcely appreciate. Where private vehicles are a rare luxury and transportation for most people is walking, riding on the back of a bicycle taxi for distances of a few kilometers, or squeezing into an overcrowded minibus for longer distances, geography matters enormously. To live in a village is usually to live without electricity, running water, or roads, connected to the larger world perhaps by a cell phone (which must still be charged at a kiosk in town) or bicycle but otherwise by a foot path and then a dirt road to the nearest market. To live in a district town is to have access to a market and a few shops, to electricity and running water, a hospital, and a secondary school. Newspapers, with their vital job advertisements, may arrive in town erratically and are shared. The expense of transport, however, leaves even town dwellers very far from the opportunities for jobs and contacts that a city can provide.

For those who get jobs with large NGOs and international organizations in the cities or district capitals, a major perk is access to a project vehicle and driver, not as a European or North American might imagine, to avoid the tedium of driving one's own car, but simply to have convenient transport—to be able to go back and forth between Lilongwe and Blantyre in a white 4x4 with a UN, EU, or NGO logo on the side. The project vehicle can also be used unofficially for personal trips and to do a favor for a friend or relative who needs transport. Family and neighbors may expect to get rides for themselves, animals, and goods, thus creating tension for the broker who risks being reprimanded by the project director for unauthorized use of the vehicle.

WHAT DO BROKERS DO? AND NOT DO?

Whether NGO brokers live in a city or district capital, whether they have a PhD, an MA, or just a diploma, whether they work for a large international NGO or a small local one, what they do in the office is much the same: manage a chain of paperwork that links the offices of the brokers at the top to the offices of those at the bottom. To translate donor dreams into activities, brokers produce action plans with budgets, documents monitoring the progress of the project and its spending, and mid-term and final project reports. A district broker described the chain of documents succinctly: "Because we have a hierarchy, we cannot talk direct to USAID; we can only talk to our bosses and our bosses send this request to donors."[11]

The cosmopolitan and national brokers we interviewed seemed to be very busy; they were constantly interrupted by a co-worker coming with a question, by phone calls, or by foreign visitors such as ourselves. When they leave the office, it is either to take care of their other obligations, such as to visit a relative in the hospital or to attend a meeting, usually at a hotel. If the meeting is to be short, it is likely to be in the same city as their office; if it is a several-day meeting, those with offices in Lilongwe prefer to meet in Blantyre and vice versa, because traveling justifies allowances and per diems. When we were in district offices, the brokers seemed to be less busy and more interested in learning whether we might become patrons able to assist them personally. When district brokers leave their offices for professional reasons, it is for a meeting at a nearby venue with representatives of the district NGOs or district government officials or for a trip to Lilongwe or Blantyre for a workshop.

What district NGO brokers rarely do, however, is go to the villages where their project beneficiaries live. When they do, it is to announce a new project, to organize an event for a visiting dignitary, or briefly to monitor local programs. Because they do not visit regularly, they do not see the full range of the project problems, particularly because the responsible locals are reluctant to alert them to any issues while the money is still flowing. Thus, even when district brokers make monitoring visits, the trips are often of little use. When we interviewed district elites, we asked them about their experiences in the villages. Almost invariably, they explained that they wanted to go to the villages but were too busy to visit because they had a report to finish or a proposal to write, and besides, their vehicles did not have petrol or were broken. Of course, sometimes the vehicle is not broken and there is money for petrol, but the roads are bumpy, there is no place to eat, no electricity, and no toilets, only pit latrines.

District brokers are therefore unlikely to know of problems with donor projects. For example, a maternal, infant, and child health project distributed mobile phones to community volunteers so that the women in the villages could call a hot line for advice from a health worker. Not until the project was evaluated by outside evaluators did the INGO learn that the village chiefs, who are very influential in rural Malawi, were angry that they had not received phones and thus did not support the project.

Another problem—and we think a more serious one—is that even when brokers know that there are problems with a project, they are unlikely to tell their bosses. One project provided nurses with tablet computers to book appointments electronically at antenatal clinics for pregnant women. The nurses would know how many women were to come each day and setting appointments would avoid having the women wait for hours to be seen. Two Americans from the stateside NGO, Marjorie and Helen, introduced the booking system to the staff at the health facility. The introduction was a complete failure. First, the nurses did not want to learn how to use the tablets; they said they had their own system. Second, there were only three nurses, and since one had to be on maternity call each night and might have to go home to rest the next day, two nurses typically faced a waiting room packed with women coming for antenatal care, a sick child, or their own health problems. Moreover, using such a system and letting

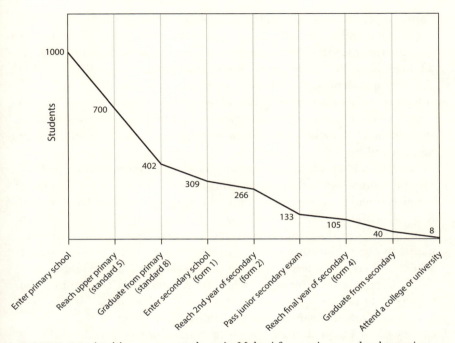

FIGURE 5.2. Attrition among students in Malawi from primary school to university. Although most children in Malawi start primary school, attrition is steep. *Based on Margaret Frye, "Bright Futures in Malawi's New Dawn: Educational Aspirations as Assertions of Identity." American Journal of Sociology 117 (2012), figure 3, p. 1578.*

what few others do: they have a secondary school degree. But they have not yet found jobs, so many remain in the villages they long to leave. For them, the NGOs are both a lifeline—a link to possibilities beyond the village—and, all too frequently, a source of disappointed hopes. Their aspirations and the uncertainty with which they live make them particularly sympathetic actors in the NGO drama.

Unlike the cosmopolitan, national, or even most district-level brokers, the interstitial elites have not gone beyond secondary school, either because they were unable to pass the exams for admission to a university or because their parents could not pay the fees. Figure 5.2 shows just how few Malawians have attended a college or a university, or even completed secondary school.

The figure was produced by Margaret Frye using UNESCO data.[13] As of the early 2000s, when many of the brokers we interviewed were in school, of one thousand Malawian children who began primary school, only forty would attain the prestigious secondary school credential—the

Form 4 diploma—and only eight would attend a college or university. Parents in rural Malawi aspire to have their children attend secondary schools and describe the sacrifices they have made to pay the fees. They consider it an investment that would benefit the family over the child's lifetime. One survey respondent in rural Malawi said, "But school should be their future, if there is an opportunity that they will get a good job or will lead a better life then let it be what God gave him. If that happens, it will be up to the child to think how they can help the parents" (John, fifty-four years old, ten children).[14]

Not all children of subsistence farmers aspire to more education. They may be content where they are, they may prefer to advance through commercial activities, or they may simply be resigned to the likelihood that they are unable to climb the ladder of credentials. For those who aspire to a job in the formal sector, however, the path is narrow. The dreams stimulated by the aid industry turn out to be fantasies, and most drop out of school. Others, our interstitial elites, keep hoping against the odds.

The interstitial elites play a key role in the romance of AIDS altruism. The objects of the donors' intentions are the villagers, whose behavior they wish to change. Only through the media—radio and the national newspapers—can the donors hope to reach the villagers more or less directly, and even then, many villagers do not have a radio, and a much-read used newspaper makes it to a village only rarely. For anything that requires actually delivering programs to the village, there is a "last mile" necessary to connect donors' dreams with village realities, much as the post office depends on mail carriers to deliver a letter to a house. The interstitial elites are valuable to the district brokers who implement projects since most actually live in the villages or are at least willing to go there; they are valuable to the donors because they are willing to work for free, at least for a while.

These young men and women enter fervently into the romance of the AIDS enterprise. One of our earliest, most enlightening, and at the time astonishing encounters with interstitial elites illustrates how imaginations were being transformed by the AIDS enterprise. At the guest house where we were staying, we met two well-dressed young men, both secondary school graduates with aspirations for social and economic mobility, attending a training on HIV prevention. They told us of having applied through the district World Vision office for funding for their AIDS youth club. When they returned to the office some months later to inquire about the application, they were shouted at and told to go away. We expected that they would have been angry. Their response was that, no, they were not angry. They said, "For us, World Vision is a glittering castle."[15] Their story was that the glittering castle (the mirage) World Vision held out is what led them to form their AIDS prevention youth group and to pursue their mission. World Vision, like other NGOs, offered them the trainings that kept alive their sense of themselves as modern—in their clean, pressed shirts and slacks, discussing decision-making, the physiology of sex, and the morality of condoms—in the absence, but still in the hope, of jobs in the formal economy.

It is among the interstitial elites that donor dreams and local aspirations both mesh and clash most forcefully. The aspiring elites are the front-line cadres in the AIDS fight. They typically begin as volunteers for an NGO project. Some, the lucky ones, eventually find a paid position in a small NGO, but many remain volunteers. From the perspective of the donors and the NGOs, volunteers make a project "sustainable."

The term "sustainable development" originated in the search for ecologically durable forms of economic development, but the ideal of sustainability has increasingly become a conscious policy of donors in a more comprehensive sense. Donors seek projects that they hope recipients will be able and willing to sustain after the donor—and the donor's funding—departs.[16] For this, they need volunteers who do not have to be paid; the interstitial elites provide the volunteers who sustain the donors' dreams.

Donors might imagine volunteers as ordinary poor villagers so committed to caring for their fellows that they will work for NGO projects without pay. But ordinary villagers do not normally become volunteers. They do not have the level of literacy (and certainly not the mastery of English) that most NGOs require of participants in a "training," and they are busy trying to manage their insecure rural livelihoods—farming, petty trading, gathering firewood, pounding maize, repairing their huts, and making the sometimes long walk to a health clinic or trading center. So it is the interstitial elites, with education and wider ambitions, who make possible the image of sustainable projects staffed by "volunteers."

The interstitial elites are geographically situated in the villages or small towns and trading centers, but their aspirations reach far beyond. These aspirations are defined by the education they have (an MSCE, the tough post-secondary school exam) and the education that they do not have (a university degree or beyond). They were born and raised in a village, but, unlike most others with that background, managed to complete secondary school and thus consider themselves—and are considered by their families and neighbors—as an educated elite. Some, like Maxwell Honde in the next chapter, have remained in their home villages, and some may have made it to a town after years of volunteering. Most of the ones we met were precariously balanced between a village, where circumstances still kept them, and a local town or district capital where they sought wider possibilities. While they are categorized as "youth" and may participate in an AIDS youth club or be trained as youth peer educators, their ages range from early twenties to forty or more.

The channels that carry donor resources and opportunities through the meeting rooms of the capital's hotels and NGO offices narrow to a sludgy stream in the district capitals. But however slight the trickle of actual resources and opportunities, this thin stream sounds like a babbling brook to the thirsty hopefuls clinging to worn copies of their MSCE certificates and looking for a way out of agricultural drudgery in the village. While the interstitial elites are meant to be the ultimate intermediaries who transmit government and donor programs to the beneficiaries of international altruism, in fact those local brokers, the interstitial elites, are often where the trickle of benefits donors have to offer actually finishes up.

Volunteers

Why would young men and women with precarious livelihoods work without pay for an NGO? In many of our interviews, they say it is to "benefit my community," but there are other motivations as well. Much as university graduates in the US will take an unpaid internship with the hope of getting experience that makes them more competitive in the job market, they volunteer, hoping to parlay that into a job. In addition, the interstitial elites are eager for whatever bits of information, education, and traces of cosmopolitan discourse have filtered downstream to them. As volunteers in HIV prevention and in care for the sick and for orphans and as beneficiaries of NGO trainings, they embrace donor-sponsored themes, explaining to us with enthusiasm how they have learned the principles of "decision-making" or debated the morality of condom use in an AIDS training. They also embrace training. A young man says earnestly, "we need gender sensitization"; a woman living with AIDS explains how her support group is being trained about the problem of "stigma." It is as if all the currents of thought from upstream wash down to these eager recipients, who drink deeply of whatever they can imbibe.

Interstitial elites demonstrate a flexible opportunism, a restless search for ways to survive economically.[17] Although they are being trained to be volunteers, they, like the brokers above them, also benefit materially from the allowances that accompany a training: a per diem and allowances for food, accommodation, and transport. Thus, volunteering becomes another livelihood strategy. The trainings also usually provide a certificate that the volunteers can display to a potential employer as evidence that they are knowledgeable and worthy.

As we mentioned above, in the early 2000s, youth groups were in fashion among the HIV prevention community. Initially, brokers approached headmasters to organize youth clubs in secondary schools. A representative of an NGO (or sometimes the government) would encourage students to create a club to put on HIV-prevention dramas in the villages. The broker would then return and conduct a training for which the participants would receive an allowance—highly prized by young people who had very little access to cash.

In 2005, we interviewed students and headmasters at eighteen school-based youth clubs and learned our first lesson about the unsustainability of volunteers. Although the headmasters said the groups were active, that "they just needed more resources," the students said that the youth clubs no longer functioned because members dropped out when they realized there would be no further resources. One said

> ... that he dropped because he did not benefit from the club there were no allowances given from NGOs and he said he expected to be getting at least a financial support from well-wishers or NGOs. These organisations just know to tell us to educate the people on HIV-AIDS perform plays but they do not think of us they just use us.
>
> They come here in expensive vehicles fooling us here in the village, in some towns people are at least supported even with uniform, bicycles why not here?[18]

Apparently, the sponsors did not return to the schools after the training and so they did not know that many of the youth groups were no longer functioning. Still, NGOs continue to form volunteer groups, not just for school youth but for secondary school graduates in the rural areas, our interstitial elites, and also for village adults.[19]

Trueman Uzeyani's very mixed career illustrates the aspirations and insecurities of the interstitial elites as they try again and again to gain a toehold on the unstable terrain of programs and volunteer projects. We spoke with him many times, following him from a stint as a survey interviewer to a youth volunteer, then to a paid position with an NGO, then to unemployment, and, the last we heard, to enrollment in a course to learn accounting.[20]

Trueman's erratic career began in 2004, when many donors were funding youth clubs. His uncle, a village chief, advised him to create a club, which he did. Trueman invited six boys and girls, good friends within his village, and two from a nearby village. They wrote a constitution and set up a bank account—preconditions for funding from NAC and other donors.

> After we agreed there is a need, I created some posters about the group, invited people.... Forty-five came for first meetings, [we] elected president, secretary, treasurer, I was the treasurer. We agreed each member should contribute 5 kwacha a month. [We] agreed to do some *ganyu* [day labor], we had land to grow maize and sweet potatoes.

They sold the crop and opened a bank account. "At that point we didn't know how to write a proposal." When asked whether the forty-five who started still came, he said no. Like other educated youth who aspire to paid NGO positions, he criticized his fellows for their mercenary motives:

> The problem in villages is when you are trying to organize such things they have a different mentality, they say "perhaps this one can get money somewhere, perhaps we can get some," but when it doesn't happen little by little they are dropping, twenty are left.

At the time we talked with Trueman, fifteen were active, mostly those who had some secondary education and might thus hope that an NGO would include them in a training. Trueman did well. His group received money from NAC to educate youth, and he was hired as a paid coordinator for YONECO (Youth Net and Counseling), a very successful Malawian NGO, which built its appeal to donors on its ability to reach village youth. Trueman's job was to hold trainings for other villagers to disseminate global messages:

> They should take part in advocating messages of HIV, stigma and discrimination, sometimes we go as far as human rights, we look into the areas of poverty which is fueling the spread of HIV, we tell them how they can keep well financially and whatever. We promote sports.... In the time back it was hard to get people to a meeting of HIV/AIDS so we try another way around, organize football, net- ball.... [I]t is working, they come in large numbers, this way we get a multitude of people.... Mostly they are interested in sports, but we say "you have to do this as well." Sports keep them busy.

When asked whether the youth already know what they need to know about AIDS—that it is spread by sex and is fatal—he presented the villagers as ignorant:

> in fact all of them know much of HIV/AIDS, but there are misconceptions, some say they can't use a condom because it is infected with the virus. And they don't know the difference between HIV and AIDS.

By 2006, Trueman no longer had a job because YONECO was "not operative anymore because of a misunderstanding." The "misunderstanding" turned out to be that donors discovered that the leaders of the group stole money from NAC; they "didn't use it to fulfill the group's objectives." YONECO was supposed to "empower the community," Trueman said, by giving cash to "CSWs" (Commercial Sex Workers) so they could change professions and to youth clubs to do dramas. "But YONECO didn't perform well in the community." YONECO was later rehabilitated and became more successful than ever, but by then Trueman had lost his position and moved on.

Without a job, Trueman took an accounting course. Although he said he would prefer to study community development, the accounting course was cheaper. Even after years of volunteering and NGO work, Trueman still did not have a stable job, although he did have enough resources to pursue a credential that he could at least hope might led to regular employment.

Others who similarly started as volunteers, got a job, and then lost it when funding dried up nonetheless remained hopeful, sometimes for years. We found them in "shell" NGOs in district capitals, and occasionally in or near a trading center, waiting and hoping for the appearance of a new sponsor to bring their small organization back to life. After a donor-funded HIV counseling and testing organization that we encountered first in 2004 lost funding, its former employees, now volunteers, kept working for years. They continued counseling and testing, getting test kits from the local hospital, carefully keeping records in a heavy log book, and approaching every visitor to see whether the funding for their youth center might be restored.

In 2006, when the building no longer had electricity or water and was basically derelict, these "youth," no longer so young, applied for and eventually received a grant from NAC for an AIDS prevention youth group, but the main activity was a ten-day training for twenty-eight people. In 2009, the same group again applied to the NAC for a grant to resurrect their building as a youth center where they could train youth about AIDS. They received the money, but after the first tranche, NAC insisted that the rest of the money be used to train chiefs and other influential "traditional leaders." Despite this setback, the group managed to get a grant from the MTV-sponsored Staying Alive Foundation,[21] which they found on the web. It gave them a year-long grant to pay for a VCR, TV, DVD, and a night watchman, so they could use their building to educate youth, their own priority. As of the last we heard, in 2013, one of its key members (by then in his forties) had finally found a permanent job and had moved to Lilongwe. The rest were still occasionally volunteering; several were again unemployed.[22] Thus volunteering, even when it never leads to a paying job, can sustain the volunteers' hopes for years.

Despite the differences between the cosmopolitan, national, district, and interstitial elites, there are three striking commonalities. One is that, although broker jobs exist to bring the benefits of donor projects to the villagers, brokers' views of villagers are a strange mixture. On the one hand, brokers seem convinced that the villagers enthusiastically participate in NGO activities even without material rewards. But brokers also contrast the identity to which they aspire—that of being educated and modern—with village backwardness. From their point of view, villagers are ignorant, superstitious, and irrational.[23]

Second, although all brokers consider themselves fortunate to have a job with an NGO, they constantly have to juggle competing obligations: to bosses at work, families at home, professional and personal social networks on which they depend for information about new job opportunities, and responsibilities to their patrons and their clients. The most vexing obligations, and the ones we heard most about, are not their obligations to their jobs, but to members of their extended families. The brokers in the aid industry are among the lucky few Malawians who have a salary. As we noted in the preface, anyone with a salary is considered by his relatives and himself to have a moral obligation to provide funds for a funeral, for a nephew's school fees, for transportation to a hospital in an emergency, and for grain during the hunger months. Anyone with a salary thus has to parse carefully to whom she or he will give, how much, and how frequently.

Third, what concerns brokers most is the insecurity of their jobs. Unlike employment in the civil service—a civil servant is rarely, if ever, fired—NGO brokers can be fired or their jobs can just vanish. World Vision may decide to pull out of a country, or Denmark may withdraw funding because of corruption it considers outrageous, or a three-year project simply ends, leaving the broker adrift. Since the 2008 financial crisis, many donors have cut their aid budgets, and the pages of Malawi's newspapers are full of stories about how to cope with the fall in donor support.[24] Brokers are also vulnerable to global donors' quest for the next new theme. AIDS is no longer the urgent new priority. Interviews with Malawian NGO brokers found that they were frustrated that donors had not set a new post-AIDS theme. They believed that the government also was waiting to see what donors would do. Without a donor agenda setting out clear development priorities, neither the government nor the NGOs can position themselves to take advantage of a new funding stream.[25]

The degree of job security parallels the hierarchy of elite brokers. Cosmopolitan brokers with a PhD are the most secure, followed by the national-level brokers with an MA. Yet even they may not quickly find another job that provides enough money for first-world health care and education for their children. District-level brokers without exceptional skills, such as the ability to write a report in good English, may not be able to find a job at all. And, of course, even interstitial elites with a paying gig, as Trueman had at YONECO, have no job security at all.

BUFFERING INSECURITY

Trying to defend against uncertainty is a continuing preoccupation for many of the brokers. Frank, an NGO Monitoring and Evaluation Officer, interviewed in 2014, had parlayed one short-term NGO position into another, moving from data entry clerk to an NGO working on women's empowerment, to a project persuading farmers to substitute manure for fertilizers. He repeatedly used his salary to upgrade his educational credentials but had only managed to earn a "diploma," a two-year post-secondary credential. When we met him, he was again enrolled in school seeking a degree. Despite the insecurity, he said that people prefer NGOs to government employment because NGOs pay more. But he noted that at NGOs "any mistake you make you are gone." You are "always shivering at the end of projects, wondering how you will pay for your children's school fees if they let you go."[26]

It is hard to overstate the importance of education for buffering insecurity. For Malawians at all levels, educational credentials determine access to economic mobility; the higher the degree, the higher the income.[27] Correspondingly, the higher the degree, the higher one's social status. Some jobs, such as sweeper or night guard at World Vision, require no more than a primary education. National elites must have a university degree, and even better, a post-graduate degree. It is not that a cleaner must have the skills associated with a primary education nor that the deputy director of a UN agency must have a PhD to do her job, but rather that the degree signals moral worth. Not to have any education at all defines one as at best lazy and at worst backward, uncivilized, and foolish—terms that elites often use to refer to "the rural masses." Other jobs, such as a driver, require a secondary education and an expensive training course. Even to be selected as a volunteer for an NGO typically requires having passed the rigorous exams at the end of secondary school, a sign of ambition and energy, of devotion to enlightenment.[28]

And so it goes up the ladder. Those working in a position for which secondary education is a requirement aspire to a further degree that would make them eligible for a higher-level staff position; someone with a university degree can aspire to a job doing monitoring and evaluation for World Vision programs in rural areas, or with merit and luck, a job at headquarters in Lilongwe or Blantyre. And the pinnacle to which one can aspire, a PhD, would make one eligible to head a large NGO or be second-in-command in a UN agency. At each level, acquiring the relevant credential becomes more expensive, so Malawian elites, as soon as they land one job, start saving to invest their resources in the next credential.

At all levels, both work experience and credentials matter for getting a job, but credentials matter especially for job security. In 2014, talking with a friend who had been repeatedly hired, let go, and rehired by the same NGO, we asked why he was again going back to school to try to attain a (very costly) four-year degree, especially now that he had a wife and children to support. He said "for security." If an NGO project ends, he insisted, and they have to let someone go, they will let the one with the diploma go and keep the one with a degree.[29] He seemed unsure why, but speculated that the NGOs have to report their staff's qualifications to their donors. Chatting over dinner, a group of five young people, including Frank, the NGO Monitoring and Evaluation Officer, and four of his friends in school or with entry-level NGO jobs, made an identical point. When asked why so many people are going back to school to get diplomas and degrees, they said that "it is for job security." Even those who claimed that "experience matters most" for getting a job agreed that another degree helps with job security.[30]

Brokers commonly also buffer insecurity through entrepreneurship. Many attempt to supplement their salaries and meet their many obligations by engaging in a wide variety of business activities. Some have land in a distant region that must be visited and tended to. Many manage a village plot that provides at least some of the food for their household. Although we did not study civil servants, Gerhard Anders' picture of Malawian civil servants describes very well the array of activities the cosmopolitan and national brokers engage in to make their lives more secure.

> Virtually all civil servants were engaged in business and trade. Their business enterprises ranged from selling second-hand clothes (*kaunjika*) and raising poultry to running restaurants, bars and resthouses, as well as taxis or minibuses, maize mills, saw mills or tailor shops. Others traded tobacco or travelled to neighbouring countries and to South Africa to buy wholesale goods. Most of them did so "to make ends meet," as they said. It was also common practice to cultivate a plot or "garden," either in the home village or near town, where they grew maize and vegetables mainly for subsistence. Some had more land and cultivated maize and cash crops. Especially in the central region and the North, many senior civil servants owned estates where they cultivated tobacco and maize.[31]

One district broker we met is a successful, talented NGO contractor. Although he had the education and experience to be a member of the national elite, he dropped out of the NGO scramble. Rather than seeking yet another NGO contract, he decided to stay in the district where his most recent position had been. He then undertook numerous entrepreneurial efforts to stay in the area: he purchased a bar, where he could drink and chat with his compatriots; he used his ties to the Town Assembly to acquire office space to set up a computer school; he sold internet access in a small room at the back of his bar; and he planned to expand his entrepreneurial reach by establishing his own NGO. Each of these activities in itself might succeed or not, and he continued to be available for short-term NGO jobs tied to the local area, but his main investment was in cultivating his ties to the other town fathers whose friendship and cooperation would help his local enterprises succeed.[32]

To defend against insecurity, brokers have to maintain their networks, which are a mixture of professional and personal connections forged at school, at church, and at work. These connections matter at every level of the broker hierarchy. Cosmopolitan brokers maintain contacts in important government ministries and participate in churches or ethnic associations where the politically influential gather. National-level brokers, many of whom formed tight friendships at the elite Chancellor College of the University of Malawi, watch out for one another, sharing information about such vital matters as the salaries at different INGOs or anticipated changes in donor priorities. Someone who is concerned about his job may contact a friend to line up another one; similarly, someone who hears of a job that would be a promotion for her friend will inform her. Local networks matter even more for district-level brokers. We saw this when, at the end of a large research project, a colleague wanted to host a celebratory lunch to thank the dozen or so district officials and others who had helped with the project. A key district official insisted that the luncheon could not go forward unless numerous other local NGO heads and other local influentials were included. Since the host lacked the budget to more than double the guest list, the luncheon never happened. For the district broker, maintaining local networks was a higher priority than rewarding the particular people who had helped with the project.

FREELANCE BROKERS

Up to now, we have described the hierarchy of brokers who are employed, or aspire to be employed, by the large national or international NGOs and their myriad subcontractors. But as we have pointed out, any foreigner in Malawi needs at least one broker to show him or her around, and any Malawian, from a taxi driver to a waiter, can become an impromptu broker. The following recounts the story of the young American couple that established Good Futures (introduced in chapter 2) in Balaka town. It is pieced together from interviews with Teresa, their broker, and with Moira, a board member of Good Futures, who visited several times. We also draw on the organization's website.[33] Good Futures' story shows both the key role brokers play in nurturing donors' images of the good they are doing for orphans and other Malawians in need, and from the broker's point of view, the unreliability of donors' generosity.

In 2004, the American couple came to volunteer for an NGO that turned out to be a sham, so they decided to do a project on their own. They met Teresa. Impressed by her energy, they chose her as their trusted broker and provided about $900 a month to pay Teresa's salary and the rent for a house for project activities. The couple initially wanted to help grandmothers caring for the orphans of their own children who had died of AIDS by providing seed and fertilizer so the grandmothers could grow food for the orphans. But this was a time of famine, Teresa noted, and "many they refused, they wanted cash at hand." Then the couple tried to do the same thing but with a different group, but "this next group refused." Then, Moira recounted, the couple decided to form a youth club to "help on the sensitizing on HIV/AIDS and other activities they'd like to be doing." But only a few people initially came and "it didn't work out." So they decided to go for the very young youth ("thinking they'd grow into the program and stay with the club as they got older").[34]

Eventually, the emphasis shifted to teaching English in an after-school program, which, according to the blog posts of the American director (the husband in the couple), was popular with both parents and students. His posts from 2007 and 2008 offer enthusiastic and sometimes poignant reports:

> On Wednesday, Thursday, and today we visited with Teresa, Mr. Domani, and James to see how activities at the youth centre have been going. We are delighted by the progress we have seen. The children have been learning lots of skills like pottery and basket weaving. The staff have strongly emphasized having the children learn and practice English. And the children's drama skills are said to be the best in town.
>
> We have been talking to the parents and guardians of the children who attend the centre, who have given us a lot of positive feedback. One woman had persuaded her grandson to come to our program to improve his English skills. He had been failing English at school. After weeks of coming and learning with the staff, he is now the Number One English student.[35]

In November 2008, when he was again visiting, the project director wrote enthusiastically of Good Futures' many ongoing programs.

> As I write this, I sit at the kitchen table of the ... house.... If I look through the kitchen window and listen hard, I can overhear the group of about forty children who are busily debating deforestation here in Malawi ("The Environment" is the theme of the week at the Centre). If I look to the right I see a group of 16 women, ranging from 20 to 65 years old, sitting in our shaded, thatched-roof "hut." They are busily learning to read and to write. This "Adult Literacy" group is a part of our recently added "Adult Education" Program. Looking directly into the yard, I can wonder with delight at the ingenuity and talent of the young people in our CREATE Program who have built in our side yard a beautiful shed from local materials, where they can grow edible mushrooms. Growing mushrooms is one of the income-generating projects that will help Good Futures move to a self-sustaining future. All around our Good Futures house, we

101

can sense the excitement and the sense of community that has developed around this house and these projects.

This project was unusual because its founders, who were also its major donors, visited Malawi repeatedly for two or three months at a time. While they were on the spot, they were able to monitor activities and to see that the building they rented for a youth center was being used. When Moira, the board member, visited, Teresa could show her adult literacy classes (even if the numbers who actually showed up were fewer than the numbers the organization claimed) and the library, garden, classrooms, and some youth activities.

Teresa's involvement with the American donors illustrates both the impossibility of donors really knowing what goes on in the organizations they fund, and from the broker's point of view, the impossibility of relying on donors. Moira began to be concerned when on one visit she found that the library was "messy," and worse, that when her foreign patrons weren't around, Teresa was using the youth center to house her relatives. After all, with her salary from rich Americans and a house, how could Teresa not take care of her relatives' needs? Just as the funders of Good Futures were Teresa's patrons, Teresa, like every successful broker, had become the patron of her sons and daughters, siblings, nieces, nephews, and grandchildren.

Teresa also discovered that she could not really count on her American patrons. Fully occupied with a new baby, they stopped coming to Malawi, and by 2011 they had decided that they could not commit themselves to fundraising or donating from their own assets to support the organization. They brought Teresa to the US for a fundraising visit, which was unsuccessful. So the organization and its staff were on their own. The blog posts stop after 2009, and the organization's website and Facebook page have no further activity.

Thus even a successful broker, who, in a working collaboration with a donor, built what could be presented as successful programs, is insecure. Teresa eventually found herself unemployed. After Good Futures collapsed, Teresa drew on her contact with the local NGO community in the district to look for other work.[36] That network, and if things got desperate, the reciprocal obligations she had maintained with her relatives in the village, were Teresa's real security.

Unlike committed missionaries, or behemoth aid organizations with more-or-less permanent offices in the capitals of poor Third World countries, most individual altruists are not prepared to spend a lifetime supporting even the best of good causes in Africa. Thus the career of a broker—

particularly a low-level district broker like Teresa—is necessarily precarious. Like other brokers, the brokers for butterfly NGOs often turn entrepreneurial, making pitches to anyone they meet who could be a donor and consulting friends who had been successful in getting a proposal funded.

An adventurous practitioner of NGO entrepreneurialism, a cashier at a small grocery in Balaka town, illustrates how the themes of the global AIDS enterprise and the heady fantasies it fuels percolate through Malawian society. We met him in 2009 as we were paying for our groceries. He asked, "What do you think of Malawi?" When we answered that we had visited many times and liked it, he repeated the question, finally in frustration offering the answer he presumably wanted, that "Malawi is very poor"—an opening to talk about needy orphans or widows. A few days later, a friend who was staying with us at the Catholic Women's Association brought us a proposal that the cashier was circulating. The proposal, for an NGO to be called Village Hope, jumbled the full array of donor themes in one big mash-up—agriculture, health, education, the environment, rural development, AIDS and gender—and promised donor favorites: empowerment, participation, and sustainability, all for an NGO that as yet existed only on paper. The flood of NGOs had stimulated high aspirations for improving Malawi, but those, much like the aspirations of many institutional altruists, were unlikely to be fulfilled.

The cashier's proposal begins with a statement of goals and mission:

MISSION
Its mission is to help rural communities to identify solutions to problems that impede growth and development through participatory approaches.

VISION
We envisage, healthy and empowered rural communities with sustainable livelihoods.

OUR GOAL
The ultimate goal is to enable community members to make informed choices from a range of appropriate options for sustainable growth and development.

Despite promising that "VILLAGE HOPE has a sharp focus, clearly defined objectives and a consistent approach to its work," the proposal promises to "concentrate" on "agriculture, health, education, environment, rural development HIV/AIDS and Gender." Replete with terms like "sustainability," "participation," and "partnership," the proposal also promises

FIGURE 5.3. Sign for Youth Impact Organisation, Liwonde, Malawi. This NGO, like many others we studied, promises to address an implausibly broad array of issues. *Photo: Donald J. Treiman.*

more solid-sounding objectives like facilities for "water storage, irrigation, infrastructure, soil conservation/forestry and agricultural storage facilities." When we Googled this last phrase, however, it turned out to be lifted directly from a proposal by the Aga Khan Foundation for a development project in India, not Malawi. Village Hope's proposal also borrowed other sentences, including these: "In Malawi, gender determines both domestic and productive roles. Women generally have responsibilities for both, but their ability to contribute to society is constrained by social, cultural and political traditions," simply substituting "Malawi" for "India."

The proposal concludes with the contacts of the executive director—the shop manager's wife—who would be the only salaried person in Village Hope. This imagined NGO was not, however, as purely aspirational as it seemed. The small-town world of district brokers has its own local patronage system, and our hopeful store clerk, we learned, had been encouraged to form his NGO by a friend employed in the local branch of a large, well-funded British NGO, who wanted to help the clerk with the burden of his obligations to his poor relatives in the village. She had guided the writing of the proposal and was helping him raise the initial capital he would need. He claimed to be already providing village children with soap and school uniforms, and his friend was encouraging him to register the organization and apply to NAC for funding.

Much of the language of this proposal, as well as the language in interviews with the international and national elites and with district NGO brokers, echoes international definitions of the problems of poverty, women's disempowerment, and AIDS and their prescriptions for the solutions.[37] As we shall see in chapter 8, however, while district elites may know some of the global rhetoric, they are in many ways less committed to these global solutions than are either the national elites or the eagerly aspiring interstitial elites. For the district elites, and especially the town fathers, problems of local moral order such as controlling prostitution and pornography trump global concerns with gender equality and human rights.

AIDS money clearly altered the landscape of aspirations for the cosmopolitan, national, and district brokers and the interstitial elites. Many aspired to careers as NGO brokers, some successfully, some temporarily successful, some not successful at all but still hoping. In the next chapter, we show that at all levels brokers have very different experiences of the three forces through which they understand their careers: merit, miracles, and malice.

CHAPTER 6

BROKERS' CAREERS

Merit, Miracles, and Malice

MALAWIAN BROKERS TELL THEIR CAREER histories by drawing on three narratives: that of Merit, emphasizing their objective achievements and the ways their hard work, intelligence, and honesty are rewarded; that of Miracles, emphasizing the remarkable coincidences or the unexpected help from relatives or strangers that make success possible, which they almost universally attribute to God's help; and Malice, or simply misfortune, when anyone from capricious donors to envious co-workers can undermine or sabotage a career. To fully understand brokers' aspirations and their disenchantments, we describe the ways brokers themselves perceive that merit, miracles, and malice structure their opportunities and thus their outcomes.

In the preceding chapter, we focused on the uncertainty with which brokers live and their attempts to buffer it. Here we take a closer look at the ways that the career aspirations of brokers at all levels can suddenly be derailed by the death of a parent, salvaged with the help of a benefactor, or altered by any number of others who have the power to help or harm. Indeed, where patron-client ties are so important, life can have a roller-coaster feel. Leston, a district broker whom we met in 2015 at a UN-sponsored meeting in a Lilongwe hotel, described his career: he grew up poor in a village. A good student, he reached secondary school, but his father was barely able to pay for his tuition, so for food he ate what was left on the plates of other students. A girl at the school told her mother, who then stepped in to support Leston. After finishing secondary school he took a job as an agricultural extension agent, but he had higher aspirations: he wanted to study accounting. Out of nowhere, a "well-wisher" appeared. He had seen Leston on MBC TV talking about the dangers of alcohol and called him (the number was on the screen), saying, "Leston, can we meet on Friday? I have good news—do you want a BA of any kind?" Of course Leston said yes. But then malice struck: someone told the well-wisher that Leston had just gotten a job in the district office so that it would be a waste of resources to support him, and the donor withdrew his offer. Leston said, "After this, I was very desperate but I still had hope."[1] Despite frequent disappointments, many Malawians persist in hoping that some combination of merit and miracles will help them overcome the difficulties and dangers they confront.

MERIT

Malawians have a dominant narrative about the route to success, which is defined as, at the least, having a regular salary and living in a city. This narrative emphasizes merit—the talent and hard work that lead to degrees and diplomas. The examinations that successful students must pass are rigorous in the sense that they require a lot of preparation and only a small number of students achieve a passing grade. They are also arbitrary and capricious in the sense that crowded schools with high failure rates do a poor job of assessing student achievement.[2]

The discourse of schooling in the media is that education leads to a bright future through merit alone, that nothing is required other than commitment and hard work.[3] For many, however, the dream of a bright future is not realized. As we showed in chapter 5, the majority of students entering primary school leave during the first eight years. And despite the extraordinary achievement a secondary school degree represents in Malawi, having completed secondary school offers very little in the way of employment, especially for villagers without connections in the city. Money also matters. Primary school is free in principle, but there are costs for uniforms, fees, and time lost to family responsibilities, a major reason for leaving school.[4] For secondary school and university, where the cost is higher, those with outstanding scores may get help from a scholarship. For most, however, someone must pay for tuition plus other expenses: boarding school for secondary students, accommodations, food, and miscellaneous fees at university. Understandably, those who complete each stage proudly emphasize the signs of their merit—their marks, the various examinations mastered, their degrees—but say less about their good fortune in obtaining resources, whereas the stories of those with less schooling emphasize the lack of resources—a father died, a cash crop failed. Most Malawians we interviewed about their careers first said that merit alone matters: they applied for a job and were chosen. What are less often credited are the enormous advantages of those who come from more privileged backgrounds, as do virtually all the members of the national and cosmopolitan elites.

James, a high-level broker whom we interviewed in 2010, had a charmed career—it appears to be all merit—but it is a career that was built on the foundation of well-to-do parents. James worked as the "right-hand man" of the American country director of a big INGO. Although James' father grew up in a village, the father became an officer in a regional bank. James himself is a city boy: primary school in Lilongwe; secondary school in a prestigious school in Dowa District, then the University of Nairobi. When we asked why he had gone to university in Kenya, he said it was because his parents moved there and they sponsored his fees. After finishing, he worked in businesses in Nairobi and then in Malawi, completing an MA in England. He joined the INGO in 2007. He read an advertisement, and was interviewed and selected. When we asked why he moved from business to an NGO, he said, "You know the job market in Malawi, NGOs are some-how dominant." James said that he would soon need to find another job since the contract for the organization was to end in 2011. Asked whether he was confident he could get another job, he laughed and said "hope-fully" and "I have gotten used to the NGO sector."[5]

Not all the cosmopolitan and national brokers that we interviewed had such smooth careers, but almost all of them had the advantage of at least one relative with a good job in in the government, an NGO, or a business organization.

MIRACLES

Many Malawians also emphasize the role of miracles in their careers. Where so much is arbitrary and uncertain, any good fortune—being hired for a job, hearing from a friend about an opportunity, or being offered personal help—can be interpreted as evidence of God's miraculous intervention. A district broker explained that his mother had died when he was six, and his stepmother had thrown him out of the house when he was a teenager. He had gone to live with an uncle, but that uncle had died, so he was on his own. "With God's help," he got a job and then was able to save enough money to finish his Form 4 degree.[6]

Some miracles are more miraculous than others. A young man, Mphatso, hoping that we might become his benefactors, told us wistfully of his friend's accidental encounter with an American tourist: the tourist took a liking to the friend, thought it was a shame he hadn't been able to go to university, and left saying "trust me, you're going to hear from me very soon." Amaz-ingly, three weeks later he received a ticket in the mail; she had arranged for him to go to a junior college in her New England town and, Mphatso told us, his friend was already studying there.

The moral of these stories is that however unlikely it is that any particu-lar contact with a foreigner or even a sympathetic Malawian will have great benefits, the fantasy is always there. Not unlike characters in nineteenth-century novels who suddenly had their lives transformed by a bequest from a distant relative, Malawians live in a capricious world where miraculous good fortune—or bad fortune—can strike at any moment.

The same element of chance can derail a career. NGOs come and go; funding is provided for a specific project and then ends. A friend told us a particularly sad story of seeing a former NGO colleague selling tomatoes in the market—her luck was bad, the NGO left the country, and she couldn't get another job.[7] For elite brokers, such misfortunes are like the vagaries of the weather for subsistence farmers: sometimes it rains too much, sometimes too little, sometimes just right. The brokers, would-be brokers, and intermediaries of all sorts are like corks—continually bobbing to the surface but with little control over their direction—in the churning wake of billions of dollars of foreign aid.

MALICE

The other side of miracles and merit, as Malawians well understand, is the threat of malice or simple misfortune.

Mphatso, whose friend had miraculously been given the chance for education in the US, had suffered repeated disappointments, some of which seemed malicious as well as unfortunate. After scoring very high on his MSCE and the university entrance exam, he found that when the newspapers published the names of the students admitted with fellowships to prestigious Chancellor College, his name was not on the list. He suspected that perhaps a politician or administrator had used pull to have a relative admitted instead, but there was no appeal and no way to find out what had happened.[8] Longing for more education and the chance to better himself, Mphatso leapt at the chance to be trained for a career as a ferryboat pilot on Lake Malawi. He was accepted into the program, given notebooks and books (on such subjects as trigonometry, physics, and meteorology) which he still treasures, but after six weeks the program was abruptly cancelled, with no explanation, and all the students were sent home. Many years later, and after many reversals, he rebounded with the help of a patron who admired his persistence; in 2015, he received a degree in business from a private university.

Others told us of betrayals: opaque processes in which even those who have demonstrated their merit are suddenly and inexplicably fired, or their requests are turned down by a superior without explanation. Although such things do happen in the US, in Malawi, the possibility of having one's aspirations thwarted by corruption, patronage, envy, and simple arbitrariness seems more pervasive and makes the promise of merit and the hope for miracles seem fragile.[9]

Sometimes the concatenation of merit, miracles, and malice gives a fantastic quality even to what is in other respects a straightforward story of success. Richard Mkandawire became a monitoring and evaluation specialist for a large INGO, enthralled with planning and spreadsheets. The son of a civil servant, he grew up in Lilongwe, so he did not have to cope with walking long distances to an overcrowded, under-resourced rural school. He also experienced misfortune: when he was in boarding school, just ready to come home for vacation, his father was killed, murdered by robbers ("hacked with pangas") as he walked on a road back to his house. "It was very traumatic, gory." His uncle then took over paying his school fees. Although Richard did well on the high school leaving exams, his scores were not quite high enough to qualify for university, so when he saw jobs advertised in the newspaper, he applied. His application for an internship with the tax authority was successful, apparently purely on merit, as he had no contacts there. Asked why we sometimes heard from Malawians that they needed contacts and at other times not, he said "sometimes there is a level field," and sometimes there is "nepotism." In this case, he thought the hiring process may have been relatively fair because his department was expanding and they were hiring many people at once, "so maybe all their relatives had already been hired."

For Richard, the miraculous element of his story involved his being accepted, finally, into university, on his third try. Unable to afford special tutoring, he had studied with a group of friends who "encouraged each other," but he failed the exams on his first two tries. However, one day his supervisor's daughter (who had heard his name because he "used to joke around with the girls in the office") asked her mother, "didn't I hear Richard Mkandawire's name on the radio on the list of people accepted to Bunda [the agricultural college of the University of Malawi]?" His supervisor asked him "had I sat for the examinations," and he told her he had. She was excited and told him to call Bunda right away. They looked for his name on the list and said, "yes, and your classes start Monday." Here we might say a miracle was needed because there was no direct procedure for notifying candidates, and the miracle was a chance communication through a personal relationship. If the daughter of his supervisor hadn't happened to hear his name and mention it to her mother, he would have missed his chance to attend university.[10]

In a world where so much depends on personal relationships—the uncle or older sister who steps in and pays school fees, the brother who puts one up in the city until one can find work, the mother who takes care of one's children—there is also profound fear of the malice of others. Misfortune happens, but not to everyone—why did this promiscuous person get AIDS but his equally promiscuous friend did not? A common answer turns good fortune into bad: witchcraft provoked by envy.[11] In a conversation with Frank and his friends, whose career aspirations we described in the previous chapter, one of the friends brought up the topic of witchcraft, saying that

> people will use witchcraft against you if you go to get education.... It depends on the village, but if you are from a remote village and you go to university to get an education, people will be very jealous and put curses on you. Sometimes the curses kill people and, they assured [the interviewer], this really happens. People with education will die in car accidents because someone cursed them. They also said that you are shunned from your village when you become a village elite.[12]

Good fortune—particularly if it is not shared with those to whom one is obligated—incites envy and witchcraft. The possibility of witchcraft and witchcraft accusations means that your neighbors and friends might also be your enemies. If you are denied a promotion, or your organization is suddenly out of funds, perhaps it was a colleague or even a supposed friend who betrayed you. Thus, along with other sources of instability, people live with what Adam Ashforth, a leading Africanist, has called "spiritual insecurity": "the condition of danger, doubt and fear arising from exposure to the action of unseen forces bent upon causing harm."[13]

In the careers of Maxwell and Estele, which we describe in detail below, we can see all these elements: the effort and talent that constitute merit, unpredictable and unexpected good fortune or misfortune, and actions of malicious others all jostling to shape, derail, or reorient the career paths of brokers.

SUCCESSFUL CAREERS

Maxwell Honde: Mostly Miracles

Unlike many interstitial elites, Maxwell did not keep trying to leave his village. After completing Form 4 and passing the MSCE, he returned to his village to take up farming and to support his widowed mother, his girlfriend from secondary school who had "unfortunately, conceived," and their child, as well as the orphans of all three of his deceased brothers. He was not discouraged, however:

> Whatever happens to me, most of the time I accept it. I say it's o.k. After mother died I said how long do I have to mourn, I have to do things. If I had money I maybe would have gone somewhere and done things, but it's fine, it's o.k.[14]

When he came in contact with Peace Corps volunteers from abroad, it seemed to him like a miracle—a term that captures the accidental quality of such encounters, even though such accidents are much more likely to happen to some people than others. Maxwell's merit in completing secondary school, his mastery of English, and his personal virtues, including having volunteered for his village CBO, placed him in a situation where something miraculous *could* happen. When the Peace Corps volunteers arrived nearby, Maxwell's chief asked him to be their local "counterpart": "It just happened, I didn't even plan to be taken by those guys, but I was the only young person in the CBO."

When we met Maxwell at a guest house in the capital of Mchinji District, in the center of the country, he had a temporary job entering data for a research project. He was relatively well off: he had inherited land that his mother's brother, a village chief, had given him after her death. Asked how it happened that the chief had given him such a large parcel of land, he answered, "God is good. My late mother's brother ... has a big land, I went to him and talked with him, told him I didn't have a big land to use, please help me, so he had to help me, gave me five hectares." Thus, he could grow maize for subsistence and tobacco for sale, and when an opportunity arose, take a part-time job.

Maxwell's good fortune was also structured by the opportunities that institutional altruists have created. When, the next evening, we spoke with him again, he explained that in 1996 a Peace Corps volunteer had helped neighboring villagers establish a CBO, Pamodzi, which became "international," Maxwell said, when it successfully connected with a foreign donor. Maxwell's chief then asked him to start a CBO (presumably to bring resources to *his* village). For a young man like Maxwell—talented, energetic, devoted to his community, educated but without prospects in the formal job market—forming a CBO was an obvious step. As Maxwell described his involvement, the CBO began when "the chief, his headman, asked those who are willing should join hands, we will be working for the benefit of our own community." There would have certainly been groups already working for the community—church groups to visit the sick, funeral groups to prepare food for the mourners and to bury the dead, rotating savings groups. Unlike such spontaneous products of village culture, a CBO follows an internationally sanctioned model. Maxwell's fledgling CBO, Tsogolo, wanted to follow Pamodzi's "advanced" model: "We asked them to train us how to sensitize the community about HIV/AIDS. Then it was AIDS, AIDS, AIDS, but we didn't know much. They taught us how to form subcommittees, how to write a constitution, a strategic plan," and that they should form subcommittees for various activities such as caring for OVCs and home-based care for the chronically ill.

When Maxwell's CBO started, it had forty-two volunteers because, he said, people assumed that a group associated with the *azungu*, the Whites from the Peace Corps, must have resources.

"They were saying ah we hear the PC brought a lot of money but we haven't seen anything. They thought the azungu were just giving out money. When the last PCV was leaving, many withdrew, then we were only 27. Now the ones who are active are 15. They don't come always; they are volunteers, you can't make them come." Asked if he gets discouraged, or if he wants to get paid, Maxwell insisted, "No, this is my community, my relatives will benefit in the future. I'm not discouraged."

Thus the newborn CBO Tsogolo joined the myriad of government and donor-funded programs that twinkle alluringly on the edge of rural Malawians' subsistence economy.

A crucial part of the training of Maxwell's CBO was learning proposal writing, which he did. The organization's first support came from MANASO (Malawi Network of AIDS Service Organizations), a national NGO partly funded by USAID, which supports PLWHAs. Maxwell's group got 180,000 kwacha (about US$1,500 at the time) to buy pails for the PLWHAs in his CBO's catchment area:

They were too poor to buy both food and pails for carrying water and they needed the food more because they were sick. We also bought them towels—3/4 of our patients were using their clothes to dry themselves. We bought them soap. Then we wrote a proposal to World Vision for blankets, they gave us about K93,000 for 80 blankets, these were supposed to go to the orphans, the elderly and the positive living [people living with AIDS]. Then in 2001, during the

113

famine, we asked them for money for maize, they gave us K53,000. We used it to buy maize. Then two years ago we asked World Vision again for an income generation activity, they gave us K80,000, we bought timbers and then resold them. We used this money to buy little things like soap, fish to bring when you visited the sick, you have to bring something. And we ask what do you think we should bring you next time? Sometimes they say a pack of sugar or a pack of rice.

Another donor, Every Child, funded the CBO to buy cloth to provide uniforms for children so they could go to school—at that time, he said, every organization was implementing projects to get kids in school.

Maxwell became the "go-to guy" for the NGOs in his neighborhood that need to reach villagers. He and his CBO were important assets to World Vision, MANASO, and other NGOs implementing programs in the local communities in his area. After 2004, however, when the Global Fund and other donors funded AIDS prevention on a massive scale, the activities of many NGO programs changed from providing material resources to programs viewed as "sustainable," such as training for youth clubs or home based care groups.

In Maxwell's story there is no mention of malice—of envy or jealousy. At the time we spoke with him we did not think to ask, but we assume that he was aware of the potential for malice and took steps to circumvent it. One such step would have been not to hoard his good fortune, but to teach others to follow in his footsteps, and indeed he has done this: just as a more "advanced" CBO gave Tsogolo a start, Tsogolo has produced progeny. At his chief's suggestion, Maxwell helped six other villages create CBOs to bring resources into their communities. Working always as a volunteer, with the occasional per diem from a training as his only material reward, Maxwell has become the coordinator for the seven CBOs and secretary of Tsogolo CBO.

Maxwell's career also exemplifies other elements of the broker experience. Despite a run of successful proposals, and with more in the pipeline (a proposal to teach local people to cook nutritious foods for those ill with AIDS, a proposal for a paraffin pump so they can sell it in small amounts to generate income for the CBO), and despite his overall optimism and a sunny disposition, even Maxwell criticizes the ways many large NGOs operate. First, the NGOs all want to support AIDS activities:

In Malawi there is this thing—now I'm generalizing—if I'm selling *mandazi* [donuts] and I do well, everyone wants to sell *mandazi*. It's the same with these CBOs, there are lots of things CBOs can do, but people were saying no, we want to be like you.

He would prefer to work on planting trees: "in our area, many trees are cut down, in five years time, the area will have no trees." But most NGOs weren't interested in that issue.

Very few, and to pass a proposal would take much time. A project came for this ... They said we are here, we want to start planting trees because in this area there will be no trees, we want you people to know you need trees. They were here for two months, then we found that project has phased out.

A successful broker like Maxwell, who shows the flexible opportunism to take advantage of shifting donor priorities—willy-nilly seeking pails, food, trees, or school uniforms to bring resources to his community— nonetheless remains mistrustful of his NGO partners. Even World Vision, which has funded several of his group's activities, arouses suspicion:

A child in UK can fund a child in Malawi, but he does not know the address of the person in the UK, so some people think this is dishonest. It has been happening that those children in UK are sending money say £50 to their friend in Malawi, the World Vision person comes to the child and says your friend in the UK has sent you this bag of sugar [made in Malawi]. But if you criticize World Vision they say you are not a good person. But there is no way you can send sugar—Malawi sugar!—from the UK to Malawi.

Estele Zgambo: Merit and Malice

Estele Zgambo[15] is older than Maxwell, married with three children, and by the measures Malawians would use, much more successful. With a degree from Malawi's Chancellor College and an MA, she has the credentials, the connections, and the skills to work for international donors and to claim a place in Malawi's national elite. Hers is definitely a story of merit—but, again, with a bit of help.

Although Estele went to primary school in a village, she did well enough to be selected for a top national secondary school and then to be selected for Chancellor College. Her parents are poor, but an uncle who was a village headman helped with her school fees all the way up to university. As she tells the story, even her apparent lucky break—the chance to go to Uganda on a fellowship for an MA—came not from personal connections, but when, while working at a temporary research job, she happened to see an announcement for a fellowship funded by the United Nations Development Programme (UNDP) through the African Economic Research Consortium. Estele applied and was selected.

This emphasis on merit—on open competition for jobs and fellowships—does not, however, create the straightforward career path one might assume. Those Malawians successful enough to enter the world donors have made find themselves on a zigzag path with jagged breaks, as a job or organization disappears or a short-term project is not renewed. Jobs and fellowships are sometimes allocated in a meritocratic way, but once someone finds a job, it is insecure. Those in Estele's position must constantly envision the possibility that the positions they hold might abruptly end or that a malicious superior may undercut them. The only apparent security is the alluring, if uncertain, promise of the next credential. Again and again, Malawians told us how they grabbed any fellowship possibility that came along—traveling to a different country, changing fields or directions—to take advantage of a possibility of bettering their circumstances. Such is the longing for degrees and credentials that, as the Malawian writer Steve Sharra notes, "Many who do not make it after Form Four spend the rest of their lives sweating to find an alternative route to university education."[16]

This preoccupation with credentials is in part due to the way donors have structured the world brokers inhabit. Worried about corruption and nepotism, donors have put in place elaborate (if often ineffective) controls, so that jobs have to be formally advertised with minute specifications of credentials, years of experience, and skills. One advertisement we saw took up a quarter-page with a list of degrees, experience, and skills required for a two-week job designing an organization's web page. The exaggerated emphasis on formal credentials means that in many respects actual job performance doesn't matter.

The organization of foreign aid further exacerbates the sense of unpredictability and caprice in Malawian brokers' lives. From the donors' point of view, short-term demonstration projects meant to prove the value of a new approach to AIDS prevention or agricultural development may seem like a logical way to leverage their money and influence. From the point of view of Malawians, however, such short-term projects, driven by donor priorities and the latest remedy donors imagine will solve Africans' troubles, create a chaotic, unpredictable environment. Organizations arrive with ambitious agendas and suddenly collapse or depart for no apparent reason. Even where there is a reason—a failure to keep proper records or account for funds somewhere up the line, for example—staff suddenly find themselves out in the cold when a project is abruptly cancelled. A newspaper account from 2011 tells an all-too-familiar story: "Morale at Malawi Aids Counselling and Resource Organisation (Macro) is at an all-time low following management's decision to send staff on an indefinite unpaid leave."[17] In such a world, flexibility and resilience are virtues, while planning and a clear sense of direction may lead only to disappointment and heartbreak.

Such a disjointed path is evident in Estele's and her husband's careers. After receiving a BA from Chancellor in Economics, Estele relied on her network from college, doing contract research for a couple of years ("piecework" she jokingly called it, using the word "*ganyu*," used for agricultural day labor). Already married, she saw an announcement for a UNDP-sponsored MA fellowship combining study and research in Malawi with several months at a Ugandan university, and she applied. By the time she learned she had won the fellowship, she was six months pregnant, and she had to leave for study in Uganda when the baby (her first child) was only four months old. While it was "worth it,... when I returned, she was seven months old," which was very hard, especially with her first child. Just as she finished the MA (choosing a research project whose major attraction was that it was funded, "that's why I liked it most"), her husband got a job in Lusaka, Zambia. She went with him but returned after a few months when she was offered a research position in a three-year project funded by a European donor. But the project collapsed when its Malawian director used part of the budget to buy an expensive car, against the strong advice of her board. The director resigned, the project was shut down, and all eight staff members were thrown out of work.

The director, whose malice—or perhaps just mischief—had cost everyone else their jobs, moved on to another "very good" job, while Estele, now pregnant with her second child, was left with her finances in shambles. By this time her husband was pursuing another degree at a theological seminary in Malawi where salaries were "very, very poor." His relatives helped them out "a lot," and Estele got work with a friend and then with a consulting group which bid for various donor projects. But the work wasn't steady. Nonetheless, she and her husband had free housing at the seminary, where her husband worked part time while pursuing his studies. Eventually Estele was offered the seemingly long-term job she was holding at the time we talked with her—doing proposal development for a large INGO, but even then malice could again upend her life. When her husband won a fellowship for seminary studies at a university in Kenya, the fellowship was supposed to pay for his accommodation and expenses in Kenya, while the seminary in Malawi supported his family. But "within a month of his leaving they said we had to move out of seminary housing and they stopped his salary." So she was supporting the family, with their plans again thrown into turmoil. They made a "big sacrifice" in hopes that with the additional degree her husband would be able to find a position such as director of research for a relief organization. She herself aspires to move up—perhaps even to her dream job with a UN organization—so that she and her husband could send their children to good private schools, assuring that their children in turn could earn university degrees. Meanwhile Estele herself is searching for a way to go abroad for a PhD, either in the United States or England, while she takes advantage of every opportunity her current job offers for additional training and certificates that make her more marketable. In 2014 she dropped by the hostel where we were staying in Lilongwe and said she was looking for a job that was better paid. The next year, she emailed that she was working for another INGO.

The instability of NGO funding, and perhaps the many opportunities it creates for corruption, can also contribute to brokers' experience of malice. We met Arthur Matemba in 2009 when he was leading a series of trainings at the Catholic Women's Organization, funded by international donors through a local Malawian FBO. Deeply religious, an inspired preacher, and an engaging personality, he had been traumatized by his treatment by the FBO. We had gotten to know him quite well because he returned several times for various trainings, and as we got to know him better, he was eager to tell us his story. Several years before we met him,

> Arthur had been fired in a "humiliating" way. He seemed to remember every detail, including what day of the week and what date it was. On a Thursday he was called in by the Director of [the FBO] who said that they had lost their grant from the Danish church group, but that he would keep Arthur, no matter what, because he belonged with [the FBO]. . . . Then on Friday they had morning worship and again on Monday, during which the Director said the same thing in front of the entire organization—that they had lost the Danish church grant but that Arthur was going to be kept. After lunch he had to go into town, and when he came back in the late afternoon (just about time for "knocking off"), his office mate said that there was a letter for him. He saw a sealed letter on his desk and opened it to discover

one line, that he was terminated. It was August 4, but the letter was backdated to July 1. Arthur had only recently moved to Lilongwe. He had to move back to Blantyre, where he had friends [note the importance of social relationships as insurance]. A "brother" [in Christ] took him in and eventually gave him money to rent his own place. Then he got a short term project with Save the Children. When that ended, he was asked by [the FBO's] department of ministry to come help them out (preaching is his greatest love and apparently a real skill). He did so as a volunteer, very aware of being a good Christian and doing good to those who have wronged you, but also because he had nothing better to do. Then he got a call from the Director—the same one who had fired him—saying they had a "gap" in the Southern region and offering him his current job.[18]

Both malice and misfortune may also be self-inflicted. Envy and ill-will are more common where people have not invested adequately in creating and sustaining ties of personal loyalty. Sometimes brokers cheat their NGO employers and lose their jobs. Alternatively, the one honest employee in an organization riddled by corruption may be shunned—and even have his career threatened—by his peers.

Like the director of Estele's NGO, who bought a luxury car for herself with donor funds and brought down her organization, Malawian brokers do not always do what their patrons want or expect.[19] The demands of family members, the temptations of alcohol and romance, and the powerful aspiration for a comfortable life—with electricity, running water, nice clothing, or at another level, the luxuries that give prestige among the elite—have led more than one broker we know to go off the rails. Occasionally such a broker is caught and fired. More often, it appears, a broker who has maintained his network ties, who is an established member of a group, will be forgiven for even serious misbehavior.

BEING A BROKER

Despite their very different situations—Maxwell, a farmer in his home village, and Estele, a successful professional in the capital—Maxwell and Estele are both brokers, and the essence of that role is very similar. In her current job for a large INGO, Estele, like Maxwell, writes proposals to donors to fund her organization's activities. Unlike Maxwell, she is a professional, paid for her time, and her proposals are for much more money.

Nonetheless her basic role, like his, is to mediate between donors and potential recipients. She scans the many donor requests for proposals and tries to match them to projects her organization could pursue at the village level.

Maxwell also tries to mediate between what his community needs and what donors will fund. Since he recognizes that resources in any form are valuable to his community, he has developed the knack of writing proposals for whatever donors might have on offer. His consistent success perhaps indicates how much donors emphasize correct proposal-writing form, so that from plastic jerry cans to school uniforms, Maxwell and the CBOs he has assisted have succeeded in their funding requests.

Estele and Maxwell have very different kinds of careers, although their histories also have a great deal in common. Maxwell had help from his uncle and his chief; Estele and her husband relied on assistance from their families and their school networks. Both Estele and Maxwell achieved success in their respective worlds through academic merit and hard work. But the deeper similarities and some of the important differences in their experiences and perspectives come from the different ways their lives as brokers are shaped by the practices of international donors.

Estele's occupational world has neither the uncertainties of farming—weather, pests, the sporadic availability of fertilizer subsidies—nor the security of being able to fall back on subsistence agriculture. She and her husband lead lives very different from Maxwell's in that they aspire to much more, and in some respects they are more insecure—just at the verge of achieving the international standard of living, with its good private schools, access to a vehicle, travel to conferences abroad, and comfortable housing, but vulnerable to sudden shocks that threaten to derail their plans.

Maxwell encountered a jumble of donor programs in which opportunities for funding appeared seemingly at random. Indeed, Maxwell's delighted rendition of his string of successful proposals has the quality of a child on an Easter-egg hunt: "oh, I looked under a bush, and there was another one!" While concern with AIDS was the unifying theme of most of these grants, neither he nor his fellow villagers were picky. Any opportunity for funding had the possibility of bringing resources into the community, both material goods like water jugs or a paraffin pump, or, more personally, opportunities for per diems and transportation allowances associated with "training." Maxwell had an extraordinary run of proposal-writing successes compared to most of the village-based Malawians we met, but his experience is like theirs in confronting an unpredictable realm of alluring possibilities. The particular projects of various altruists, whose larger plans and strategies are utterly opaque to those on the ground, lead local youth like Maxwell to grab whatever miraculously comes their way.

Maxwell's broker activities, darting from paraffin pumps to school uniforms, have the same frenetic hummingbird quality as that of members of the urban elite like Estele and her husband, scanning newspaper job advertisements or fliers announcing fellowships for foreign study. Both are grasping at the opportunities that donors, for inscrutable reasons, make available. But the nature of their aspirations and the sources of their insecurities are very different. Unlike Maxwell, who can continue to farm despite its uncertainties, Estele and her husband, while wealthier and more privileged, have become dependent on donors' constantly shifting priorities in a way that Maxwell has not. On the other hand, many aspiring brokers in Maxwell's situation—educated, but without jobs that would allow them to leave the village—have the worst of both worlds. They are dependent on donors' meager and scattered offerings, but without the pay and the credentials that give Estele, despite her insecurities, realistic hopes for a prosperous future.

We have noted that donors, rather than promoting the modern rationality they hope to teach Africans, create a capricious, unpredictable world in which an opportunistic approach to both careers and shifting donor priorities makes more sense than careful planning. One small donor website posted this wistful quote from a Group Village Headman in Malawi: "We hope you are going to come back and in time because lots of Donors promise but they don't implement in time or come back at all."[20]

But the effects of donor projects on the experiences of brokers go deeper. Donors have fundamentally altered the landscape of aspirations through which Malawians make their way. For Malawians at all levels, "development" is not aggregate but personal: a condition to which they aspire.[21] And "development" implies both material progress and modernity. Villagers seek chiefs who will bring "development," which they understand to mean local NGO or government projects. Cosmopolitan and national elites seek ever-enhanced educational credentials and a modern, Western standard of living, even while they try to manage their local networks both to buffer the insecurities donors create and to establish themselves as important people who can take care of their own clients and kin. District elites try to preserve their roles as guardians of their local communities, while they hope to take advantage of the new resources donors provide. And the interstitial elites, those educated and talented enough to imagine leaving the

CHAPTER 7

THEMES THAT MAKE EVERYONE HAPPY

Fighting Stigma and Helping Orphans

HOW DO BROKERS AND DONORS manage to work together? There are conflicting motives and complex misunderstandings between donors and brokers, and between both of these and villagers. Each arouses fantasies in the others that cannot be fulfilled. Nonetheless, because it is in the interest of each to do so, brokers and donors, and sometimes villagers, fumble toward "working misunderstandings"—ways of accommodating one another that allow them, however uncomfortably, to get along.[1] In this chapter, we examine themes on which the two parties have worked well together; in the next chapter, we explore themes where reaching a working accommodation requires more rhetorical skill.

We begin with a story illustrating the misunderstandings and accommodations that brokers and donors make. Like many stories in the world of African aid, this one is a funny, almost surreal, cultural mash-up. It is an extreme example of the creative accommodations people reach when they need each other and want to make some joint enterprise work, even though their interests and understandings conflict.

In June 2008, UNICEF and several other donors organized a daylong event with music and speeches to launch a newly redesigned female condom. To publicize the launch, the sponsors took out a two-page advertisement with photos from the event in a major Malawian newspaper, *The Nation*. In an accompanying article, one of the speakers at the launch, a district-level broker, told her story:

> As Esnat Mbandambanda, a master trainer with the Médecins Sans Frontières in Chiradzulu would have it, the female condom can also keep women safe, even when they are raped. She has a story to tell on how she was protected by the female condom.
> "It was on 22 December, 2007 when robbers came into my house. They took away everything. Then, they told me that after getting away with my property, they had to sleep with me. They tied my

hands to the bed. I told them I was ready for them, knowing that I had my female condom on. When they saw the condom, they said to each other: 'She is deformed, let's go,'" recalls Mbandambanda, a widow who has been on ARVs for the past eight years.[2]

Taken as "fact," the story is nonsensical. Why was this widow who had been on ARVs for eight years "protecting herself" by wearing a female condom? Are her listeners to imagine that she wears the condom around the clock, just in case someone shows up to rob and rape her? The donors who hoped to generate enthusiasm for the female condom surely were dismayed by a story in which rapists were so repelled by its appearance that they ran away, saying, "She is deformed, let's go." But if we consider what could have led Esnat Mbandambanda to tell this story, we gain insight into the contrasting perspectives of donors and brokers. For the donors sponsoring the launch, it made sense to ask a local NGO worker, in this case a "master trainer with the Médecins Sans Frontières," to offer a testimonial about the value of the female condom. Indeed, a photograph in the newspaper shows Esnat Mbandambanda on a dais, enthusiastically waving a female condom above her head. Yet for this broker, who had presumably already learned the value of revealing her HIV status publicly (as many brokers involved in PLWA or "expert client" roles are expected to do), some possible ways of endorsing the female condom would nonetheless have been awkward. If she actually uses the condom (which we doubt), a reasonable thing to say might have been, "I always keep one by my bed, in case my boyfriend drops by." But as a middle-aged widow, perhaps she did not want to acknowledge having a regular sexual partner or partners. Nor would she want to say she had actually been raped—another discrediting possibility. From her perspective, the best story was that the condom protected her because it drove the rapists away.

Esnat Mbandambanda's story seems lurid and absurd. But the everyday realities of AIDS-prevention efforts, while on the surface more prosaic, are no less the product of sometimes fumbling, sometimes enthusiastic efforts—by parties who often misunderstand each other's motives and expectations—to find a working accommodation. These efforts, however, rather than producing a hilarious mash-up, often produce what look like bureaucratically impeccable themes ("Fight Stigma!"), categories (OVC), and buzzwords ("psychosocial support"). These concepts and practices emerge from the awkward embrace of donors, brokers, and villagers, forced by circumstance to reach some accommodation that obscures differences among them.[3]

In this chapter we take up two themes that work very well for both donors and brokers: "fighting stigma" and "orphans and other vulnerable children." These have been perennial favorites of the AIDS enterprise, in part because donors, brokers, and villagers can unite around them as positive values, even if the meaning of that positive value differs.

"Fighting stigma" is the mom-and-apple-pie of AIDS prevention interventions. Everyone loves the idea. To Western donors and AIDS activists, stigma and discrimination were perceived as major barriers to controlling the epidemic. Peter Piot, the executive director of UNAIDS, the international organization charged to coordinate the control of the epidemic, said, "Stigma silences individuals and communities, saps their strength, increases their vulnerability, isolates people and deprives them of care, of support.... We must break down these barriers or the epidemic will have no chance of being pushed back."[4] To Piot, fighting stigma requires a commitment to human rights and the willingness of those who are HIV+ to "Break the Silence," to publicly disclose their status. To Malawians, its meaning is very different. Here, the message to fight stigma reinforces the normal obligations of reciprocity and interdependence among kin and neighbors. What donors imagine as fighting stigma in the Western sense of fighting discrimination is embraced on the ground from a very different point of view—the traditional obligation to care for the sick and to help neighbors and family members.[5]

Many donors sponsor programs to fight stigma, but the emphasis on compassion and care fits especially well with the mission of one set of actors, religious congregations. Below is a typical statement by an African religious leader:

> ... at the end of a two-day meeting in Kenya, the All Africa Conference of Churches called on member churches to lead the fight against the stigmatization of AIDS. "Churches should fight stigmatization of AIDS, which has proved to be the biggest impediment in the war against the disease," said General Secretary Melaku Kifle. "The church can no longer afford to be passive in the face of HIV/AIDS and other conflicts affecting the continent and must come to grips with African problems."[6]

Local churches embrace the appeal to fight stigma because it gives them a way to combat AIDS without having to raise awkward issues about sex and condoms or to discuss openly what everyone knows: that some women and men in the congregation (and perhaps the pastor as well) are likely to have outside sexual partnerships.[7] This strategy allows churches to maintain comity and fellowship among their members by advocating that people should "love each other," should not blame or "isolate" each other, and should treat each other with kindness.

The adjuration to be kind to those with AIDS resonates with the importance villagers place on caring for the needy and maintaining harmonious relationships among neighbors. When we studied proposals written by villagers requesting money from Malawi's NAC to fund CBOs, many of the proposals promised that the organization would "love" and care for those with AIDS, as well as for the elderly or orphans. A study of rural churches and mosques found that pastors and sheikhs strongly advised against divorcing a spouse with AIDS. The advice was not a matter of opposing divorce in general. Rather the pastors and sheikhs felt that someone had to care for the person who was ill: "the primary reason given for opposing AIDS-related divorce is the mandate to care for the sick. One leader who strongly and emphatically opposed divorce under suspicion of AIDS emphasized the wife's role to care for her husband: 'No! It is not appropriate! Who are you going to leave him with? Who would take care of him?'"[8]

A study of caregivers of rural Malawians with symptoms widely recognized as those of AIDS found that although the caregivers were reluctant to define the illness as AIDS, there was little sign that their patients were shunned:

> The caregivers do their best whatever the name of the illness. They prepare meals and medicine and feed the patient, they heat water and bathe the patient, and they wash sheets. They do this day after day, trying to help the patient improve, to be more comfortable, to avoid worrying. Members of the local community, who surely also recognized the patient's illness as AIDS, provided moral support: there was little evidence that either patients or caregivers were stigmatized. Visitors came to check on the patient's progress, and to support the caregiver. Almost all caregivers received gifts of food or soft drinks for the patient, or small amounts of money. In addition, friends and relatives provided moral and social support to the patients by sitting with them and cheering them up, and to the caregiver by sympathizing with her burdens.[9]

Similarly, writing of responses to the epidemic in Malawian villages, Pauline Peters and her colleagues report that "widows of men known or suspected of dying from AIDS were treated no differently than other widows, the same being true of widowers."[10] They acknowledge that AIDS arouses complex fears and moral judgments, sometimes including blaming the person ill with AIDS for "careless behavior" or interpreting AIDS, like other hard-to-explain kinds of illness or death, as due to witchcraft. Nonetheless, they find that the ambivalence and tension AIDS evokes do not translate into ostracism, reluctance to provide care, or interpersonal disdain.

We believe that even the claim that there has been a "silence" about AIDS is wrong for Malawi, and we think it is wrong for other African countries as well.[11] Rural Malawians talk a lot about AIDS—not surprisingly, since they know many people who have died of AIDS and they themselves are worried about becoming infected. To say, as the far-away leaders of the international response to the epidemic do, that people with AIDS must "break the silence," must "talk about AIDS," mistakes interpersonal tact, the reluctance to raise delicate issues or to say publicly at a funeral that the cause of a death was AIDS, for an actual silence about the disease.[12] In the conversations reported in our ethnographic journals, people are careful not to mention AIDS directly to the relatives of someone who has died of the disease, but they discuss the symptoms of those who are ill, and they discuss and debate AIDS at length outside the hearing of the immediate family.[13] Some of our acquaintances in Malawi talk openly about AIDS in their own families—an aunt who had AIDS but took a sexual partner anyway, a nephew who refused to take medication even when his parents begged him to do so, a widowed sister whose husband died of AIDS—without any trace of embarrassment.

What does exist is an anxiety that might lead HIV+ people to hide their status from others, what Amy Kaler and her colleagues have called the fear of being seen as "walking corpses."[14] In societies in which everyone is dependent on relations of personal interdependence, someone who will not be around to reciprocate, to repay the help he or she has received, may become a less valuable member of the community. Kaler's survey and interviews with caregivers of those on antiretroviral treatment in Uganda found that most AIDS patients were treated kindly by neighbors; negative experiences often reflected pre-existing disputes over land and other matters.

When respondents did mention negativity generated by AIDS itself, the element of AIDS which figured most strongly was its perceived

lethality, rather than its modes of sexual transmission. While individuals might suspect their spouses of sleeping around, the idea that
a person with AIDS was a "walking corpse" appeared to be a more
powerful engine of ostracism than the sexual behaviour implied by
AIDS infection. One man, for instance, said that his mother kept her
HIV status hidden from all those except others whom she knew to
be HIV positive, because she did not want other[s] to "backbite her,
like that one is a moving corpse."[15]

According to Kaler and colleagues, relatives of those with AIDS feel a
strong moral obligation to help, even when this risks impoverishing the
whole kin group. And neighbors offer both help and advice—until some
begin to worry that the patient may never recover and thus never be able
to reciprocate.

Despite a reluctance to invest in ties with those who may never be able
to reciprocate, norms of mutual help and interpersonal tact among villagers often overcome pragmatic considerations, as in an incident reported by
one of the ethnographic journalists about the Seed Multiplication Group
(SMAG) of which she is the secretary. Since the members of these local
groups receive hybrid seeds and fertilizer that they are obligated to repay
after the harvest, the question of whether to admit Mr. Dumani, an agricultural extension agent with the Ministry of Agriculture who had returned to
his village with obvious signs of AIDS, aroused controversy:

It was on Saturday morning when I went to Mtetemera for the meeting about our Club of the Seed Multiplication. On that day, we had
some new members who came to join our SMAG.... Mr. Dumani
was looking very weak and unhealthy body therefore everyone knew
that he was sick. [After the meeting], the Chairman asked me as the
secretary, Mr. Lakuna the Treasurer and Miss Charles the Committee
member to remain in the room to meet with the Chairman.[16]

The Chairman urged that Mr. Dumani not be allowed to join the group
because he was unlikely to be able to repay what he borrowed, and then
the group would be left with his debts:

The Chairman Mr. Mvula asked the Committee if it was good to
allow Mr. Dumani to join our farming club. He said that he asked
that question because Mr. Dumani looked very weak and sick as everyone seen him. He said that we have to discuss first and find the

solution because farming is a hard labour and even if one have money, but it needs the owner to look after that job every time.

The Treasurer Mr. Lakuna said that the Chairman was saying the truth that Mr. Dumani was sick and in addition to that Mr. Lakuna said he saw the sores on Mr. Dumani's body. The sores were many and covered his whole body.

[The Chairman] added by saying that ours is a club and now if we allow him to borrow the bags of fertilizer from the Agora through our club, we should just know that it will be our problem because we will be forced to square that credit for him this year . . . and the Agora which have accepted to lend us the bags of fertilizer is a company and if we shall fail to square their credit, they will come to our houses to carry all the properties that we have and sell them to square their money that we borrowed.

The other members of the Executive Committee objected. Miss Charles suggested that Mr. Dumani "should just join our club for him to have the right place for selling his crops but he should buy the implements by himself and allow him to join the Club." The diarist, Alice, agreed with Miss Charles:

When Mrs. Charles finished speaking, I was asked to give out my suggestions and I said to them that there is no need to refuse him joining the club because we don't know about the type of disease that he is suffering from. We can just say that he has AIDS yet it is not [true] and though it can be that he has AIDS, we don't know when he will die. He can maybe stay for 2 or 3 years alive and maybe strong if he can get recovered very well. He has also his wife who can be working for him if he will find that he is sick and in addition to that, Mr. Dumani is a field Assistant he is receiving money every month end. He can employ people to work for him in his garden and he can even pay back the bags of fertilizer's money when he will fail to work in his garden. I can see nothing wrong there because he is not a young man, he knows what he is doing and if we refuse him, it will show that we have isolated him from our club because he is sick. Let him use his freedom of life. Nobody knows about his plan. It might be that he has enough money which he has kept for farming.

The Chairman Mr Mvula was not happy with my speech, therefore he said that the committee should think twice because our club is for business and not that we are growing our crops for food.

In the end, the committee told the Chairman that Mr. Dumani should be permitted to join the club.

A comparison of views about stigma in Malawian newspapers and the views of rural Malawians in conversations described by ethnographers shows a stark difference. The articles echo international messages: treating people living with AIDS equitably is an issue of human rights in general and stigma in particular. In local conversations, however, "The injunction to treat equitably those who are infected is more often interpreted as referring to the normal obligations of reciprocity and interdependence, and less often as extending a helping hand to a despised minority."[17] AIDS messages to fight stigma do make sense to Malawian villagers, but they make sense because they restate the advice they often give one another about the need to "assist," care for, support, and love each other.[18]

In contrast, it makes little sense to Malawians to fight stigma by "breaking the silence," by publicly saying "I am HIV positive," a key injunction of the international AIDS community. When we asked one of our ethnographers, who had told us that she was HIV+, whether she would tell others, she answered "No! What good would that do?" She would be a walking corpse. And if she died (which she has not), someone must be blamed, which could promote enmity and even violence.[19]

The popularity of stigma as a theme in AIDS interventions is peculiar, since there is no evidence that reducing stigma, however understood, reduces the spread of HIV in Africa. Indeed, it is not clear why advocates believe that reducing HIV stigma would reduce HIV risk. The brilliant AIDS documentary, "Miss HIV," shows the "Miss HIV Stigma-Free" pageant in Botswana: HIV+ women proudly promenade in revealing gowns and assert their right to sexuality, even as public health researchers deplore the mixed messages the pageant conveys.[20] If the goal of HIV prevention is behavior change, then persuading people *not* to condemn behaviors that lead to HIV transmission could be counterproductive for reducing HIV risk. And for local people, avoiding sex with those who are HIV+ would be a practical strategy for avoiding infection.[21] Indeed, Malawian villagers, when first offered confidential HIV testing, quite reasonably suggested that the University of Pennsylvania researchers who were doing the testing post a list of all those who tested HIV+ so that others could avoid having sex with them. Stigma, where it exists, might be a barrier to seeking treatment and to programs like the prevention of mother-to-child transmission. But at least before antiretroviral treatment was widely available, a straightforward public-health analysis of programs most likely to reduce HIV transmission would have placed fighting stigma far down the list.[22]

Nonetheless, stigma looms large in the arsenal of AIDS-prevention interventions because it sounds good all-around and offends no one. Everyone, from donors and their sponsors, to brokers, to churches and villagers, can get on board. But even though donors, brokers, and villagers have all signed on to the same program, they "misunderstand" each other in the sense that the fight against stigma means something quite different to each group.

FROM ORPHANS TO "OVC"

The journalist John Donnelly, writing about the idealistic Christians who streamed into Africa in the wake of the AIDS epidemic, observes that, "As the members of these faith-based groups boarded planes for faraway destinations like Lilongwe, Addis Ababa, Nairobi, and Dar es Salaam, they imagined themselves building orphanages."[23] Orphans were the big draw. As we show below, the term "orphans" morphed into the broader category of "Orphans and Vulnerable Children." The expanded terminology works for everyone in a different sense than stigma does. Rather than legitimating an intervention, it defines a category of people who are especially deserving of help.[24] As child sponsorship organizations have long known, the image of orphaned children touches altruists' hearts (and opens their pocketbooks), so the more capacious category makes donors, brokers, and villagers very happy.

In Malawi, we frequently met altruists who had come to help orphans and heard their stories of why they came and how they had helped. From a busload of World Vision sponsors bearing gifts for "their" orphans to church groups awaiting the local broker who would take them to village orphans, altruists sought the emotional high of an encounter with orphaned children. Linda Richter and Amy Norman describe how heart-rending images of "AIDS orphans" can motivate encounters that are satisfying for visitors but can have problematic consequences for the children:

> Short-term volunteer tourists are encouraged to "make intimate connections" with previously neglected, abused and abandoned young children. However, shortly after such "connections" have been made, tourists leave; many undoubtedly feeling that they have made a positive contribution to the plight of very vulnerable children. Unfortunately, many of the children they leave behind experience another abandonment to the detriment of their short- and long-term emotional and social development.[25]

131

Imagining Orphans

For international organizations, the image of "orphans"—those bereft of both parents, alone in the world, facing desperate poverty and the emotional devastation of terrible loss—is a perfect lure for attracting funding. But in many ways, neither the category "orphan" nor the image of children alone in the world makes much sense on the ground in Africa.

Orphaned children in Africa are rarely abandoned. In Malawi, when a child has lost both parents, members of the extended family meet to determine where the child should live.

When an anthropologist, Anat Rosenthal, was studying orphans in Malawi, she asked her Malawian broker to talk about some specific cases of orphans. The broker said:

> B: We have some child headed households, but some of them, like in the villages, it's not totally a child-headed household. There is someone looking after that child-headed household like an aunt or a granny or an uncle only that they [the children] are staying in their own house.... so they stay in their own house but they are being managed by an adult ... or a grandparent. They live in the same compound.
>
> AR: Do you see households that are totally independent?
>
> B: Yes but they are not many, they are not many because culturally they [the relatives] don't abandon their children.[26]

Another informant, Maggie, said much the same thing:

> M: Automatically this [the family] is the best place, immediately relatives take care of the children. Sometimes you'll see a plan that the relative sits down and discusses who is going to take this one who is going to take this one. So if there are three or four children, they just share them.[27]

While most orphans remain in their own village or the village of a relative who is caring for them, if there is a wealthy relative in a city, the child may go there. Many of the elite brokers whom we spoke with were caring for the orphaned children of their brothers and sisters. Thus, parentless children may be better off economically and in terms of education than children who are still living with one or both of their biological parents.[28]

Despite these facts-on-the-ground, orphans in orphanages loom large in the donor imagination of those looking at Africa from afar, even though very few orphans end up in institutional care.[29]

Western charitable organizations see supporting orphanages as an unalloyed good—building clinics, classrooms, and dormitories, as well as visiting to hug and comfort the children. But even these acts of generosity may have perverse effects: Linda Richter and Amy Norman note that as in "the highly publicized case of David Banda, the Malawian boy adopted by Madonna in 2006, destitute families sometimes place children in orphanages in the hope that their child will receive food and be educated."[30]

Counting Orphans

Small-scale altruists are moved to help a grandmother caring for her grandchildren who have lost their parents. Institutional altruists necessarily operate on a far larger scale. Reports on AIDS orphans often acknowledge the enormous influence of the 1997 report: *Children on the Brink*. Its "breakthrough" was a new methodology for estimating paternal and maternal, as well as double, orphans. It estimated a total of twenty-three million orphans in twenty-three developing countries in 1996, and projected thirty-five million by the year 2000 and forty million by 2010. The report provided "the first comprehensive global estimates of orphans of HIV and other causes, [and] helped raise world awareness of the impending calamity of the HIV/AIDS pandemic in developing countries."[31] By including children who had lost one parent in the category "orphan," the report created much higher figures for the total number of orphaned children than if only double orphans had been counted.

For example, an analysis of survey data from Malawi records that 3.0 percent of children 0–17 had lost both parents, while 13.2 percent of children aged 0–17 in 2004 were orphans by the wider definition.[32] Thus, the more capacious "orphanhood" definition allows international organizations to win the sympathy that the image of a parentless child evokes, while claiming very large numbers of children as orphans in need of help and support.

International Organizations and Villagers Collaborate to Create a New Category

Incorporating children who were not orphans but were considered by donors and international organization to be "vulnerable," further expanded the number of children who needed help:

133

UNICEF played a vital role in further broadening the category of children in need. After some years of pursuing an approach focused on "AIDS orphans," UNICEF and its associated international agencies spearheaded a shift in terminology for the sector from analysing the impact of AIDS on children by referring only to "children orphaned by AIDS" to referring to "orphans and other children affected by AIDS," and subsequently—in a move away from explicit reference to AIDS—to referring to "Orphans and (other) Vulnerable Children" (a phrase that was rapidly abbreviated to "OVC"). In its application, it is widely acknowledged that the phrase refers to the context of AIDS.[33]

Thus international organizations built on the global concern for AIDS orphans to launch a set of initiatives that not only included a much broader category of orphans but also all poor children.

The expanded definition of orphan to OVC also suited villagers well, as it permitted them to fold the problematic term "orphan" into the larger category of "vulnerable children." For villagers in Malawi, as elsewhere in Africa, the term orphan, which arouses compassion in donors, is unappealing.

In most Malawian languages the terms used to define an orphan and orphanhood include loss of parents; the rupture of social bonds; lack of family support; the process and situation of deprivation and want; and the lack of money or means of livelihood.[34]

The anthropologist Patricia Henderson, writing about Kwa Zulu Natal, makes an almost identical point about the meaning of the term "orphan" in isiZulu:

[T]he condition of orphanhood in an African context embraces existential dimensions, and has more to do with destitution, alienation and a lack of belongingness. The idea of being orphaned may accrue theoretically, therefore, to a person who still has parents but who has experienced profound displacement, for example, through war. To be orphaned in this sense is to be without moorings, social support and place.[35]

Since the condition of having lost one or both parents is not what distinguishes children in need of care, there is resistance to singling out children who are orphaned for special benefits unavailable to other needy children.

As a purely practical matter, local understandings determine the distribution of resources to village families. Since there are no official records of the economic status of children in a village, and since interventions rarely begin with a survey that distinguishes between poor orphans and other poor children, the village chief, or a pastor, or a village committee is given the task of determining who deserves aid. For them, however, singling out those who happen to be orphans makes no sense.

Nor does favoring orphans make sense for district NGO brokers. World Vision found that its child-sponsorship program created problems of inequality and envy in the villages: why should one poor child be favored over another just because that child was an orphan?[36] The flexibility offered by the term Orphans and Vulnerable Children means that brokers working on the ground can fold child sponsorships into broader programs meant to help whole communities, as World Vision does. They thus avoid creating envy, envy that may lead to accusations of witchcraft against families with orphans, who are seen to benefit unjustly.

Henderson describes an example of conflicts over singling out some children for extra help because they are "orphans" in a World Vision–sponsored organization for orphaned youth:

> Members of the project had lost one or both of their parents through death. The group was constituted in this way despite the fact that in setting it up, Zanele [a community worker for the project] was challenged by adults who came forward to form a children's rights committee. They pointed out the similarities between "orphans" and non-orphans in their community, particularly the fact that many children shared extreme poverty. The adults suggested the unfairness of distinguishing between orphans and non-orphans—a distinction thought to be unfair not only in terms of some tangible similarities between children but also in terms of the opprobrium with which the term "orphan" was burdened in metaphoric usage in isiZulu.[37]

Thus the term Orphans and Vulnerable Children or OVC is not simply a random piece of organizational jargon. Rather it represents a strategically calibrated, if unacknowledged, compromise among a number of agendas, meanings, and interests. Like many other awkward neologisms and acronyms that litter the AIDS landscape, the term also illustrates enormous cultural creativity as program beneficiaries and donors try to find an umbrella large enough to cover their multifarious needs, while retaining a symbol powerful enough to legitimate their activities.

REWARDING ORPHANHOOD

Even where the category "orphan" is problematic in local terms, local brokers have learned that the way to an altruist's heart is through offering "orphans" to visit and help. Sometimes these brokers are actually looking mainly for help for their own mothers or grandmothers, who may be raising numerous children or grandchildren. Indeed, the broker may be eager for assistance for children he himself is otherwise obligated to support. Brokers have learned that for altruists, being offered the opportunity to visit orphans, as we saw with Hopes and Prayers for Africa, is the most gratifying aspect of a mission trip or other forms of "voluntourism." Whatever the pejorative implications of the term "orphan" in local languages, and whatever the administrative difficulties of restricting assistance to actual orphans, entrepreneurial brokers—as well as chiefs and villagers—have learned to describe the assistance they seek as help for orphans, and on the ground, some children have learned to speak of themselves as orphans as well.

Anthropologists Helen Meintjes and Sonja Geise, who conducted extensive fieldwork in South Africa, show how the donor-defined category "orphan" has altered local understandings: "We document the emergence of children as 'orphans' who prior to the AIDS pandemic and its donor-driven responses would have been unlikely to have been considered as such in their communities."[38] Even though the traditional term for orphan in Xhosa, Sotho, Zulu, and other African languages is "synonymous with being unloved, uncared for, and destitute, [carrying] with it stigma and pity," when NGO resources focused on "orphans" arrive, "the word appears in places it had not previously circulated, as the concept is rhetorically deployed in a struggle to accumulate basic resources." In the Zulu community of Ingwavuma, "the one English word—besides basic greetings—that rolled off the tongues of residents of the area was 'orphan.'" After a foreign doctor founded an Orphan Care Project offering "food and school fees and to assist with foster care grant access for children under 18 whose parents had died," the authors report:

> Sunday afternoon in Ingwavuma, and there was a gentle knock on the door. Gentle but persistent. Nokuthula entered my host's house. "Auntie," she said to her over a cup of sweet tea, "Can't you help? I am an orphan." My host has known Nokuthula and her family for years. Nokuthula is "parentless": her father was never present, and her mother died when she was a tiny girl. She has been raised for 14

years by her maternal aunt. My host observed that for the first time ever Nokuthula labelled herself an "orphan."[39]

The fight against stigma and support for orphans and vulnerable children are staples of the AIDS enterprise. Whatever their merits for preventing AIDS or mitigating its effects, these themes and categories are popular with both donors and locals because—despite differing and sometimes contested meanings—they can be stretched and adjusted to make everyone happy. To Western publics, fighting stigma suggests heroic struggle against discrimination and for universal human rights; to religious leaders, it suggests an extension of their message of compassion and universal love. Combating stigma does not raise the awkward issues about criticizing others' sexual practices or the controversies over abstinence versus condoms that have long roiled the AIDS-prevention world.[40] And for villagers, being told to love and care for one another fits well with the advice they give each other and with expectations of care, helping, and reciprocity within village and extended-kinship systems.

The category "orphan," as we have seen, is problematic on the ground in sub-Saharan Africa. But the aspirations of both donors and local brokers can be satisfied—and the material need of some villagers served—by broadening and softening the category of orphans to include "orphans and other vulnerable children." Here there is a working accommodation that satisfies, for the most part, the interest of donors in serving the widest range of poor children while invoking the sentimental appeal of orphanhood.

CHAPTER 8

THEMES THAT MAKE EVERYONE ANXIOUS

Vulnerable Women and Harmful Cultural Practices

UNLIKE IMAGES OF VULNERABLE ORPHANS and stigmatized AIDS sufferers that rally donors, elite brokers, and even villagers to the same cause, images of vulnerable women and harmful cultural practices fascinate and disturb both brokers and donors, but leave them working at cross purposes. Donors and brokers agree that "vulnerable women" and "harmful cultural practices" contribute to the spread of AIDS, but underneath this surface agreement, the anxieties these issues arouse are very different for the two groups. The two themes are similar in that both brokers and donors manage to find common language, echoing the importance of each other's concerns. Yet in both, the issue that seems to one group a major driver of the AIDS epidemic arouses anxious reservations in the other.

The first theme, "vulnerable women" is a passionate concern of the global AIDS enterprise. It has justified many interventions, in Africa as elsewhere, to empower women so they can protect themselves from infection. The role of women in the AIDS epidemic is viewed quite differently, however, by both elite and rural Malawians: they see mercenary women who seduce and infect men in exchange for material resources, and favor constraint rather than empowerment. The second theme, "harmful cultural practices," refers to cultural traditions, such as sexual cleansing of widows or sexual initiation of girls at puberty, that are imagined to create AIDS risk. Concern about such sexual practices has long been deeply meaningful to Malawian elites who have embraced modernity and Christianity. To them, these practices are not only a sign of the backwardness of rural villagers, but are also immoral. The global AIDS donors, in contrast, speak the language of respect for cultural differences, and hesitate to back programs that seem like Western assaults on native traditions.

Because ultimately donors control the money, vulnerable women have become central to AIDS policy and programs, while the harmful cultural practices that concern educated Africans receive more limited and specialized attention. The donors and brokers nonetheless strategically manage to find a common language, in the case of women by focusing on women's poverty, and in the case of cultural practices, by promoting what are seen as universal human rights, especially of women and children.

LINKED IMAGES: WOMEN AND GIRLS AS VICTIMS

From the beginning of the AIDS epidemic in Africa, global donors have defined vulnerable women as central to the crisis.[1] Women and girls are portrayed as victims of men's lust: innocent wives infected by heedless husbands or poor women coerced into risky sex by men's money and power. The image of the vulnerable woman is often accompanied by statistics showing that in sub-Saharan Africa, women comprise 58 percent of all adults living with HIV and that among young people ages 15 to 24, women are between two to three times as likely as men to be infected.[2] The focus of many AIDS interventions, from the persistent effort to develop a female-controlled method of preventing HIV transmission (a microbicide or female condom), to efforts to empower women through training to learn how to negotiate safe sex, to attempts to transform men into model domestic partners, highlight the preoccupation with women as victims.

Images of women's desperate vulnerability are particularly vivid in the discourse about "harmful cultural practices." In the Western press, disturbing, lurid stories paint women and girls as at the mercy of primitive, even depraved cultural practices, purveying a prurient blend of the exotic and erotic. Newspapers carry horrifying stories linking AIDS to the rape of infants in South Africa[3] and outraged reports of widows forced to marry a dead husband's brother.[4] Similar stories have appeared in Malawi newspapers.[5]

Even when the images are less lurid, institutional altruists are convinced that African cultural norms stifle women's agency. Thus, norms that deny women full equality—in education, inheritance, marriage and divorce, economic opportunity—have to be transformed if AIDS is to be stopped, and more generally, if Africa is to develop. Thus issues of culture and vulnerable women are intertwined in the AIDS imaginary, even if, as we shall see below, the fates of these two themes differ in important ways.

CONTENDING MORAL VISIONS

Images of vulnerable women or harmful cultural practices mean different things to foreign donors, brokers, and villagers. These differing views are powerful because they embody competing moral visions.[6] Secular,

139

progressive advocates of human rights, gender equality, or empowerment seldom recognize just how morally infused their visions are, just as are the commitments of Malawian brokers and villagers to their images of proper behavior.

We found that in some contexts Malawian brokers enthusiastically embrace modernity, whereas in others they criticize donors who do not appreciate, or even understand, the moral visions that both brokers and villagers believe uphold social order.[7] When brokers speak formally—in our interviews in their offices, to the press—they support human rights and individual autonomy, and deprecate the backward practices of villagers. When, however, our conversations with brokers are informal, they, like the villagers, blame the Western values of the donors: "nowadays there is too much freedom," especially for women and young people. Rather than worrying about violations of human rights, brokers and villagers are more likely to be worried about moral disorder.[8]

VULNERABLE WOMEN, MERCENARY WOMEN

Of all the themes that stimulate the imaginations of donors and brokers, one of the slipperiest is that of "vulnerable women" (often "vulnerable women and girls"). Here, Malawians and their international partners appear to be singing the same song: because of poverty and culture, women are particularly vulnerable to HIV infection, and as a result, "something must be done." But although the melody is the same, the lyrics are different. Both partners seem to identify the same problem, but each has a very different conception of *what* must be done. Western donors imagine women as victims who urgently need training in empowerment so that they can "just say no" to unsafe sex. Malawian brokers and villagers acknowledge that women are "poor," but they are anxious about mercenary women in miniskirts who tempt good men. To end the epidemic, mercenary women need to be restrained rather than empowered.

The Perspective of International Elites: Empower Vulnerable Women

A special meeting of the United Nations in 2001 declared its commitment to a global response to AIDS.[9] The Declaration of Commitment labeled women and girls as particularly vulnerable to AIDS, "[s]tressing that gender equality and the empowerment of women are fundamental elements in the reduction of the vulnerability of women and girls to HIV/AIDS" (Article 14) and that "The vulnerable must be given priority in the response … Empowering women is essential for reducing vulnerability" (Articles 62–64). "By 2003, all nations are expected to address factors that make individuals particularly vulnerable to HIV infection," including "lack of empowerment of women." In the Declaration, young men ("boys") are sometimes mentioned, but in a brief, *pro forma* way, as if the authors did not want to be seen as not respecting gender equality.

The goal of empowering vulnerable girls and women has become the Holy Grail of development policy more generally.[10] In the AIDS world, a focus on the benefits of empowering women is complemented by an image of women as the main victims of the epidemic. Thus, donors must help by empowering them in their sexual and marital relationships: women must always have the right to refuse sex, even with their husbands, and they have to be empowered to set the terms of sex, including condom use.

The image of women as too powerless to refuse risky sexual encounters is linked to a broader understanding that women lack economic power, along with educational and legal equality. In imagery adapted from the US and European women's movements, the argument is that if women had economic and social equality, they would be less dependent on men, and thus less likely to engage in risky sex. Women need power so that they can bargain sexually as equals. It is taken for granted that giving women resources (such as education and the ability to earn their own livelihoods) will reduce their vulnerability to HIV.

Improving women's condition is good in itself, and we heartily endorse it. But the assumption that increasing women's autonomy and power by improving their economic status will protect them from HIV is not borne out by data from Africa, which shows that HIV prevalence is often higher among the urban and the wealthy, both men and women.[11] Overall, if a donor's only concern were HIV prevention, it should probably encourage girls to stay in the village and marry early to a man too poor to have girlfriends.

The Perspective from Rural Malawi: Mercenary Women

From afar, Western altruists see desperately poor women, without legal or social rights, engaging in survival sex to feed themselves and their starving children. Malawians, close to the epidemic, recognize that many women are poor and have few alternatives to depending on a sexual partner. What preoccupies both Malawian villagers and brokers, however, is the threat

posed by rapacious women who divert men's money from their moral obligation to support their family, and in so doing, bring a fatal disease into
the home, a disease that, it is assumed, will be swiftly transmitted to the
men's innocent wives, and ultimately, leave their children orphans.

We begin with the villagers' views, then the brokers'. Below is a conversation reported by a local ethnographer among men at a trading center,
lounging in front of a minimart, who see a woman they know to be a prostitute. The conversation is tinged with envy at the amount of money she
earns, more than many men in the area. The ethnographer wrote using his
own form of anonymization:

> B started raging against the lady C that she is a prostitute she is dis-
> turbing people marriages, she is going for married couples within
> the villages that is why she is not getting married. See she has bought
> a lot of bananas paying a K200 note all those notes she is being given
> by the men within the area. Mr. B continued talking about the lady
> C that that's why *Kachilombo* [Chichewa for HIV, the "little wild
> beasts" in the blood] is not going to finish. It will not go away be-
> cause of these (*ANAMASUPUNI*) meaning prostitutes. He Mr. B said
> that "we men are stupid when we see a woman prostitute even if she
> demands a lot of money we still have to pay forgetting that we have
> left our homes without household needs we can pay a lady K100 or
> K200 while our family is starving this is common. This lady C shall
> not [need to] get married because she is getting cash daily and at the
> end of the months she gets thousands of kwachas."[12]

Here, and in many of the more than twelve hundred ethnographic journals
written over the years by rural Malawian observers, the problem of wom-
en's poverty is perceived as less important than the danger posed by their
success in extracting resources from helpless men.

Domestic violence (variously called "gender-based violence" or "intimate partner violence") is another intense focus of donor concern. But it
too looks very different from a Malawian perspective.[13] While donors condemn violence against women, Malawians see *women* using violence to protect their legitimate claims to men. In the ethnographic journals, the most
common form of violence is between a wife and a girlfriend. Typically, the
wife attacks the girlfriend in order to defend her property—that is, her husband and the resources he provides for her and her children. While some
watching the fight blame the husband and others the girlfriend, no one
questions that the wronged wife is justified in defending her claims:

This morning I went to Mangochi Turn Off where I found women fighting and after investigation, I heard that the fighting was between three people.

A certain business man is married and has got four children but he has also a sexual partner who is well known for having sex with married men. Today the man went to chat with the girl friend who has spent the night at Isha Allah Rest House.... He thought that nobody has seen him because he used a certain path which is behind the market and it is through a certain bush but the friend of his wife who was going to the market saw him.... She saw the man entering the rest house and she rushed to her friend and tell her the whole story that her husband has entered the rest house.[14]

When the wife and her friend see the couple coming out of the rest house "holding hands," "talking lovely," laughing and kissing, they start after the girlfriend, while the husband runs away:

Many people come to witness the fighting and encourage the women to beat the girl because it is her behaviour of having sex with other women's husband and that always she said that she is queen of the town and that every man in the market has sex with her....

Many people rushed to the scene of the incident and supported the two women. The two women beat the girl seriously and tore her clothes. The girl cried with pain for she had several wounds on the face and she managed to cut the finger of the wife of her boyfriend leaving it about to fall down and the wife cried with pain then she touches the breast of the girlfriend and cut it with her mouth....

Several people were still at the place of incident talking to each other. Some people said the women were wrong for they have beaten an innocent person because the girl did not propose the man but is the man who had proposed her and the woman should have beat the husband. Others said that the girl is a wrong person because she knows that the person who is proposing her has got a family and she did not refuse him so she must receive the reward from her behaviour.

Both wives and girlfriends and their neighbors understand well that a fight over who should be having sex with whom is also a fight about how a man's resources should be distributed. It is also a moral issue: no one questions a wife's right to defend what is hers and her children's.

FIGURE 8.1. Village women socializing. Malawians spend a great deal of time gossiping about the moral and immoral behavior of their neighbors. Here, a group of women are laughing and chatting on the veranda of the home of one of them. *Photo: Gerald Cotts.*

Another dramatic incident in a market center drew a crowd of onlookers who laughed and jeered. The ethnographer describes a wife storming into a bar looking for the bar girl who has been sleeping with her husband. The bar girl and the husband have run away, but the other bar girls attack the wife and defend their right to do business on their own premises. The wife, her lip bloodied, insults them, calling them "prostitutes" and boasting that she gets the husband's "whole salary" while they receive only a paltry sum. The bar girls taunt the wife for not being able to satisfy her husband, with one shouting, "You have the big problem, big mum, your husband is not for you alone! He was born not for you special, and indeed he will be sleeping with all of us here, because we also need what he has, we need the penis as well, for once it enters on us, we just know that we are to eat that day. No penis, no money!"[15]

Against this background, it is perhaps understandable that Malawians' image of vulnerable women differs from that of international donors.

The Perspective of the Elites: Awkward Contradictions

The gap between the ways altruists from afar think about women and the ways Malawians do is by no means peculiar to rural villagers. The awkward contradictions for Malawian elites who adopt the rhetoric of global feminism are vividly illustrated by Patricia Kaliati, from 2007 to 2012 variously Malawi's Minister of Gender, Child Development and Welfare, Minister of Information and Civic Education, or Minister of Information and Tourism. Kaliati was celebrated for her support of women and girls' empowerment, as at this Girls Empowerment Network workshop called "Empowerment girls can do wonders":

> Kaliati received a hero's welcome on arrival and departure at French Culture Centre, with hundreds of excited school girls and orphans shouting *Akweni! Akweni!* while rushing to hug her.
>
> Kaliati said her ministry will ensure the girl-child is protected and empowered starting in homes and the community.
>
> She appealed to all abused girls including incest crimes to report culprits and pleaded with mothers not to protect husbands who defile their daughters.
>
> Kaliati, a former teacher also received overwhelming applause and chanting during an inspirational talk bluntly telling school-girls to finish school and avoid the evils of early marriage.[16]

In the formal context of a speech on empowering girls, Minister Kaliati's rhetoric was impeccable. In another context, however, she, like rural wives, speaks as a wife seeking to protect her marriage. In 2007, an article in the *Saturday Nation* reported that Kaliati had kidnapped and beaten a maid, Elizabeth Ngalawa, who she believed had had sex with her husband.

> Ngalawa, 33, who once worked for Blantyre-based women rights lawyer Seodi White, claims the group took her to Nkando (the minister's home) where Kaliati allegedly stripped the victim and the minister asked the men to lay with her as punishment for going out with Mr. Kaliati.
>
> When contacted for her side of the story late last month, the minister said Ngalawa could not have been harassed without having done any wrong.

Said Kaliati: "Wasn't she caught with my husband? Go and ask her if she wasn't found with him [Mr. Kaliati]. She must face me and we must find out all about this."[17]

Three years later, Minister Kaliati said to the press:

If you are a celebrity or a prominent person in society and you indulge in gender-based domestic violence; forget about using your fame to escape the wrath of the law, Gender Minister Patricia Kaliati has warned.

"I am bitter with prominent figures that are at the centre of domestic violence. But what I can tell them is that no one is above the law. We will deal with them."[18]

As of June 2016, after several years as Minister of Gender, Children, Disability and Social Welfare, Kaliati is now Minister of Information, Communications Technology and Civic Education and the official Government Spokesperson.

Many Malawian elites, like villagers, see seductive women as at fault for threatening the moral order by making themselves irresistible to men. Despite the rhetoric of women's vulnerability, they seek to restore order by suppressing vice, reducing temptation, and—especially—restraining women's behavior.

Policy Solutions

Where the Malawian donors and brokers differ most is in their conceptions of what fuels the AIDS epidemic and how best to prevent AIDS. For the donors, it is campaigns to change intimate behavior, especially by empowering women, particularly young women. For the brokers, it is stopping immoral behavior that is associated with Western modernity. For villagers, the solution is to restrain women who have been influenced by "democracy" and now have "too much freedom."

It is not that the elite brokers are forced to use the rhetoric of "vulnerable women." Sometimes this genuinely resonates with them, as when they imagine poor women in the village—their grandmothers, perhaps—or the general poverty they know villagers experience. But when they think about solutions closer to home, they think about the prostitutes and seductresses who are after men's money. Both women's poverty and women's desire for money are realities for the elite brokers.

So how do NGO brokers, who see themselves as threatened by disorderly women but who also partake in the globalized discourse about vulnerable women, manage? Again, as with Minister Kaliati, one solution is to speak in different voices in different contexts. In our experience interviewing brokers in both formal and informal contexts, when they leave their offices, they spontaneously talk of predatory women. For example, brokers from several southern African countries, participating in a meeting in South Africa on an intervention to empower poor women who have to sell sex to survive, were fully on board; at the tea break, however, a broker said to his colleague, "But what can a man do if a woman dresses in a way that tempts him?" No one disagreed that "sexy dressing" was tempting: the shared assumption was that a man approached by a woman in a mini-skirt could not do other than have sex with her.[19]

Restraining Women

Western donors are often appalled when African legislators pass laws that, in the words of advocates, "criminalize AIDS." The concept behind the laws is that those who know they are HIV+ but nonetheless have unprotected sex are willfully endangering others. Global donors counter by urging respect for human rights. Elite brokers have responded to the global pressure by enveloping the issue of controlling infected women in the rhetoric of human rights. In October 2009, a police sweep in Malawi's Mwanza District arrested sex workers and men and took them to the police station. The men were released; medical personnel gave the women a mandatory HIV test, and then gave the names of the HIV+ to the police. A magistrate charged the women with violating a section of the criminal code that penalized spreading venereal disease. As reported in the newspapers, the government official who had final responsibility for AIDS policy, Dr. Mary Shawa, began by criticizing the police. Even as she invoked "human rights," however, her focus returned to mercenary women who endanger their fellow citizens:

> Dr Mary Shawa, Secretary for HIV/Aids and Nutrition in the Office of the President and Cabinet, said while Malawi had to employ every available and legitimate way to contain HIV/Aids, testing the sex workers alone, and not their clients as well, was not justice enough. . . . "We all know the importance of human rights. But when we are demanding our rights, we also have to keep in mind our responsibilities. It is the sex workers' right to make money but if we are all careful, we

will not make that money at the expense of another person's right to life," Shawa said.[20]

Thus in an unbroken flow of rhetoric, threats to the human rights of sex workers morphed into the threat sex workers posed to the "right to life" of men they might infect.[21]

Another high official, the director of the Malawi Human Rights Commission, speaking of the need for mandatory testing of sex workers, put it more bluntly. He said, "It's not easy to take a human rights lens to some of these issues. It's like having a person with a machine gun with bullets. The bullets shoot out, bang! bang! bang! And many people are dead."[22]

In the case of vulnerable women, then, the misunderstandings that separate the perceptions of Malawian brokers (and villagers) from those of international donors are harder to bridge than in the cases of stigma or orphans. Here, the "working misunderstandings" often don't work, as local actors use the rhetoric of empowerment and human rights while continually returning to policies that would constrain rather than enhance women's autonomy. In all three of our examples (and we could provide many more), gaps between expectations and understandings of different participants in the AIDS enterprise are finessed, sidestepped, or obscured. Categories and concepts are unstable in their meanings, and groups with very different agendas "get along" because they do not confront the different meanings they attach to the same words.

The elite brokers usually manage to elide the contradictions between the international rhetoric and their own views. The district-level brokers and town fathers are less deft. They repeat, and we think believe in, the international messages, but they also have concerns that are not on the international agenda. In 2000, the government asked each district assembly to develop an HIV prevention plan. For the Balaka District Assembly, high on the list of objectives was to "promote cultural values, beliefs and practices that prevent the spread of HIV/AIDS" and "to effectively promote abstinence and mutual faithfulness among youth and adults." The document also listed problems. Most were standard, such as "increase of patients with HIV/AIDS related illnesses," "unavailability of antiretroviral drugs," and "inadequate resources." But the district elites were also concerned about controlling promiscuous sex—"social and religious gatherings at awkward hours" [i.e., at night, when people could have sex in the dark and would not be observed]—and controlling the "proliferation of pornographic materials in the district."[23] These district leaders, while echoing some standard global rhetoric, accentuated the positive meaning of

148

"culture": not the practices of backward villagers, but traditional values—
the good culture that needs to be restored (along with the authority of
parents, elders, and one assumes, the local elites themselves). Here, then,
in a document on HIV prevention prepared by town fathers, we see how
donors' standard objectives are blended with local concerns about late
night religious gatherings and the availability of pornography, both of
which are seen as creating sexual temptation.

Other suggestions emerged from regional meetings organized by NAC
to get the views of district-level brokers and town fathers. Again, the policies and programs of NAC hewed very closely to international policies
and programs. The district brokers repeated these, but they were also concerned about moral order. In the following list of suggestions taken from
the minutes of the meetings, we find the participants concerned about a
decline in proper sexual behavior, an increase in immoral sexual behavior,
and the abandonment of good cultural practices while bad ones persist.[24]

In response to a question asked by the NAC organizer of the meeting,
"What is fueling the epidemic?" most answers were based on the widespread understanding that when husbands and wives were separated for
an extended period, each was likely to take another sexual partner, and,
conversely, when men and women were together at night for functions
such as dances and prayer meetings, they would inevitably pair up. Other
responses showed concern about the decline of moral order:

Abandonment of cultural practices that were promoting delayed
    sexual debut
Uncontrolled prostitution
Misunderstanding and misapplication of human rights (eg dressing by
    girls and young women attracting older men hence increase risk of
    contracting HIV)

For older villagers and townspeople, there is a direct line from the first
multiparty elections, in 1994, to "sexy dressing," and from there to AIDS,
as in this discussion in a bar. An older woman says

You know what, democracy has destroyed everything see the way
they have dressed, see the min-skirts this makes men to get attracted
with the legs, ending up proposing them and sleeping with them
others put on tight clothing, trousers which all these things during
our time was not happening since 1960's, 70's 80s, but since 1990's
Oh![25]

149

In the face of the anxiety felt by men and wives, the solution to AIDS is not to empower women as the United Nations demanded: they are all too empowered. In another conversation among rural Malawians, a man disagrees with the human rights approach and proposes what he considers a more appropriate solution:

> What is necessary is for the Government and the Judiciary to put a law in place to get rid of prostituting in Malawi to stop girls in bars once found they must be arrested throughout the country.... why can't the police be arresting all women and girls moving in town at night and conserve the lives of men who are public figures, professionals.[26]

While the elite brokers, who join policy workshops or meet with donors to formulate strategic plans to combat AIDS, do not openly express such views, it is programs that fit local aspirations—providing bursaries to secondary school girls to finish school, forcing pregnant women to get tested to prevent transmission of HIV to their babies,[27] or encouraging young people to abstain from sex—that receive enthusiastic assent. Other approaches, which donors may see as more empowering, may end up sidestepped as Malawian brokers drag their feet on programs that don't really fit their understanding of the world.

HARMFUL CULTURAL PRACTICES, DELICATE CULTURAL SENSITIVITIES: "THE SEXUAL AREA IS A CULTURAL MINEFIELD"

When we were newcomers to Malawi, one of the first things we heard— often literally the first thing an educated Malawian said to us—was about the *fisi*. In the villages, we were told, the *fisi* ("hyena") is a man hired by a woman's brothers to sneak in and impregnate her if her husband is not doing the job; the *fisi* is also frequently described as a "sexual cleanser," paid to have intercourse with women whose husbands have died to drive away their spirits from the village, or to "cleanse" a woman who has miscarried. We also often heard about the practice of labia stretching; a Malawian friend (and elite broker) seemed both bemused and appalled as she explained that some Malawian women have labia long enough to tie around the man's penis to enhance his sexual pleasure.[28]

At first we were fascinated, a bit titillated, and a little embarrassed by these tales. But then, as we realized how frequently we heard about these and other exotic practices and the role our informants insisted these play in spreading AIDS, we were simply puzzled. Why were Malawian brokers so eager to regale a foreigner with shocking stories? Why did we hear so little about these exotic practices in the villages? And what role do these stories play in prevention policies and programs?

We focus not on whether these practices really exist (many do, or have existed in some form within the memory of the elders), but on the responses they evoke in donors, brokers, villagers, and visitors from the West.[29] Images of harmful cultural practices carry meanings about African backwardness, about cultural authenticity, and about the mysteriousness of the AIDS threat. These meanings also differ for those in different social worlds: for educated elites versus the villagers whose world the elites have escaped, for international staff versus country nationals in their battles for autonomy and influence, and for donors who desire to be "culturally sensitive."

To convey a flavor of the brokers' views of cultural practices—often transmitted to donors and other visitors—here is a June 2014 e-mail from a friend working in Malawi:

I just had a conversation that I thought you would find interesting. I was talking with a doctor from the UK who is working in Blantyre and received a 4 day training on medicine in Malawi. One of the days was dedicated to "cultural factors impacting health in Malawi." Of course the training discussed cultural factors influencing the high prevalence of HIV (or bad culture). The trainer, an upper class Malawian who worked at the College of Medicine Hospital, said that one of the main contributors to the continued epidemic is the beliefs held by Malawians. As reported by the UK doctor, the trainer said, "these beliefs are especially a problem in the villages. Many people in the village believe that if you have sex with a child or a virgin then it will rid you of the virus. This keeps giving the virus to the Malawian youth and children, especially young girls who can't protect themselves."

Of course the UK doctor bought the entire spiel and told me how "backwards beliefs" are still such a big problem for HIV in Malawi and how difficult it is to "get uneducated people to believe the facts" about the epidemic.[30]

The belief that "sex with a virgin will cure AIDS" has not been documented, either in Malawi, or in South Africa, where the claim apparently originated.[31] In the more than twelve hundred ethnographic journals we have, there are many outlandish claims about AIDS—government or donor conspiracies to spread the disease and hide the existence of medicines to cure it, witchcraft accusations, and claims early on that condoms either harbored the disease or could cause cancer—but the claim about sex with a virgin never appears. So we have to ask why elite Malawians would make such a claim about village beliefs and why international aid workers would so readily believe it.

What Do Elite Brokers Consider "Harmful" Cultural Practices?

The peculiarity of Malawian brokers' concern with harmful cultural practices is highlighted by the contrast with the standard public health approaches to HIV prevention. The public health view of the key sexual practices that drive the AIDS epidemic in sub-Saharan Africa has changed over time. Initially, epidemiologists and others saw the main transmission routes as sex workers, mobile men such as truck drivers, and urban migrants with wives in the villages. As the epidemic became generalized rather than confined to "core" or "high risk" groups, and as Uganda appeared to have developed a successful approach to curbing the epidemic, the international advice to Africans became the ABCs: Abstain from sex before marriage, Be faithful afterwards, and, if that is impossible, to use Condoms consistently.[32] Voluntary HIV testing (VCT) and treating sexually transmitted infections also became part of the standard "prevention package."[33] Discouraged by the persistent high prevalence in the region, in the last few years the international prevention community has identified other sources of risk—multiple concurrent partnerships and lack of male circumcision are now considered key drivers of the epidemic.[34]

These are not, however, the sexual practices that fascinate Malawian elites. They are convinced that exotic cultural practices transmit HIV, but are ambivalent about programs that would show a lack of respect for Malawian traditions. Multiple reports have been commissioned to describe the cultural practices that put village Malawians at risk for HIV; the first one we have is from 1997.[35] These reports focus on what the elites consider tribal, or ritual, or exotic practices—those that Malawians themselves define as "cultural."[36] The most thorough we have found is a 2006 report by the Malawi Human Rights Commission, funded by NORAD, a major donor to Malawi.[37]

The report begins with a defense of "culture" in universalistic terms:[38]

Like any other society in the world, Malawi is governed by a culture whose beliefs, values, customs, and a host of social practices have a powerful influence on community life. Culture is very important for national identity. Each nation has some ways of life that are unique to it. Culture is also important for national development. As it is rightly argued, people without a culture are like a tree without roots. Culture is at the root of national development, and for that development to be sustainable that culture must be vibrant. At the same time it is worth noting that, some elements of culture can be obstacles to development. (p. 7)

The report then goes on to describe the "customs, values, and traditions" of Malawi's various ethnic groups, focusing on practices considered to violate human rights and to transmit HIV. Its catalog, culled from focus group discussions and interviews around the country, describes a multitude of rituals and practices. It lists fifty-six practices, described as an anthropologist might, with their names in local languages and their "frequency" assessed through a survey. Many practices are described in great detail, with comments from the focus group discussions. The beginning of one such description conveys the tone of the document as a whole:

4.5.4 KULOWA KUFA / KUPITA KUFA

Kulowa kufa, a practice by which a man slept with a woman whose husband or son had just died, to put to rest the spirit of the deceased, was mentioned as a practice that took place in the areas of 12.9% of the interviewees.

In Chitipa, for example, *kulowa kufa* was said to take place in isolated cases. The revelation that it took place came from women's FGDs and not men's. The latter insisted that in their area no practice involving sexual intercourse took place as a means of appeasing the spirit of the departed man. According to the women, where it happens, a meeting of relatives of the deceased husband was organized where a man was chosen to sleep with the woman. In most cases the chosen man would be the one who would eventually inherit the woman as his wife (*chokolo*).

Kulowa kufa is common in Nsanje where generally it would start three days after burial when the widow or mother of the deceased would sit at the veranda of her house with maize husks in one calabash, and water in the other. Those relatives that had sex during the period of mourning came and confessed their wrong deeds, by touching the husks. While touching the husks, they whispered: "I stole your death so I have come to give it back to you." After the exercise, the woman would take some of the husks and put them under the mat or bed, where she would have sex with a cleanser. The process would last for three days. (p. 63)

Often the description of a "cultural practice" is accompanied by a recommendation for change, also conveyed from the focus group discussions, which seem to represent the voice of reasoned appraisal:

4.5.9 KUPITA IMFA YA MIMBA (MATERNAL DEATH)

... Among the Ngoni, if a pregnant woman dies, her stomach is speared in order to kill the unborn baby. It is believed that burying the pregnant woman with a live unborn baby is an abomination. This practice is referred to as *nthumbi*. FGD participants recommended that this practice should be modified because it does not make sense to spear a dead body. (p. 66)

Not all the practices are considered "harmful," however. Some are regarded as essential to the culture of various groups, and sometimes the focus group members advocate a practice for hygiene, or, as in the case of labia stretching, for promoting sexual satisfaction in marriage:

Makuna [stretched labia] are said to serve the following purposes:

- Stimulating both the man and the woman during foreplay as the man caresses them....
- Holding the man's member in place during intercourse.
- Making it easy for the penis to penetrate thereby avoid hurting the woman during intercourse.
- Reducing problems on delivery as the birth canal is properly opened.
- Making the labia cover the inner female private parts, especially for women who have given birth....

In most of the areas covered by this study therefore *makuna* were held in very high regard and most respondents were of the view that this practice should be maintained because, among other reasons, it helps strengthen marriages. (p. 40)

Many cultural practices were also condemned for increasing HIV/AIDS risk, with recommendations that they be abandoned:

> ... in most of the sites people were advocating for the abolition of wife inheritance. They contended, among others, that the practice contributed significantly to the spread of HIV/AIDS as many go into it without ascertaining the cause of death of their relatives. As one female respondent in T/A Mbenje in Nsanje recalled with bitterness:
>
> *Two brothers died one after the other in a period of less than three years after they each inherited a certain woman. The society in general thought that the brothers died because of witchcraft, but I have no doubt in my mind that it was because of the HIV/AIDS scourge.* (p. 23)

The very different take villagers have on the practices condemned by elites emerges in notes from an AIDS training that a member of a Village AIDS Committee, also the neighbor of one of our local ethnographers, attended in 2003. The ethnographer borrowed the manual and copied it for us, along with the notes the neighbor wrote in the margins during the training.

The first lesson was about the epidemiology of HIV; the second addressed the question "*Zikhalidwe ziti zimene zingathandire kfulitsa matenda a edzi?*" translated by the ethnographer as "What are the kind of behaviours that might help the spread of AIDS?" This is followed by a list of seven practices, along with the neighbor's notes of what the trainer said about each practice (or in a few cases the ethnographer's notes). Since the manuals are distributed nation-wide, the list presumably represents the view of the Ministry of Health about "harmful cultural practices." The only practice concordant with the drivers of the epidemic the international prevention community recognizes is the last on the list. From the notes the diarist's neighbor took (for reasons of space, we omit the third and fourth items on the list, the *fisi* and widow inheritance, both condemned for spreading HIV):[39]

1. *Mitala* (Polygamy): "Notes said that a polygamy behavior system is what encourages the rapid spread of this disease AIDS because when a man has AIDS and marries two wives or more like the Moslems he normally has a fixed time table like sleeping at one wife's home a week and then another week at another wife as well and it's very risky because one never knows that the time he is at another

wife then behind him an extra marital partner comes in. And that one who comes in she never knows that he has HIV/AIDS"

2. *Kuchita Chinamwah Mwa Umbuli* ("Doing initiation with illiteracy"): "The notes stated that there are a lot of initiators (*Angabila*) who are uneducated and they did not attend civic education[40] concerning AIDS and they have their own beliefs regarding AIDS, as a result they help in the spread of AIDS because these uneducated initiators tend to use one knife or razor for many young boys and if one young boy has AIDS and the same razor is used for other young boys it means the other boys will contract the disease AIDS during that circumcision they undergo at *jando* (male boys initiation)." ...

5. *Chidyerano Chmwanamwaye*: (Wife swapping): ethnographer's notes: "This means the system of exchanging sexual partners even wives because men are best friends. For example I can have a sexual partner somewhere or I am married and because I have my best friend Chamboko and he is also married and since we are best friends then we should agree both between his wife and my wife while we are all of us together that we will be exchanging these wives whenever we want to.... And this is what is called *Chidyerano* (or *Kapena*) *Chimwanamwaye* currently happening in Malawi by other tribes I assume to be the Tumbukas and the Sena and other related tribes."

6. *Kugwinits a Ntchito Lezala Limodzi Kwa Asiung'anga*: ethnographer's notes: "Using one razor blade especially at the traditional doctor"

7. *Kusakhulu Pinka* ("Not faithful"): "The notes said that when one is unfaithful it means that he/she normally does whatever he/she thinks like having extramarital sexual partners and don't trust his or her husband or his wife and eventually contracts AIDS."

What did the trainee think of these? When the ethnographer returned the manual with the notes, the neighbor was building a grass fence for his pit latrine, so the ethnographer helped him as they talked. The ethnographer asked his neighbor what he had learned. The neighbor said that he had learned very little that was new during the training because these things "are well known to anyone as of now because that issues are very common in Radio and talked everywhere, and that there is AIDS in this world even a young child knows."

There was one thing that the two men did not know that fascinated them. While they worked side-by-side they had a lively conversation about *chidyerano/chimwamwaye,* or "wife swapping." This, they joked, sounded like a really exciting idea. The friend said:

> ... what he really saw very strange was about *chidyerano/chimwamwaye.* I laughed. And he laughed and said that if it really happens then it's a good system because there are some friends who really have beautiful women (wives). I laughed and he laughed and said that if a friend of you he had married a dull woman and you had/ have married a beautiful woman then as of him [in his opinion] *chidyerano* the exchanging of sexual partners cannot happen.[41]

They continued discussing the pros and cons of wife swapping, the dangers of jealousy, and the possibility that one's wife might prefer the other man and seek a divorce ("[the neighbor] added saying that the end result it may happen that your/his friend is very sweet [a term for good sex] and his wife will be distinguishing with his sweetness and admiring his friend and eventually they come to agree each other to marry each other so that she should divorce her husband and the husband divorcing his wife and marry each other. I laughed."). Thus these villagers whiled away a morning contemplating the possible delights of an intriguing cultural practice they hadn't previously heard about. For villagers, as well as donors and brokers, exotic practices are the practices of others.

The town fathers in the districts recognize some of the same exotic practices as do the national elites in the capital, and like the national elites, they attribute these to "villagers" and not to themselves. They sometimes refer to local practices and propose local solutions. But as with the Balaka town fathers' views that late night meetings and pornography fuel the epidemic, when it comes to harmful cultural practices, the district elites are worried not only about AIDS but also about moral disorder in their communities.

All the players, from donors and elite brokers to villagers and district elites thus employ the concept of "harmful cultural practices" in a similar way: to identify practices that can be seen as the province of exotic others. But since they identify very different practices as "cultural" in this sense, they necessarily talk past each other, and each group therefore risks offending the sensibilities of the others.

CULTURAL SENSITIVITIES AND HARMFUL CULTURAL PRACTICES

Concerns about harmful cultural practices reverberate in various strata of Malawian society, but, as we have seen, with very different meanings. Here we try to explain why the issue of cultural practices intrigues so many different kinds of actors, and why those in different social locations define what "culture" is, and more important, what is potentially dangerous about it, so differently.

WHY DO THE ELITES CONSIDER CULTURAL PRACTICES TO BE DRIVERS OF THE AIDS EPIDEMIC?

Elites' concern about villagers' cultural practices is not due to epidemiological or clinical evidence that such practices are important contributors to the HIV epidemic. There simply is no such evidence.[42] While the exotic practices may sound dangerous, the basic epidemiological reality is that risk of HIV transmission from any one act of sexual intercourse is very low, estimated to be substantially less than one infection per one hundred unprotected acts of intercourse with an infected partner, and in some estimates, less than one per one thousand.[43] Even widow inheritance, when a widow is forced to marry her dead husband's brother, which sounds dangerous epidemiologically, adds to overall AIDS risk only if one assumes that the widow would remain unmarried in the absence of widow inheritance. But where a woman remaining single is unlikely, as in rural Malawi, widow inheritance probably adds no more to overall risk than leaving widows to marry or not as best they can.

Other indicators that exotic cultural practices are not the major drivers of the epidemic in Malawi are that many new infections occur in stable heterosexual partnerships (357 out of every 1,000 new infections) or in casual sexual relationships,[44] and that in many countries in sub-Saharan Africa, including Malawi, HIV prevalence is substantially lower in rural areas, where these practices are thought to be still in force, than in the urban areas where the elites themselves live.[45]

Malawian elites assume (without evidence) that what they consider to be harmful cultural practices transmit HIV. But when they talk about cultural practices, it is evident that they are also conveying to us their conception of themselves and their place in Malawian society. What is the core of that presentation of self, and why does it emphasize the role of harmful traditional practices? We have already described the way some elites use their knowledge about local culture to assert their expertise with foreigners, making the implicit (or sometimes explicit) claim that only they can provide real insight into the peculiarities of local culture. But such careerist motives provide a very incomplete understanding of Malawian elites' motives and ideas.

Modernity

The cosmopolitan and urbanized elites have an ambivalent relationship to "culture" and "tradition." On the one hand, they want to differentiate themselves from their "backward" kin in the villages.[46] These elites tell stories about exotic sexual practices as a way of differentiating themselves from what they see as the poverty, superstition, and ignorance they have left behind. But it is more than that. Such stories also provide pleasure as elites connect themselves to "tradition," which represents both what is distinctive about them in the community of nations and, in nostalgia's gaze, what might protect them and their countrymen from the mercenary individualism and the abandonment of traditional obligations that seem to threaten their society. Talking about cultural traditions is simultaneously titillating (if one hears about exotic practices), affirming of one's modernity (as one enacts her difference from backward villagers), and comforting (as one evokes a world of lost solidarities). And by criticizing harmful cultural practices as modes of transmitting HIV, the elites can see themselves as engaged in fighting AIDS.

In the end, our conclusion is that Malawian elites focus on harmful cultural practices both because they want to assert cultural authority and because they genuinely feel that these practices must explain why Africans are at such risk of HIV and AIDS. A focus on cultural practices offers them an opportunity to make a distinctive contribution to the battle against AIDS by educating villagers about the harms of their cultural practices. This is something that international experts who come to advise on HIV prevention policies and programs cannot do.

A signal that the brokers who tell us stories about *fisi* are uneasy is that they almost invariably add that of course there is also "good culture" in the villages: traditions that should be maintained and strengthened.[47] One hears that in the past girls stayed virgins until marriage, children respected their elders, and sexual morality was upheld.

For elite Malawians, the ambivalence about traditional culture is particularly acute. They simultaneously identify with the universalized standards of rationality and public health according to which many of Malawi's cultural practices are deemed harmful, but they also sense uneasily that they themselves are in danger of losing their identity as Malawian. They speak English, send their children to "international" schools (if they can afford it) where English is the language of instruction, and carry out, as best they can, the projects that donors envision. A focus on harmful cultural practices thus links them to what is distinctively Malawian, gives them a way to uplift their village brethren, and simultaneously asserts their own enlightened modernity.

WHY DO WE HEAR MUCH LESS ABOUT HARMFUL CULTURAL PRACTICES FROM THE VILLAGERS WHO ARE SAID TO PRACTICE THEM?

Another puzzle faced us when we realized that we hear virtually nothing about exotic cultural practices when we talk (through an interpreter) with Malawians while visiting a village, or when we hear at second-hand what villagers talk about through semi-structured interviews and ethnographic journals. For them, there is value in their customs. For many villagers, their own practices do not appear as "cultural practices," but rather, a familiar and often very important aspect of the context in which they live. For those who believe in them, practices that elites consider harmful are moral injunctions. Among the matrilocal Sena, a widow who is not "cleansed" puts herself and her relatives in danger of death; among the patrilocal Tumbuka, widow inheritance, where a male relative of the deceased incorporates the woman into his household, ensures that she and her children will be supported; among all ethnic groups, initiations are implemented by elders who advise young people reaching puberty that they must now leave aside childish things and become adult members of society. But as we saw earlier when two villagers were laughing about "wife swapping," they are fascinated by stories that emphasize the peculiarities of *other* groups' cultures.

Laments for an earlier carefree time when people could enjoy sex without dying are a constant refrain in the village conversations that we have read in the journals. But the notion of harmful sexual practices is exciting to villagers only when it evokes other salient issues, those of tribal differences, or, more commonly, the boundary between sexual restraint and sexual license. They worry about dances held at night because these are seen as encouraging licentious behavior. They may see the practices of other groups as strange or immoral. And in response to the epidemic, they want to change practices—like circumcising many boys with the same blade—that they have come to understand are dangerous. But they are not concerned with harmful cultural practices as manifestations of backwardness, nor are they using the issue to demonstrate their own enlightened modernity.

AND WHY DO INTERNATIONAL DONORS NOT RESPOND TO CALLS BY THE ELITES TO BANISH THESE PRACTICES?

While donors hear a great deal about exotic sexual practices, and a few donors have funded studies to catalog such practices, few donor resources have gone to attempts to change or eradicate what the locals clearly see as an important problem. While early campaigns urged traditional circumcisers to use a clean blade for each boy, and there were some "chiefs campaigns"[48] aimed at changing dangerous cultural practices, much more typical was the fate of cultural practices in a 2003 document that was preparatory to a potential World Bank grant to Malawi for addressing AIDS.[49] The document, developed in a "highly participatory process" with private sector, public sector, NGOs, CBOs, faith communities, and PLWAs involved, urged action on nine issues, the first of which was "facilitating changes in cultural values/norms to reduce spread of AIDS." Other themes included youth, "empowering vulnerable groups," and "promoting love, care, and support for those infected by or living with HIV/AIDS." The key donor, the World Bank, however, ignored cultural practices, concentrating on promoting a "multisectoral approach," "fighting communicable diseases," and "social risk mitigation," along with medical waste management and injection safety.

The same pattern was repeated in the 2003 report of a USAID consultation to develop a strategic plan for combating AIDS.[50] The report combined the concerns of national elites—those brokers who deal directly with donors—and donors themselves to develop a strategic plan for Malawi's battle against AIDS. The document's introduction gives substantial attention to harmful cultural practices, reflecting the concerns of the Malawians. But the concrete details of the plan in the subsequent chapters—what donors are actually going to fund—contain no mention of these dangerous practices. In document after document one sees the same pattern. The country nationals write and talk about what they see as dangerous cultural practices, the things about which they are experts as interpreters of their countrymen's mores, but again and again, donors do not translate such concerns into action.[51]

Donors have several reservations. First, addressing cultural practices that differ dramatically by ethnic group and region makes it difficult to roll out the sort of standardized, industrial strength, high-payoff program donors aspire to develop. But more significant, we think, is that donors are worried about their own "cultural sensitivity." While Malawians may criticize the backwardness of their own villagers, foreign donors feel uncomfortable about criticizing Malawians' sexual practices. This is the ground on which Malawian elites feel the most competent, but it is the territory where donors see dangers lurking everywhere. It is one thing to be titillated by an exotic story, but quite another to support a program for changing a Malawian "cultural practice."

Malawians can themselves feel uncomfortable raising issues that threaten to exacerbate ethnic tribal or regional tensions. As one Malawian interviewee noted, "The sexual area is a cultural minefield." In Malawi, politically dominant groups may consider other groups' customs and rituals backward or dangerous, but the politics of attacking those practices are difficult.[52] In the end, Malawians feel most comfortable addressing these issues by delegating them to the chiefs, who are seen as responsible for their own people's cultural traditions, or by coopting those such as traditional healers who may be persuaded to adapt or change traditional rituals.

Thus in the end, elite fascination with exotic cultural practices generates a great deal of talk and many reports, but without producing much at the level of policy, action, evidence, or, most important, donor funding.

Harmful Cultural Practices as Violations of (Children's) Human Rights

More recently, donors and brokers have been able to find some common ground, meeting on the elevated plane of universal human rights rather than in the muddy trenches of such practices as sexual cleansing, *fisi,* or widow inheritance. The campaigns that have succeeded with donors are on global issues that resonate locally, such as sexual exploitation or violence against children. The currently active issues are campaigns against child labor, and, especially, child marriage. Donors still do not address the exotic sexual practices and tribal customs that most preoccupy elite brokers. But they are willing to confront "harmful cultural practices" when those practices have to do with the human rights of vulnerable children.

In 2008, Malawi saw an extraordinary national campaign, organized by UNICEF and funded by NORAD, with advice from a group of Malawian NGOs and support from the Permanent Secretary for Gender.[53] Its slogans, in both Chichewa and English, appeared everywhere: on brilliant cherry-red banners at roadblocks, splashed across the front or back pages of both daily papers (as seen in figure 8.2), and on ubiquitous bumper stickers on minibuses. The "STOP!" campaign proclaimed the right of every

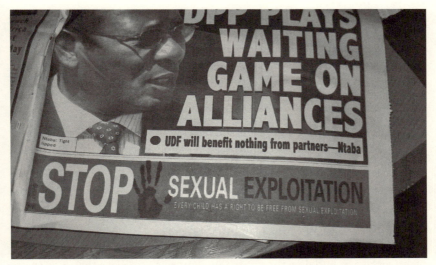

FIGURE 8.2. Front-page banner from Malawi's daily paper, *The Nation*, June, 2008. Sponsored by UNICEF and funded by NORAD, the Norwegian aid agency, these banners promoting human rights appeared on newspapers, bumper stickers, at road-blocks and city halls across Malawi. *Photo: Ann Swidler.*

child to health and education, condemning violence against children, sexual abuse, and other ills: "STOP Child Trafficking: every child has a right to their childhood"; "STOP Sexual Abuse: every child has a right to be free from abuse and violence"; "STOP Harmful Cultural Practices: every child has a right to good health"; along with exhortations to stop "Early Marriages," "Child Labour," "Property Grabbing," and "Sexual Exploitation."

This remarkable initiative was followed by aggressive campaigns, financed by an array of global organizations, against child labor (ILO) and especially child marriage (UNICEF). Despite years of opposition in Parliament, a recent burst of NGO advocacy about "an epidemic of child marriages" has resulted in legislation outlawing marriage for those younger than eighteen and has mobilized chiefs to fine those who marry before age eighteen. For donors and NGO brokers who advocated for the legislation, the outcome was hailed as a success. Given the realities of rural Malawi, however, the consequences of donor and elite broker advocacy may be perverse. There are few opportunities for girls, or even adult women, to earn an income to support themselves; thus, when girls drop out of school, as nearly half of those who begin primary do before they reach age 18, they and their relatives consider that the best alternative is to marry. And when a girl is pregnant, her partner is pressured by the two families to marry his pregnant girlfriend in order to avoid shame. Thus, we expect that the new law, promoted by donors and elites, would, if enforced, be likely to create an epidemic of births out of wedlock.

CONCLUSION

Concerns about vulnerable women and harmful cultural practices simultaneously engage and frustrate donors, brokers, and villagers. The frustrations they generate for donors and Malawian brokers are in some respects mirror opposites. Donors deplore the plight of poor, powerless women, while elite brokers often appear to go along, only to slip into an anxious preoccupation with mercenary women who need to be regulated and controlled. In the case of harmful cultural practices, elite brokers urge attention to the dangers these practices pose, while donors, even if tales of such practices may scandalize them, are reluctant to act in ways that they see as raising sensitive issues about local culture. Vulnerable women and harmful cultural practices thus lead to policy foreplay, but rarely to a satisfying consummation.

What are the effects of these unresolved misunderstandings? One important effect is that both donors and brokers end up focused on issues that are only weakly related to actual HIV risk, while the key social practices that transmit HIV go largely unaddressed. Because both donors and brokers focus on what stirs their moral imaginations—poor and powerless women for the international donors and backward, irrational cultural practices for Malawian brokers—neither focuses on the more mundane, more important sources of HIV risk. In a stable marriage in which one partner is HIV+ and the other is not, for example, the risk of HIV transmission is much greater because sex is far more frequent than in one-off encounters with mercenary women.

Donors and brokers may know at some level what the epidemiologists know: that it is the ordinary sexual lives of regular people—not desperately poor women, sex workers, or villagers with exotic sexual practices—that really drive the epidemic. But both donors and brokers find it awkward to address this. So they keep talking about the exotic practices of others, whether sex workers or village cleansers, "sugar dads" or women driven to "survival sex." Villagers, ironically, while they too are preoccupied with those they see as threats to moral order—girls in mini-skirts, sugar dads, and bar girls—are nonetheless more realistic. In the journals, most of their stories about AIDS are about unfaithful spouses, about men with money (such as fishermen) who take extramarital partners and then infect their wives and children, and, as they advise each other, the virtue of "depending only on each other" to avoid the risk of AIDS.

There is another irony about themes such as vulnerable women and harmful cultural practices that both inflame imaginations and inhibit action. International donors have had no concern about cultural sensitivity when it comes to the issues they really believe in: universal human rights and gender equality. For them, equalizing the position of women, persuading men to desist from gender-based violence, equalizing educational opportunity for girls and boys, or protecting the rights of children and adults against sexual violence and exploitation are manifestly right—not cultural issues, but simply the right things to do. Hence local concerns become validated largely when they can be made compatible with the international donors' conceptions of the universalized morality of human rights and gender equality. Here again, it is moral conceptions that drive policy, even when those moral understandings appear to be simply unassailable, natural truths.

CHAPTER 9

A PRACTICE THAT MAKES EVERYONE HAPPY

Training

WHY DO DEVELOPMENT PROJECTS, SUCH as those to prevent or mitigate the effects of AIDS, take the forms they do? We have described "themes," basically words (categories, slogans, and buzzwords) that allow altruists and brokers to imagine themselves joined in a common enterprise. The ability of donors, brokers, and villagers to develop working misunderstandings at the level of verbal formulas, however, provides only one answer to the puzzle of how they manage to get along. The deeper answer isn't about words, but about *practices*—the routinized activities that allow people to cooperate even when they have very different goals and understandings.[1] These practices bind the three groups together in a collaborative effort, but they also bind them by sharply constricting the range of activities that AIDS projects actually implement on the ground.

The necessity of uniting actors with divergent agendas gives development projects their static quality. International and national NGOs seeking funding promise the moon, claiming that they have innovative themes, with new categories, new slogans, and new buzzwords. But there is monotonous uniformity in what they actually do. On the ground, NGOs employ a very narrow set of practices that "work"—work not in the sense that they effectively prevent AIDS or meet the needs of the villagers for clean water, better health services, better schools, food security, or jobs, but in the sense that they satisfy the varied agendas of the actors. These ubiquitous practices are conducting a "training" and "monitoring and evaluation," known as "M&E." In this chapter we write about training; in the next, we write about M&E and other practices through which donors and brokers create success.

TRAINING: OMNIPRESENT, INFINITELY ADAPTABLE, EASY, AND CHEAP

It is hard for those who have not worked in the development world to comprehend how ubiquitous "training" is as a central activity. From a distance, the citizens of rich countries can imagine that "development" means providing tangible public goods. Clean water *does* get to some homes, roads do get built, and some villages do get a clinic or a school classroom. But when the task given to NGO brokers is to transform the lives of ordinary people, the technology they deploy is to conduct a training. In temporary emergencies, donors feel authorized to give real resources to humanitarian relief organizations that provide shelter, food, and medical care. For virtually all other development goals, donors have settled on training volunteers as the central practice.

Why do donors favor trainings? Above all, they believe it makes their interventions to achieve lofty goals sustainable—if they can end the epidemic by teaching village women better sexual decision making, these women can, presumably, make better decisions today, tomorrow, and into the future. There is also a multiplier effect: the trainees will volunteer to teach their neighbors how they too can practice better decision-making.[2] Moreover, trainings are cheap compared to providing clean water or more school classrooms.[3]

The brokers who lead the trainings reap many advantages: they have a valuable job with an NGO that provides income to support their families and their personal aspirations for social mobility (usually more educational credentials) but does not require technical skills their educations have not provided. They also feel that they are improving the lives of the poor and that by disseminating messages formulated in world capitals they are becoming members of a global community of experts. The trainers are often low-level NGO brokers. The trainees fortunate enough to be invited to a training are typically the relatively educated young men and women whom we call the interstitial elite or the village elites—the chief and his relatives and clients. Both trainers and trainees consider themselves lucky to participate in a training, since they receive small allowances for travel, accommodations, meals, and per diems. Plus the trainees are pleased to learn new things, such as the physiology of sex. And they have fun.

It should be clear from this introduction that we are cynical about the ability of the donors to achieve their HIV prevention goals through trainings. We are, however, empathetic with their efforts to bring about transformative change—but even more empathetic with the low-level brokers doing the training, who are trying to achieve a middle-class life, and with the interstitial elites trying to find a place in the alluring NGO firmament.

What Is a Training Like?

We have seen trainings at the inexpensive guest houses where we stayed, and interviewed participants about what they learned, their satisfaction with the allowances they receive for attending, and their aspirations for the future. Some trainings impart substantive information, as when clinical officers are trained in a new procedure for resuscitating infants. Most of the trainings we saw, however, were intended to achieve ambitious but amorphous goals. These fascinate us because they seem unlikely to have any impact at all: the goals are either impossibly lofty, such as such as creating "AIDS competent communities" or making communities "resilient to the impacts of climate change," or redundant, such as teaching women how to do "home based care" for the sick and elderly, something they routinely did long before the institutional altruists arrived. Most of the participants we met at trainings are interstitial elites, but occasionally the trainees are villagers—not the poorest of the poor, however, but village elites, chiefs, or those with one or two years of secondary school.

For the participants and would-be participants in a training, it is mostly about money. But after observing many trainings of young men and women, it was evident to us that they loved attending a training. Trainings are fun: away from home, young men and women trainees could pool small amounts of their per diems to hire a boom box and dance the night away (keeping us awake), or sing hymns into the early hours of the morning (waking us up). More importantly, the youth were deeply convinced that through the training they had become "enlightened," a word that has religious overtones.[4] At first we were incredulous: the trainings disseminated information that our systematic survey and qualitative data show was already well known to young adults in rural Malawi. But we became believers after talking with the trainees.

Our enlightenment began when we asked a young man of twenty-two what he had learned from his four days in a workshop on "Life Skills." He answered "decision-making." We joked, "*Surely* you knew about decision-making before you came here!" No, he insisted, he learned it here. After probing, he agreed that he had made decisions in the past, but he didn't know it was called "decision-making." Another participant, age twenty-four, enthusiastically told us that he learned "that semen and urine came out of the same place." Such obvious information seems newly important when it is displayed in anatomical drawings on the trainer's flip chart, but we were struck that none of this information—about male anatomy or fallopian tubes or menstruation—has any relevance to HIV prevention.[5] What it did do was make young people feel that they were in school again, becoming more enlightened. As an interviewee said of the things she had learned: "Yes, I knew them, but not officially."[6]

At another motel where young people were being trained to deliver AIDS prevention messages to their peers in the villages, we sat in on a training session. It was in English and the template was that of a schoolroom. Participatory education has not caught on in Malawi: teachers lecture and from time to time ask a question to test the students.[7] When we entered, the young men and women were sitting at a long table, and the facilitator was standing in front of them lecturing, pointing to a flip chart with words and anatomical diagrams, occasionally interrupting her talk with a question. She then called on a student to show the others how he would teach villagers. He stood up and lectured solemnly, pointed to the flip chart, and asked his peers questions.

Later, we asked the broker—an enthusiastic young woman just out of university—what part of the training did the kids like best? The sessions on body parts, she said. We said they must have already been familiar with body parts. She answered yes, "You find they know a lot more than you thought, they come up with the Chichewa words for vagina, you think 'where do these kids learn this stuff?'" Then she went on to talk about the trainees as foolish and backwards: "They believe there is a big egg that breaks, causing menstruation. You say no, no, no, it's the lining; it's so funny I keep laughing. It's interesting how these little minds put things together, they think they know a lot but they don't. I'm giving out correct information. Before that, they just got myths and misconceptions."[8]

Trainers can graduate to be Trainers of Trainers. One of these proudly showed us a video he had made of an AIDS-prevention training of trainers. The participants were educated, well-dressed elite brokers, yet they clearly enjoyed children's games. Much of the time was spent playing circle games, and to great laughter, taking turns performing AIDS-prevention skits of the sort that secondary school students have been putting on since NGOs began promoting AIDS youth clubs. Children's games are considered appropriate, even for well-dressed, educated elites in the capital, on the assumption that the ultimate recipients of training are villagers—villagers whom these elites indeed imagine as children. When a successful Malawian broker, herself a well-educated professional living in the city, demonstrated her organization's AIDS prevention kit for training villagers—a kind of felt game board with Velcro-attachable characters representing the town drunk, the bar girl, and others at risk of HIV who could fall out of a tree to be eaten by the lion of AIDS—she assured us that putting these characters up and discussing which were at risk for a fall into the lion's jaws delighted the villagers.[9]

Observing trainings and talking with the brokers conducting the trainings, we could not doubt their commitment. Taziwana, who was conducting a training, was a secondary school graduate who aspired for more. Starting as a volunteer, she eventually became a paid facilitator, teaching other youth:

How can we be quiet, it's us the young people who are infected.... We train them so that they can resist pressures from their friends, so they can negotiate. We teach them assertiveness, self-esteem, decision-making, communication skills, so that they can know that their friends are getting the messages we are giving them, they can learn how best to deliver the information we can give them. Information on relationships, how can they have better relationships with parents, friends, friends of opposite sexes.... [N]ot all of them went to school. So we have to train them how their bodies work, each and every part of their bodies, so they don't have a pregnancy.[10]

From the perspective of the donors, the aim of such trainings is to produce volunteers who will walk the last mile to spread the NGO messages in the villages. It is this that, in the donors' imagination, makes the project sustainable—i.e., no more donor money will be needed. From the perspective of the interstitial elites and the village elites, attending a training is the only way that donor money trickles into their hands. Thus, they seek to gain access to project activities such as trainings and meetings whenever they have the chance, even if they rarely benefit. A villager, Rosemary, explained to an anthropologist, Janneke Verheijen, that:

she attends the weekly tree-nursery meetings in which villagers are taught to grow trees, as well as the adult literacy classes every weekday afternoon. She does not see the benefit of either project, as trees can be found everywhere, and she has known how to read and write since primary school. Some villagers speculated, however, that those participating in the tree-planting project would in the end receive a bag of maize, and those involved in the literacy classes would later

170

on be offered a microloan. Rosemary says she doesn't actually believe that this is true, but unwilling to run the risk of missing out in
case it is true, she shows up at each meeting.[11]

Trainings Are Constituted by a Ritualized Set of Practices

Just as a Catholic Mass would not be a Mass without wine and wafers, a
training is not a training without flip charts and magic markers, a "bun"
and a "Fanta" at mid-morning and mid-afternoon breaks, and an ample
lunch (which permits the trainees to save their per diem by skipping
dinner).

The activities of a training are ritualized as well. The trainer who is
leading—"facilitating"—the training speaks of familiar concepts and behaviors in new jargon using acronyms that will distinguish those who
know from those who do not—not orphans, but "OVC," not promiscuity,
but "MCP" (for multiple and concurrent sexual partners), and "decision-
making."[12] Forms of participation are stereotyped. We often saw participants breaking into small groups, with each group taking a large sheet
from the flip chart to draw a "problem tree" with labels for the leaves, then
the trunk, and then the roots of community problems, roots which invariably turned out to be whatever the NGO's training targeted. The groups
then reassembled to share the products of their efforts. Other activities
seemed more peculiar: hymn singing, playing children's games, skits, and
songs. But donors and the layers of brokers who implement their projects
have become convinced that whatever the problem, training is the solution. "Project agents see it as their task to make villagers express their
problems in ways congruent with the project's program ... [T]hey provide
'beneficiaries' to the development apparatus; and they ease access to the
'development revenue' for local villagers."[13]

Below is a summary of two interviews (2006 and 2007) with Robert, a
young man who was, like many other members of the interstitial elite, a
"professional" volunteer. For five years after finishing secondary school, he
was a volunteer, hoping that such experience would result in a job with an
NGO. In the first interview, in June 2006, we asked why he had volunteered so much—why not go into business? "We have friends, after volunteering they got jobs. Instead of just loafing, I ventured into volunteering,
through volunteering I managed to get things, I was the youth member
of the District Assembly, I was trained as a voluntary VCT counselor, and
I was trained to be a trainer ... It was not my wish to be a volunteer, I
wanted money to go to school."

In 2007, when we returned, he had gotten a job with an NGO on a project promoting adult literacy through training. The NGO provides Robert with a motorcycle so he can conduct trainings in a village rather than in a venue where villagers would need to be paid money for accommodation, food, and per diems. The training consists of assembling residents, showing them a picture of a problem tree, and quizzing them. When Robert asks what the root problem is, they usually begin with money; when that is not correct, they guess food or orphans or clean water. With his encouragement, they eventually say that the root of their problems is adult illiteracy. Robert then asks for a volunteer to teach literacy classes and moves on to the next village.

It was striking to us how committed Robert was to the mission of his NGO to "uplift" the community so that they know how to "read, write, and enumerate" (he used that phrase again and again in the interview). "Uplift" is wrapped in the language of ownership and participation—communities defining their own problems and coming to their own solutions.[14] But the only problem that the NGO addressed was "ignorance" and the only solution it offered was to have the relatively educated people in a village volunteer to teach their fellows how to read. Once again, the volunteers get allowances, but the poor and relatively uneducated villagers have to take what is on offer—AIDS education, negotiating condom use, literacy, whatever.

When we read that NAC had received US$41,751,500 from the Global Fund to Fight AIDS, Tuberculosis, and Malaria, we wondered whether NAC would also favor trainings for HIV prevention.[15] Newspapers announced that NAC would provide indigenous community groups with funding for HIV prevention and AIDS mitigation if they turned themselves into formal CBOs with executive committees and bank accounts. The response was enthusiastic. Starting in 2005, CBOs sprouted all over Malawi, energized by the possibility of actually receiving donor funds. To access the money, the committee had to write a proposal and submit it to the district office of one of the large INGOs that had been funded to review proposals and then, if the CBO was funded, to deliver the money.

The CBO's executive committee wrote the proposals. In the rural areas, the committee members typically were those with the highest status in the village: schoolteachers, pastors, chiefs, and businessmen. As a woman in a focus group with poor women said, "The rich are selected for committees, the poor are never selected."[16]

We read dozens of CBO proposals.[17] They were poignant in their attempts to translate what the committee really wanted—material resources—

into terms that NAC might agree to fund. Early on, the CBOs asked for resources to feed the sick and the elderly, but these were turned down as "not sustainable" or "not compatible with NSF" (NAC's National Strategic Framework, a document not available in the villages). When we reexamined the process three years later, much had changed. The CBOs had learned what would be funded: a lot of trainings and a small amount of resources for an IGA (income generating activity) that was to make the project sustainable after the funding ended.

The proposals are illuminating, as they show how the NAC's aims of mobilizing communities by providing funding for trainings meshed with the aims of executive committees that were trying to access the funding. A typical proposal, for Nsamanyada CBO in Balaka District, proposed nine committees for its CBO. Each corresponded to one of the internationally recognized activities to prevent HIV or to mitigate the effects of the epidemic; each committee was to be trained; each had a carefully detailed budget for the training. We show one page from Nsamanyada CBO's proposal in Figure 9.1. The proposal also included funding for an IGA that was to support the CBO after NAC funding ended. The list of proposed activities begins with a training for the HBC (home based care) committee, along with a request for a small amount of money to buy simple medical supplies such as Band-Aids and Panadol (Tylenol). Next on the list is a training for the committee on "Positive Living" (we think this was to counsel the HIV+ not to be discouraged and to eat healthy foods, frequent advice for the HIV+ before antiretroviral therapy was widely available), plus a small amount to provide them with cooking oil and sugar. After that came "Nutritious Training," an "Awareness Campaign," "Elderly and Disabled Training," "Child Protection Training," "Youth Peer Education Training," "OVC Training," and, lastly, "Business Management Training" (to support their proposed IGA). The trainings were to be for ten days, much longer than the usual two to five days (thus, more days with allowances).

Each budget included a request for funds to buy the training essentials (flip chart, pens, notebooks, buns, and Fantas) and lunch allowances for the trainees (500 kwacha/day, about $3.50 in 2008) and for the facilitators (830 kwacha/day, almost $6.00).[18] The Nsamanyada CBO's proposed IGA was raising pigs. They requested funding to build a pen, purchase three pigs, and buy feed and drugs for the pigs. But they also required "Piggery Training," which turns out to be considerably more expensive than buying the three pigs or even feeding them. The grand total in the CBO's proposed budget came to 1,500,000 kwacha (about $11,000 at the 2008 exchange rate). Of this budget, 357,950 kwacha was for bicycles, pigs, feed, and a pig

173

NO: 1. ACTIVITY	HBC - TRAINING RESOURCE	QUANTITY	PRICE/u	DAYS	TOTAL AMOUNT. K T
HBC TRAINING	LUNCH ALLOWANCE FOR - PARTICIPANTS	10	K500	10	50,000.00
	- FACILITATORS	2	K830	"	16,660.00
	- FUEL FOR FACILITATORS	20	K190/l	"	38,000.00
	- HALL HIRING	1	K500	"	5,000.00
	TOTAL FOR L.A. OF R.F.F.H				109,660.00
	REFRESHMENTS÷ -SOFT DRINKS	24	K40/b	10	9,600.00
	- SCONES	24	K8/sco	10	1,920.00
	TOTAL FOR REFRESHMENTS				11,520.00
	STATIONARIES÷ -REAM OF PAPER	1	K955	10	955.00
	- FLIP CHART	2	K700	10	1 400.00
	- MASKING TAPE	1	K230	"	230.00
	- BALL PEN	10	K250	"	250.00
	- NOTE BOOKS	10	K300	"	300.00
	TOTAL FOR TRAINING MATERIAL				3,135.00
	PROCUREMENTS OF DRUGS - PANADO (PARACETAMO)	12 b)	K500/6	4 t's	60,000.00
	- CARAMINE LOTION	12	K350/6	4 t's	4,200.00
	- IRONS	8	K4000	4 t's	32,000.00
	- NTHANZI ORS	504sa	K25/sa	4 t's	12,600.00
	- GENTIAN VIOLET	2½l	K1200/l		2,400.00
	TOTAL FOR DRUG PROCURE				111,200.00
	OTHER EXPENSES÷ - PROCUREMENTS OF BICYCLE	2	K12,000	-	24,000.00
	- TRANSPORT	K800	4 t's		3,200.00
	- IGA	2 PIGS	K4500	4 t's	9,000.00
	TOTAL FOR BICYCLE, TRA. & IGA				27,200.00
	TOTAL FOR ALL RESOURCE			14	

FIGURE 9.1. One page from Nsamayada CBO's proposal to the National AIDS Commission for training in home-based care. As is typical, most of the money goes for snacks, allowances for participants, flip charts and other items considered necessary for a training. *Scanned CBO document in possession of the authors.*

pen, as well as medicines and the sugar and oil for PLWAs, while most of the money—1,142,050 kwacha—was for the multiple trainings.[19]

In the proposals, the budgets and the lists of committee members are detailed, but the content of the trainings is not. What matters to the proposers is the number of people who will benefit by receiving allowances, the number of days of training, and the amount of the allowances. Creating multiple committees that need to be trained is in the interest of village leaders. Spreading the money widely gains the favor of important members of the community.

Even if the number of trainings requested by the Nsamanyada CBO seems excessive, for donors desperate to get people to change their sexual behavior or provide appropriate care for those affected by the epidemic, training may seem a plausible approach. But training is used to address virtually every problem, however implausible its benefits. An example from 2013 of a project to combat poverty and food insecurity demonstrates just how flexible training is. Funded by UK's Big Lottery Fund and the Development Fund of Norway for 340 million kwacha (about $1 million at the time), the "Find Your Feet (FYF) Empowering the Rural Poor Project" claimed to "increase food security and reduce poverty for 5,389 resource-poor farming households."[20] But how might it claim to have made a dent in the poverty of over 5,000 households? The answer is that NGO brokers would form groups of villagers who were to save money collectively and borrow from the savings to start small enterprises to provide them with a stream of income into the future. Its director reported: "We trained the families in management of village saving loans [*sic*], identified irrigation schemes, and conducted HIV and AIDS awareness campaigns." Note that the NGO's project did not lend money to provide the capital but only training for villagers to manage their own money. To increase food security it did not implement irrigation schemes (a public good that people cannot implement as individuals), it "identified" them. It did not provide farm inputs, but trained people "on various methods of modern farming."

Sustainability Is the End, Training Is the Means

Donors consider training valuable first and foremost because they imagine that it makes their projects sustainable. Trainings transmit knowledge, and in the donors' view, once transmitted, knowledge permanently transforms those in whom it has been instilled. The mantra, "Give a man a fish and you feed him for a day. Teach a man to fish and you feed him for a lifetime," frequently invoked by altruists of all stripes, implies not only that training is a permanent acquisition but that it is productive.[21] The one who has been trained has—almost magically—acquired the power to feed himself. This view of training as a permanent, productive endowment fits with Malawians' conviction that education of any sort is the source of prestige and status, the key to a "bright future," and more fundamentally, a source of "enlightenment."

The Irresistible Appeal of Training

Training is pervasive because it fits the needs of donors and brokers alike to believe that they have an easy, inexpensive key to the development of Malawi. Even if they didn't believe this, training has become a taken-for-granted, locally meaningful practice. A first, and obvious, advantage is that training is easy to do for the district brokers who implement programs. Unlike implementing an irrigation scheme or providing health care or humanitarian relief, it does not require much in the way of technical skills, equipment, or manpower. The only skill trainings require is a specialized kind of scripted talk. As other observers have noted, "talk" is the major intervention that most NGOs have the skills to offer.[22] Once a training manual has been written—or, more likely, adapted from a previous manual or from one developed in another country—and a trainer has been trained, a training can be replicated hundreds of times, thus producing large numbers of "villagers reached" for NGOs to report to their funders.[23]

Training is easy for brokers in a second sense as well. As donors' interests change, training is easily switched from one problem to another. "Talk" can be adapted to encourage adult literacy, to combat gender based violence, to respond to climate change by training people how to be resilient to floods and famines, or virtually any other donor priority except the expensive ones such as building infrastructure or distributing money directly to the poor. Lastly, training is relatively cheap. Expenditures for the salary of a broker to conduct a week's training are small, as are the costs of attracting a dozen or more participants with daily allowances of three dollars or so, five dollars a night to stay in a bare-bones motel in a trading center, Fanta and buns for mid-morning and mid-afternoon breaks, and the favorite lunch, chicken and chips or chicken and *nsima*.

SUSTAINABILITY HAS PRACTICAL AND MORAL ADVANTAGES FOR DONORS, BROKERS, AND VILLAGERS

The use of the term "sustainability" in the context of development became frequent in the 1980s, when it was used in the sense of preserving the natural environment. It then became a central component of development more generally. Why did this happen? Why is it so important to donors that their projects are "sustainable?"

Practical Advantages of Sustainability

Sustainability is especially advantageous for donors because they do not need to make long-term commitments to any project. Donors thus maintain their freedom of action. They can move from project to project, innovative idea to innovative idea, without getting bogged down in paying for recurrent expenses. We described in chapter 3 the chaotic world of NGOs and brokers in poor countries as they scrambled to keep up with the welter of programs and projects promoted by the deep-pocketed foundations and bilateral and multilateral donors. These donors pride themselves on using their money for "leverage"—to create innovations that, if successful, governments (or other donors) will sustain. They do not want to become responsible for providing services that they believe governments should provide; they do not want to constrain their ability to provide "new" solutions by being tied to earlier projects, even the most successful ones.

Organizations further down the funding chain—the beltway bandits, behemoth NGOs, schools of public health, and smaller foundations—write proposals pitching their own projects precisely by promising creativity and innovation. Dependent on an ever-changing array of funding opportunities, the successful NGOs strive to meet constantly changing themes and demands, while maintaining the livelihoods and cumulative expertise of the brokers. The belief that programs will become sustainable—and the corresponding faith in training and in the willingness of volunteers to work without pay—maximizes donors' flexibility by minimizing their commitments on the ground.

Moral Advantages of Sustainability

Sustainability is practical, but donors and NGOs justify it on moral grounds. Donor programs should make beneficiaries self-sufficient, both as empowered, self-reliant individuals and as communities that should be empowered, participatory, and democratic. Income grants would create dependency, thus stifling the entrepreneurialism, self-reliance, and creativity of the poor. Only responses to humanitarian emergencies are exempt from this logic, precisely because emergencies are defined as temporary: those suffering from a sudden outbreak of disease, war, or natural disaster are seen not as in danger of "dependency," but as legitimately in need of help until the famine or epidemic is over.[24]

As we have shown, NGO brokers are ambivalent about sustainability. They should object to the doctrine of sustainability, since they depend on the continued funding of projects for their jobs. But the doctrine fits elite brokers' own moral vision of poor Malawians. Like the broker in chapter 2 who said, "Do not make us a nation of beggars.... Do not do for us what we can do for ourselves," elite brokers share with donors a disdain for the "dependency" of villagers. When we asked a district broker who was complaining about the dependency of the poor "aren't you also dependent on donors?" he was nonplussed—it had not occurred to him that the doctrine of sustainability applied to him.[25]

We were equally baffled when we read a 2013 article in a Malawian newspaper titled "Poor Malawians Do Not Know of Their Poverty."[26] The Malawian director of a research NGO measuring Malawi's poverty level described the value of its "tool," the "basic needs basket"—a technique for measuring poverty—in terms of self-reliance:

In an attempt to explain poverty levels in Malawi, the Centre for Social Concern (CfSC) has said the poor, generally, do not know of their own poverty and hence fail to take measures to liberate themselves. The tool challenges the community to organise people to proactively improve their own conditions before seeking assistance. It is also a policy guide to establish a poverty line, a minimum wage, and a fair tax code.

Even more succinct—but difficult to interpret—was the national executive director of a faith-based youth organization in Malawi, who said of AIDS, "If a person is self-reliant then the chances of getting the disease is low."[27]

Malawian elites' criticism of villagers' "dependency" echoes the emphasis of global actors on sustainability, but experiences in brokers' own lives make their criticism more understandable. Because the brokers have a regular income, they are constantly badgered by relatives from the village who need financial help. Below is a moving lament from a district broker for a large NGO:

They [his relatives] look up on me and some expectations are even unrealistic. They go beyond the realities ... [They think] "He has more than enough and if he is not giving it is because he is just not willing to do so." So it creates more, uh, expectations, more demand and, uh, I have to cater for them at the same time I have to look after my family, my nuclear family. So that pressure is there. And um, although geographically we are distant, they still contact, ask me for this, ask me for that. And, um, sometimes we choose not to share with our families everything that happens. Because when you share some successful stories, ok, sometimes you share it for the sake of making your parents, your relatives more proud of you. But sometimes what we forget is that after sharing those successful stories is the expectation of [future] sharing.[28]

While Western donors may hear in the rhetoric of sustainability an ideal of self-reliant individualism, African elites hear the importunate demands of poor kinsmen, whose needs they can never satisfy, but also never refuse.[29] It is then no wonder that elite brokers embrace the rhetoric of sustainability with conviction, imbuing it with meanings that make sense from their own perspective, as, very often, the only employed family member among numerous desperately needy parents, siblings, orphaned nieces and nephews, and others whose demands cannot be ignored. With a vehemence that we think reflects their own frustration, those sustained by salaries paid with donor funds insist that villagers should not be paid because it will make them dependent, because it is not "sustainable."

Unlike for the cosmopolitan, national, and district brokers, for the interstitial elites who have to live in a village but desperately aspire to leave it, the ideology of sustainability has no appeal at all. Indeed, just the opposite. They want nothing more than a job, ideally with a regular salary from an NGO that will never go out of business. In the meantime, however, they take advantage of the donor passion for training to become "professional volunteers."[30] One young man who had volunteered for years with various NGOs and attended several trainings remarked, "we survived on that."[31] Another said, "If donors pull out then there will be no resources left."[32]

Creating Sustainability

For donors, training volunteers is the key to sustainability. Donors imagine villagers as committed to improving the lives of their relatives and neighbors; all they require is the training provided by an NGO. Just as the knowledge transmitted through training is conceived to be enduring and thus sustainable after the donor departs, so volunteers, who are conceived as motivated by concern for their communities rather than by material rewards, are sustainable because they are expected to carry on after the donor's money moves elsewhere. In practice, training turns out not to be the permanent transmission of self-sustaining, empowering knowledge. Indeed, training creates the demand for more training. We often heard those who had attended a training complaining that it was not long enough, or that it had been so long ago that they now need to be "refreshed" by another training.

Sustainability has also acquired another, perhaps more realistic, meaning: established NGOs teach struggling CBOs and small independent NGOs how to become sustainable in the sense that they can find new donors when the first donor decamps. In Malawi and elsewhere in the region, the Southern African AIDS Trust focuses on just that: "building capacities of community-based NGOs to develop and manage effective and sustainable responses to HIV and AIDS."[33] They look for community organizations that lack the capacity to be sustainable and train them in writing proposals to mobilize resources and in doing the paperwork to account for the resources they have spent. Small, local CBOs, however, are very unlikely to find new sponsors, whereas the few successful ones become large enterprises, devoted to grant writing rather than work in local communities. Nonetheless, this image of a sustainable organization—one that a donor initiates and that other donors will then support—persists.

The donor illusion that volunteers make a project sustainable also persists, despite study after study showing that projects collapse after the money departs.[34] Although some, ever hopeful, hang on, most do not. The stories are always similar. As we described in chapter 5, many volunteers appear at the beginning of a project, but then as it becomes evident that the project is not going to lead to a paying job or even provide benefits such as bicycles for reaching the villagers or umbrellas for the rainy season, volunteers drift away. The anthropologist Ben Jones, writing about a development project in Uganda, notes that "it was a typical story of development work in the region. The community structures supported by NGOs—such as village health teams—were active only for as long as the NGO was active, but did not do much when the NGOs were not around."[35]

Actual Rather than Ideal Volunteers

Donors valorize villagers who are empowered, participate in community mobilization for good causes, and have a sense of ownership of a project; these are their ideal volunteers. The actual volunteers, as we noted in chapter 5, are often the relatively educated interstitial elites. Their home is in a village or in a small town or staying for a while with relatives in a city while waiting, and longing, for a job. In the meantime, many are ready to spend years volunteering in one organization after another, picking up a workshop or training when they can, hoping that one of their volunteer stints will lead to a job with a salary that will take them out of the village for good.

For these interstitial elites with aspirations for social mobility, trainings satisfy a variety of needs. The most obvious is cash: the per diems and travel allowances may be the only source of cash that permits young people to contribute to their family's livelihood and to buy a new shirt for themselves. A second, and to us unexpected, advantage of trainings is that at the end participants are given what they consider to be a valuable credential: a certificate that they have completed a training in X. As one participant in a workshop in rural Balaka District explained, "Life is very competitive here in Malawi, with the next credential maybe I could get a job in the city."[36] A third advantage of trainings is that they permit participants to make contacts that may, someday, be useful. In an insecure world, everyone needs as many and as well-placed connections as possible. At a training, one can expand one's networks through contacts with the trainers and with other aspiring elites who may know about available jobs, or even with foreigners staying at the same motel, who may, miraculously, offer resources.[37]

For the interstitial elites, the aspirations sustained by training and volunteering also offered something more precious (at least in the short term) than material rewards: a modern, educated identity.[38] As for the young men we described in chapter 5, who were sent away when they tried to apply for funding from World Vision, who nonetheless reported, starry-eyed, "for us, World Vision is a 'glittering castle,'" the trainings kept alive their sense of themselves as modern in the absence, but still in the hope, of jobs in the formal economy. Many AIDS clubs are formed in secondary school. After students graduate, they can use the club to stay together and affirm the educated modern identity they have worked so hard to attain. Together, they keep alive the hope for—and the networks through which they might hear of—possible jobs, perhaps first as workshop trainers, then trainers of

181

trainers, then higher-level staff. Meeting in the classroom-like settings of a training and conducting earnest discussions of important topics like reproductive anatomy or how to conduct a youth workshop, they also enact, and thus reaffirm, a central identity.

We have seen how a single practice, the training, comes to be repeated in every corner of the AIDS enterprise—and beyond, as with the project that trained poor farmers to manage their own money in order to end their poverty. We have described how trainings remain central because they work for participants at virtually every level of the enterprise, even if they work least well for the villagers who are imagined as their ideal beneficiaries. This ever-renewed, ever-the-same practice acquires its power because it binds together donors, brokers, and beneficiaries not only with a flow of material resources, but with a tangle of powerful imagined realities. While the fantasies are very different, training works as a practice precisely because different participants can read into it their own meanings and derive their own gratifications. Donors can imagine sustainable projects producing empowered volunteers; brokers can imagine happy villagers imbibing messages through fun and games; interstitial elites can imagine careers in which they become more enlightened—and less poor—as their distance from villagers increases; and villagers can imagine at least the remote possibility of material benefits from far-away altruists.

CHAPTER 10

CREATING SUCCESS

AT THE BEGINNING OF THIS book, we wrote that the foreign aid efforts against AIDS are motivated by compassion, by a passion for doing good, by an urgent need to connect with others very different from ourselves— and by fantasies of transforming the behavior of those at risk of HIV infection. But how do donors know whether their efforts were successful? In this chapter we examine another set of practices that bind donors and brokers together: the varied practices through which they assure their funders and themselves that their efforts have succeeded.

NGOs that implement interventions to prevent HIV deploy three techniques to show that their efforts have been successful: testimonials from those whose lives they want to change, listing and counting the activities they conduct to produce change, and end-of-project evaluations.

TESTIMONIALS

Many projects organize a celebration with speeches and testimonials when a donor visits or when the project has ended. Journalists are often invited by the NGO to attend the ceremony, with the understanding that they will write a feature story on the event. A key event in the celebration is when a beneficiary takes center stage and tells the audience a before-and-after story of the change that the NGO has made in her, or his, life.

Testimonials are important to donors and brokers because they are vivid and often emotional. They confirm to the donors that their goals for transforming lives in have been met, and they confirm to the brokers that although they may have had trials and tribulations in implementing a project, in the end, the lives of individuals and communities that they worked hard for have indeed been transformed. Ceremonies with testimonials serve another aim for projects that depend on volunteers in the name of sustainability: to reinforce the sacrificial spirit among the unpaid workers for a globally funded organization.[1]

Testimonials are so ubiquitous that it seems they serve both donors and implementers well. Testimonials to NGO projects appear frequently in Malawi's newspapers, produced from the press releases of the NGOs that tout their successes. Consider a feature story on a project implemented by

the Badilika Foundation in Blantyre that aims to protect sex workers' health and rights without destroying their economic opportunities. The Foundation conducted trainings: the result of the training was, the executive director reported, that "700 sex workers have been rescued from unprotected sex and are now using condoms with their clients ..."[2]
A sex worker testified:

I now know my rights. When a customer insists on unprotected sex, I show him the poster in my room and I tell him that if he is not using a condom, then I am not interested. Of course, sometimes I feel sad to see men return with their money because I have refused unprotected sex, but I now understand that it is better to earn less money through protected sex than getting more money by having unprotected sex because the latter exposes me to HIV and sexually transmitted infections (STIs).

Another more moving testimonial comes from a feature story of the success of a project funded by USAID.[3]

It's 6:40 on a Saturday evening, and Youth Alert! Mix, Malawi's most popular youth radio program, blazes across the airwaves. In a remote area of the country, a young woman is listening.
Carol Tambala, 18, comes from a poor family from Mtelera village in southern Malawi. At 16 she became pregnant and dropped out of school. For two years, she implored her parents to let her return to school, to no avail. Carol has one ambition in life, to become a nurse, and she knows school is the only way.
"During my prenatal visits I met a lot of nurses and they told me I had to complete my education if I wanted to pursue a career in nursing," she says. "That's why it was paining me to see my fellow girls carrying books going to school every morning, knowing that staying at home would take me nowhere."
One evening she was listening to *YAM!* with her parents, and the presenters talked about the importance of returning to school after becoming pregnant.
The young mothers featured on *YAM!* who managed to continue their studies and attain their goals gave Carol courage. The program also moved her parents. "The interview with a girl who had gone back to school was touching," Carol's mother recalls. "Soon after the

program, we made a decision to allow our daughter to go back to school."

Carol is elated about returning to school: "Now that I am back in school, my goal is to become a nurse one day, and I am working hard to achieve this goal."

Not visible in the feature stories in the media and on the web are the more complicated and less appealing descriptions of how testimonials are produced, as in this coming-out story from a 1994 AIDS meeting in Abidjan, Côte-d'Ivoire, told by anthropologist and physician Vinh-Kim Nguyen.[4]

... three young people came forth to "come out" as HIV positive.... "At last, to have been able to see these courageous young people affirming themselves" sighed one World Bank official, Madame Janvier, when I asked her to recount the meeting.

... So it was perhaps not surprising that the three young people ... became the darlings of the development agencies. Funding became readily available, as well as invitations and plane tickets to meetings abroad. But Madame Janvier later came to have regrets. She felt that it was all "too much" for them: "they always look exhausted, they're always on airplanes. It's too much for their health." Madame Janvier was not alone in singling out the tendency of the new activists to travel frequently. It was a source of much jealousy on the part of those who joined the new organisation, and other aid workers occasionally accused colleagues of "showing off" their "pet" Africans with HIV at international conferences in a game of one-upmanship.

For high-level officials like the World Bank's Madame Janvier, Nguyen concludes, "'real' people with HIV came to represent that 'something is being done.' Officially, testimonies by people living with HIV were evidence that 'supportive environments' were being created and with it the right context for 'effective prevention' which would result in 'sustainable behaviour change.'"

The language of the testimonials often equates the change effected by an NGO with a religious conversion experience:

These testimonies redeploy the register of transmutation common in the Pentecostal churches.... Rebirth through the disease likewise involves standardized formulas of self-declaration, a passage to new ontological certainty and transparency that claims to reverse the deceptions of prejudice, secrecy, and untruth.[5]

But there is a mercenary aspect as well. Testimonials are marketable and help keep money for AIDS flowing. "Many of those in authority were oblivious to the fact that these testimonials were emerging as a response to their policies, policies that encouraged these testimonials. These incentives went as far as outright remuneration for testimonials, in effect creating a market for them."[6]

The ability to offer testimonials to visitors is a skill. Visits by donors to poor villages are highly orchestrated, as described in a case study of NGOs and farmers' associations in Guinea-Bissau. The NGOs selected some of the farmers, "usually among the most charismatic and eloquent," based on their ability to speak the development language. "The other farmers called them the project 'bards.' . . . They also appeared to be the ones most willing to mouth donor agendas in order to gain access to the material and symbolic resources that donors provided." [7]

In Malawi, villagers eagerly welcome visitors, and from what we have seen, the dances of welcome, the visitors' vehicles strewn with flowering vines on departure, seem genuine expressions of gratitude for the help donors offer. For the visitors, whether butterfly altruists, church mission groups, or—less frequently—representatives of behemoth donors, these face-to-face encounters are the real proof of a project's success. For the brokers, it is crucial to have "the people"—or at least some of them—show up when visitors come: as we noted earlier, for the NGOs in the AIDS industry, beneficiaries are valuable commodities in their efforts to attain funding; brokers who can reach those beneficiaries are invaluable.[8]

Reaching beneficiaries is likely to be easier when the relationships between the NGO brokers and the beneficiaries are structured by the normative expectations of patron-client relationships. NGOs, like patrons, provide benefits, and the clients reciprocate by turning out for celebratory moments, but also by participating in activities donors sponsor and by echoing what they understand as donor priorities.[9]

Altruists are aware of the value of a compelling story about a life transformed. USAID, for example, encourages its partners to produce "success stories," even providing guidelines for writing the stories and for interviewing beneficiaries.[10] Moving stories of transformation in the lives of the poor and vulnerable convince donors and brokers that they have been successful in fighting AIDS: the donor's dream has been fulfilled, the brokers' efforts have made a difference. Thus altruists, brokers, and beneficiaries—from the small church group that has a satisfying experience feeding orphans in a village to the chain of NGO brokers funded by the behemoth international and bilateral organizations—all collaborate to create an experience of connection and a conviction of meaningful change.

MONITORING AND EVALUATION

At first glance, the often highly technical practices of monitoring and evaluation (M&E), such as the "logframe" (logical framework) that has become a nearly universal tool in planning, monitoring, and evaluating development projects, seem light years removed from the run-down motels where eager volunteers are trained to fight AIDS. But these two practices are deeply interconnected. They are, when one digs down, the flesh and bone of the development enterprise: what donors pay for is primarily "talk" in the form of trainings and "paper" (nowadays, electronic paper) in the form of proposals, monitoring activities during the life of a project, and—the final "deliverable"—an evaluation report, often written by a consultant hired for the purpose, at the project's end.

Mandates and money go down the aid chain from behemoth donors to small NGOs with valuable access to beneficiaries, and, occasionally, to a village CBO.

An interview with the M&E officer for a faith-based development organization in Malawi describes the reporting process:

> We have a project officer, assistant project officer, senior development facilitator, development facilitator [their position depends on their level of education]. And each and every month, the project officer is supposed to report to the main office through me, the M&E officer, then I report to the projects coordinator. But from the field, it's like the community members, the community working groups, they report to ... or, the village development committees, report to the development facilitator. The development facilitator compiles a report to the project officer. The project officer compiles a report to the M&E officer, the M&E officer compiles a report to the projects coordinator ... and the projects coordinator reports on behalf of the programs department.[11]

One stop on the passage from the handwritten numbers to a report of success is the logframe, currently the central technology of M&E.[12] Monika

187

Krause describes her bewilderment when she first encountered a logframe at a three-day workshop for relief workers.

> Initially, the themes of the discussion during the training seemed familiar, and I felt I could participate in the discussions and in group work. But my attempts to pass came to an end when the training referred in passing to the "logframe," and everyone else in the room seemed to know what it was ... [it] seemed an accepted part of everyday vocabulary. As for me, not only did I not know what it was; when I first listened to the conversations that included references to the logframe, I could not come up with any idea as to what kind of thing it might be.[13]

Figure 10.1 is an example of two pages (out of thirty-three) from a logframe used by Malawi's NAC. The key column is headed "indicators" and is primarily a count of people involved in the project. Although the goal of the project is to change AIDS-related behavior, there is no count of the number of people who changed their behavior as a result of the objectives, strategies, and funding. The "indicators" are instead "No. [number] stakeholders implementing mutual faithfulness interventions" or "No. of BCC [behavior change communications] interventions implemented by trained personnel."

At first glance, monitoring by logframe appears to be a straightforward matter of rows and columns, to be filled with numbers and percents. But how trustworthy are the numbers? Did the reported "No. of men and women in high risk subgroups" really access information and medical services?

The very framework of M&E reporting requirements, the framework of the logframe itself, often depends on reports by the people directly involved in an NGO or CBO—those who benefit, or hope to benefit, from the opportunities it offers. Sitting in a district office of Malawi's NAC one day, we saw a barefoot, shabby man delivering to the District AIDS Coordinator a tiny slip of paper, obviously torn from a flimsy school notebook, with handwritten numbers of orphans that a CBO had helped. The numbers may or may not be accurate, but they are then aggregated, digitized, and polished as they flow upward to their final destination, a glossy report submitted by the donor agency to the representatives of taxpayers in rich countries, such as the US Congress or Britain's Parliament.

Optimistic reports of numbers of orphans "reached" by a program, or numbers of CBOs founded, or numbers of AIDS dramas produced by youth clubs depend on a patchwork of messy and unreliable numbers, provided by people who, sometimes urgently, hope to have the project continue. Those numbers are accepted and then aggregated by intermediaries on the aid chain who have no way to check on the activities the numbers purportedly represent. Then the reports are stored away, perhaps never to be read. If money disappears without appropriate accounting, however, alarm bells ring, and in egregious cases, the flow of money may be cut off for a period. Otherwise, the logframe exists in its own self-contained universe, symbolizing rigorous management to donors and providing a satisfying sense of accomplishment for brokers who master its arcane technology.

We found that it is difficult even to know whether a CBO group exists. In 2006, we went out to learn whether CBOs that had received funding from NAC in 2005 or 2006 were actually active. We took two approaches. One was to enlist field supervisors and interviewers for a University of Pennsylvania survey that was already underway in rural Malawi to ask, informally, several people in each of the villages that were supposed to have a CBO whether it was, or had been, active and what it did. We found that if the respondent was on the CBO committee or related to someone who was, the answer was yes, it was caring for orphans and/or helping those sick with HIV (the two main activities of CBOs at this time). If the respondent was not directly involved with the CBO committee, he or she usually was unaware that there was any organization active in the village— even though we knew from documents at NAC that the CBO had received funding. Our second approach was to ask a student to talk informally with respondents in fifty-seven villages in a district covered by the Penn survey and to ask whether there was a group in their village that helped orphans or the sick. She reported:

In addition to being unable to calculate a total number of CBOs, the reports were characterized by contradictions. There were discrepancies around whether a CBO was active, who was funding it, how frequently activities occurred, and how resources were spent. With all of these discrepancies, it was impossible to state what was really occurring with any confidence. Even the basic question of whether a CBO actually existed was prone to contradictory reports. In 38 of the 57 villages where we conducted interviews, individual respondents gave different reports on whether there was even a CBO in their village. Some people responded that there were no CBOs at all whereas others named and described a CBO.[14]

ANNEX 1: LOGICAL FRAMEWORK

Overall goal and priority areas

Overall goal
To prevent the spread of HIV infection among Malawians, provide access to treatment for PLHA and mitigate the health, socio-economic and psychosocial impacts of HIV/AIDS on individuals, families, communities and the nation.

National HIV/AIDS Priority Areas

Prevention and Behavior Change
Goal: To reduce the spread of HIV in the general population and in high-risk subgroups in Malawi

Objectives and outcome by end of 2009	Key strategies	Key action areas	Indicators	Means of verification	Responsible Govt. agency	Collaborating agencies	Estimated cost	Assumptions
Objective 1: To expand the scope and depth of HIV/AIDS communication for effective behavior change	Scale up innovative and culturally appropriate modes of communication	Develop specific interventions for men, women, girls and boys on values of mutual faithfulness & abstinence	No. stakeholders implementing mutual faithfulness interventions	S/holder reports				Determinants of risky behavior are commonly known
			% of men, women, girls and boys reached with messages of mutual faithfulness	Comm. Survey				
Outcomes Communication materials developed and distributed		Develop target specific IEC and advocacy materials that address area specific cultural challenges	% of married reporting practicing mutual faithfulness	Comm. Survey				
		Develop IEC materials targeting parents to improve the cultural social distance with the children	No. of s/holders with IEC materials targeting specific risky cultural practices	S/holder rpts				
Increased HIV/AIDS radio/television programs produced and number of hours aired.		Support traditional leaders and chiefs to disseminate information that perpetuate the notion of community	% of parents with IEC materials and engaging their children in positive cultural values	Comm. Survey				
		Strengthen life skills instructions in schools and colleges	No. of TLs disseminating information on cultural	Comm. survey				

Prevention and Behavior Change
Goal: To reduce the spread of HIV in the general population and in high-risk subgroups in Malawi

Objectives and outcome by end of 2009	Key strategies	Key action areas	Indicators	Means of verification	Responsible Govt. agency	Collaborating agencies	Estimated cost	Assumptions
Objective 5: To promote safer sex practices among the general and high-risk subgroups	Intensify BCC interventions	Disseminate a national BCC strategy	% of s/holders implementing BCC programs	A national BCC dissemination rpt.	Common understanding of safer sex behavior			Common understanding of the BCC strategy
	Increase access to condoms	Enhance capacity of stakeholders to implement BCC strategy	No. of BCC interventions implemented by trained personnel	NAC rpts				
Outcome: Increased number of people adopting safer sex measures such as condom use	Promote mechanisms for targeting high risk subgroups	Develop visual IEC materials, videos & films	% of community members accessing visual IEC materials	NAC rpts & Comm Surveys				
		Support skills training for groups of married women	No. of women trained	S/holders rpts.				
		Develop a National Policy and Strategy on condom	% of sexually active persons reporting access to condoms	Survey rpts. on condom access				Demand for condoms will be met by supply
		Strengthen the national condom distribution system to ensure universal access	No. of condoms distributed	MoH & NAC rpts.				People who access condoms will use them
		Expand condoms social marketing programs	% of sexually active persons reporting access to condom information & materials	Survey rpts				
		Develop programs for empowering sex workers	No. of sex workers reporting leaving the trade and engaged in IGAs	Program rpts of S/holders				
		Increase facilities for high-risk subgroups to access information and medical services	No. of men & women in high risk subgroups accessing information and medical services (sex workers, prisoners,	NAC & S/holder rpts				

FIGURE 10.1. ANNEX 1 LOGICAL FRAMEWORK, National AIDS Commission, Malawi. This sample logframe (slightly truncated here) is typical of those used by donors and NGO brokers to plan and monitor project activities; it is based on an annex to the Malawi National AIDS Commission (NAC), Malawi National HIV/AIDS Action Framework (2005–9) report (pp. 42–75).

Monitoring and evaluation "works" because it satisfies crucial fantasies —in this case, the donors' fantasy that they are able to control a messy, distant, and hard-to-read reality. M&E gives substance to the fantasy that the donors have control over their subcontractors, from nearby beltway bandits, to the largest INGOs, to distant NGOs in Lilongwe and tiny organizations in a district capital. All up and down the aid chain, donors can portray themselves as responsible stewards of the resources they expend because they have enforced elaborate reporting requirements and have produced ornate, numbingly complex documents as evidence of their probity. A subcontractor organization that wants funding thus has to jump through a variety of hoops required by its donors (and their upstream funders, such as the US Congress and the World Bank), and success at this task is taken as evidence of project success.

EVALUATION REPORTS

In addition to the testimonials and logframes, donors expect monthly, quarterly, and yearly reports, as well as an end-of-project evaluation summing up what was accomplished by the project.

End-of-project evaluations are particularly important for donors and brokers. It is these reports that are meant to say whether the project was successful or not. Some reports are colorful and engaging: glossy paper, many color photos of desperately needy, or gratefully happy, beneficiaries. They can be quite long—as much as three hundred pages, including appendixes—and dense, for example for an evaluation of a complex multiyear project. The reports typically begin with an executive summary, presenting the highlights. This may be all some read. Then there is usually a chapter on the background of the project, which demonstrates why the intervention was needed, a chapter on the methods of data collection and analysis, followed by one or more chapters on the results, and, finally, a conclusion—and perhaps several appendixes.

Producing such a report may be the task of the NGO brokers or an outside consultant hired by the project who works closely with the project staff, which provides background data, suggests employees and beneficiaries to be interviewed, and supplies documents like budgets, objectives, and logframes.

Newspapers in Malawi often have at least one, sometimes several, advertisements for consultants to perform an evaluation. Even when the advertisement specifies that an "independent" evaluator is wanted, however, that independence cannot be taken at face value, since the evaluator is not paid until the organization that commissioned the evaluation is satisfied with the report—a sort of insurance against the donor receiving bad news. In many conversations with other consultants, and in our own experience consulting for large projects, we have found that consultants are routinely pressured not to include bad news in their final reports. If an intervention shows few statistically significant results (as was the case in several interventions we evaluated) the implementing organization demands that the consultant conduct focus groups with beneficiaries (who reliably produce glowing testimonials) or that the data be "reanalyzed." Even when, as sometimes happens, a promised intervention is never implemented (because nurses refuse to implement it, for example, or—as is more often the case—because its basic design was never realistic), the consultant will be expected to bury the fate of the intervention in a long, dense project description.

The conundrum for an independent evaluator is that the donors do not want to learn that their fantasies were not fulfilled—an outcome that is particularly problematic for international donors who are responsible to their country's taxpayers. For the brokers in the implementing organizations, showing success is a life-or-death matter—they need to show success so that the donor will continue to fund their work and, importantly, their jobs. Similarly, the independent evaluator may be tempted not to be quite so independent, since she also wants to be hired again. When we asked an experienced consultant about what to do if the evaluation found that the project had failed, she said: tell the people running the project your concerns privately, but make sure the final report doesn't sound too negative.

At a USAID workshop to prepare for a major multi-country effort to change sexual behavior in Africa, we suggested more rigorous studies with experimental designs, such as the randomized intervention and control groups used in medical studies, or a baseline and end line study to assess change. The representatives of NGOs were not enthusiastic—they said they had too much to do helping people. Moreover, aside from the difficulty of randomizing an intervention, NGO workers think it is "wrong" to withhold from any group a program that they are sure is effective. So the barriers to rigorous evaluations are not just cost and inconvenience, or not wanting to know whether a project works. It also seems to those who care deeply about improving the lives of others that a serious evaluation diverts time, attention, and effort from what really matters—the program the donors and brokers already believe in.

Our reading of advertisements in the Malawi papers for consultants to evaluate projects provides more evidence that the NGOs implementing projects, and the donors that fund them, do not want to learn that they were unsuccessful. Projects were almost always evaluated after the project had ended. If there was no baseline against which to measure change, it was easy to claim—and to believe—that there had been change in the right direction. Further complicating effective evaluation, beneficiaries and those who hope they might someday become beneficiaries are very likely to tell evaluators what they want to hear. Furthermore, when it comes to reports of sensitive matters like numbers of sexual partners or condom use—precisely the behaviors AIDS prevention projects hope to change— respondents have again and again been found not to have told researchers the truth.[15] And, indeed, why should they be expected to do so?

As presented in the advertisements, the specified terms of the contract advertised virtually preclude a thorough evaluation. Even if the evaluator is to conduct an end-of-project survey to compare with the (rare) baseline, the specified number of respondents may be too few to produce statistically significant results or too many to be interviewed within the specified time and budget constraints. For example, the consultant is to "interview" twelve hundred beneficiaries in eight districts—but there is no provision for the time it takes to draw a proper sample, or for transportation to the districts, or for analyzing the data. Or, if the study is based on qualitative interviews with stakeholders and beneficiaries, the time allotted—often only thirty or forty person-days—is insufficient to analyze the data before writing the report. These constraints mean that even when the stated goals of the evaluation—to see, for example, after a program has ended, whether the population it sought to reach is willing to say that it has helped them— can only be accomplished in a purely symbolic and performative way.

From the point of view of small NGOs on the ground, evaluations are an afterthought and an annoyance. The NGO is already on to the next project. From the point of view of subcontractor NGOs and donors, such evaluations are a necessity, to be shown to their own funders up the line. Really bad projects may be quietly defunded, but the larger questions—about which kinds of programs for preventing HIV transmission and for achieving other development goals actually work—remain unanswered.

If the goals of M&E are making donors feel good and keeping the funding stream flowing—"creating success"—then cooperation between donors and brokers is crucial. Donors play their part by not requiring brokers to do systematic, scientific studies of the effects of the programs; brokers play their part by allowing donors to retain the fantasy of control—dutifully sending success stories, monitoring documents, and evaluation reports up the aid chain—and by not reporting things that went wrong; villagers play their part by providing success stories. Only when large sums of money go missing does the fantasy run aground, at least briefly.

Are there better ways for donors to learn whether their goals were reached? Given the severity of the epidemic and the huge amount of money expended on HIV prevention, we concur with the current view that promising interventions should be tested more rigorously using experimental designs, for example a randomized controlled trial to assess whether providing monetary incentives changes behavior or whether early treatment with antiretroviral drugs can dramatically reduce HIV transmission. If large AIDS funders or INGOs believe that they have a promising approach to HIV prevention, or to any other development goal, there is no reason why they should not also try to evaluate their interventions in rigorous ways.[16]

When there have been rigorous evaluations of HIV-prevention innovations meant to change behavior, the outcomes have been disappointing. A meta-analysis of the literature on AIDS interventions found only seven randomized controlled trials of AIDS behavior change interventions: in none of these were the differences between intervention and control groups statistically significant.[17] Another study estimated the added contribution of behavior change interventions to reducing HIV infections (beyond the decline in infections that occurs after those at highest risk are already infected). In some countries there was an added impact; in others, including Malawi, the researchers found none.[18]

If the donors supporting the AIDS industry really wanted to know the causal impact of the projects they fund, they could require—and pay for— more rigorous evaluations, and find ways to share the lessons of their many projects so they could learn both from success and from failure. From the perspective of donors and brokers, however, there are good reasons for eschewing rigorous evaluations: both groups are bent on doing good, not collecting and analyzing data; the time required to implement a rigorous evaluation and to analyze the results is not compatible with the short NGO project cycle imposed by the donors; and the donors evidently believe that rigorous evaluations are unnecessary—or, perhaps, they do not want to learn that their projects were not successful.

Since current approaches to evaluating behavior-change interventions are so inadequate, what does that imply for future evaluations? We believe that, at the least, projects should do careful before-and-after evaluations, and donors should read the evaluation reports with skepticism informed by knowledge of the goals of the brokers themselves, their frustrations, and the insecurities with which they live. More importantly, we think that the development community would benefit enormously from an accumulation of "collective wisdom"—not quite the same thing as rigorous scientific knowledge—about how HIV-prevention and other development initiatives actually work on the ground. The difficulty is that the current structure of incentives leads NGOs to pretend that their interventions are like silver-bullet medical interventions—a single, clear project to train villagers, or to create community councils, or to discourage men from domestic violence—and then to cover up both the complex human relationships involved in how the intervention was actually carried out and its actual successes and failures.

If the development agencies and NGOs could be persuaded to keep track of how their interventions were actually implemented (what is sometimes called a "process evaluation") and to report truthfully on the things that went well and those that went badly, even in the absence of rigorous evaluation projects might benefit from cumulative wisdom about how to make interventions more successful. This would require focusing not only on the specific "intervention"—as if it were a pill that beneficiaries only had to swallow—but on all the other things that make an intervention work or not work, including the all-important role of brokers. It may be that persuading a chief to let his villagers participate, the villagers' hope of material benefits from the project, the friendship that formed between an influential villager and the project staff were more important to the outcome than the particular intervention being tested. But these are things that the current approaches to evaluation can't begin to discover—because donors, far from the site of the intervention, cannot know the variety of factors in the specific context that might influence how their interventions are implemented, and they have no incentive to acknowledge, or learn from, failure.[19]

At all levels of the AIDS industry, as well as among the butterfly altruists, those who have put their time and energies into stemming the tide of the epidemic want to believe that what they have been doing has worked. A long-time worker for large INGO active in many countries described in a conversation the current USAID-funded project he was working on (we have changed a few details so that the project is not identifiable):

> We produce a radio program that has dealt with just about everything: what is love, the danger of having multiple concurrent part-

ners, sexual networks, the importance of couple communication about AIDS prevention. I don't have a handy list of topics, but it's been running for over 2 years now. We were getting about 200 SMSes per program in feedback. We have 15 field producers living in the communities, sending in stories. We work in over 350 communities now, and will work in more by the end of this year. In each we have formed a Community Action Group to do local action planning, and we have established groups in villages that either listen to our radio program together or have other topics they discuss a few times per month. We also do trainings and encourage youth volunteers to form drama groups.[20]

When we pointed out that there is no persuasive evidence that these or other projects actually change behavior, she paused, and then replied, "But we can't give up, we have to do something." Another respondent, also a long-time worker in development aid whose task in Malawi was to distribute foreign aid from a behemoth donor to national NGOs, acknowledged that most of his grants to NGOs had produced little effect. He said, "What I am most proud of here is building the capacity of the Malawians I work with," i.e., that they are now better able to manage money and the paperwork that donors require.[21] Thus workers on the front lines of AIDS prevention either march forward under the conviction that they are "doing something," or they take solace from feeling good about what they have been able to accomplish, even if they recognize that their larger aspirations may have failed.

Transforming intimate behavior in order to lower HIV risk is difficult because there is no known technology that reliably produces success. Thus donors focus on intermediate outcomes, such as the empowerment of women or the number of condoms distributed. When the goals are not only lofty—to transform intimate behavior—but the technology to reach them is mainly exhortation through the media and through trained volunteers, success is likely to be elusive. And yet, there has been, and continues to be, creative collusion among donors, brokers, and villagers to demonstrate success.

CHAPTER 11

CONCLUSIONS

Doing Good Better

WE HAVE HAD MANY SKEPTICAL things to say about the AIDS enterprise. Our message, however, is not that the task is easy and those who do not get it right are fools. Just the opposite. We are constantly aware how hard it is to do good at long distance. It is difficult because the visions that inspire the romance of altruism are often at odds with the visions of the brokers on whom the donors depend and with the visions of those living in villages or slums who long for help that will permit them to survive from day to day. It is particularly difficult for the giant institutional altruists such as USAID and Save the Children. Their tasks are hard because foreign aid, by definition, is sent to faraway places.

The obstacles to doing good at long distance are many for both institutional altruists and freelance altruists. Institutional altruists must depend on a chain of local NGOs to reach their intended beneficiaries and on a chain of local brokers who may have their own understanding of what is needed. Where, for example, donors see vulnerable women who need to be empowered, brokers see mercenary women who need to be restrained. Freelance altruists also depend on brokers. They must find, or be found by, a broker who will guide them to an orphanage or a poor village. In both cases, the brokers may not be fully trustworthy because they have their own policy ideas and because they have obligations to the relatives, patrons, and clients who comprise their social safety net, obligations that may take precedence over their obligations to those who are paying them.

The task is yet more daunting when it comes to AIDS prevention efforts in Africa, where the goal of institutional altruists is to change intimate behaviors that for many local people are central to life's joys and to its meanings. We really do not know how to produce effective, willing "behavior change." Yet more fundamentally, altruists are caught between their idealistic aspirations and the limited, uneven, and sometimes disappointing results of their work. Experienced development professionals working for globe-spanning aid organizations know these problems, but to sell their organizations' programs to ultimate funders—idealistic voters and generous individuals in the West—they have to promise not modest, uncertain progress, but transformative change. The challenges of trying to help thus result not only from the inherent difficulties of the task, but also from the need to move distant publics, whose hearts are touched by distant suffering. Thus, practical difficulties on the ground are compounded by the need to pitch unrealistic goals with soaring rhetoric.

Many development professionals begin as deeply committed idealists; a stint as a Peace Corps volunteer is a common first step. For many whom we met, a position in international development is not just a job, but a deeply meaningful vocation. Some become seasoned realists, and yet remain morally committed. But all, from staff in large INGOs in world capitals to brokers in small CBOs in rural Malawi, are constrained by the practical demands of their situations.

Foremost is that the brokers must constantly seek funding for their organizations to preserve their own jobs and those of their staffs. They must write proposals that respond to changing donor priorities, and because most need multiple donors to survive, they must write multiple proposals, each promising that their innovative approach will fulfill the donors' goals. They must make their funders believe, even make themselves believe, that whatever approaches to transforming Africa are currently in favor will succeed, even if they are aware that past ideas have mostly failed, and even if the new projects they put forward mostly ring small changes on existing approaches. When projects end, development professionals must write reports to their donors that at least imply that their aspirations to transform individuals and communities were successful.

Small-scale altruists have more modest aspirations: to bring textbooks to a village school, to dig a borehole for clean water, to spend time with orphans. They use their own resources or rely on donations from their friends, families, or churches. Although they, too, must convince any donors that their projects will be successful, these altruists more often achieve their more realistic goals. Even so, those who want to create ongoing projects soon discover, as seasoned development professionals have, how difficult it is to operate in unfamiliar territory. While they often develop deep emotional attachments (as we have) to brokers who befriend them and guide them, those who want to establish long-term projects face challenges and disappointments. They must find sources of consistent funding, which requires them to inspire others—friends, members of their high school graduating class, church groups, or strangers—who will help fund-raise. They, like development professionals, must offer inspiring images of transformation to motivate generous giving. Both institutional altruists and freelance altruists are caught in a system that rewards those who can inspire rather than those who deliver modest realism.

Large and small-scale altruists share another set of problems: knowing what is really happening in their projects. It is relatively easy for the small-scale altruists to show accomplishments, such as a new church roof or new notebooks in the hands of schoolchildren, and to send pictures of the Malawians with whom and on whose behalf they worked. But they have little way of knowing what becomes of their help after they leave. Knowing what is really happening in their projects is far more challenging for the development professionals at the top of the aid chain. The reports they receive from their brokers will tell them little if brokers construct the reports to advance their own interests.

Brokers may themselves have little knowledge of what a project accomplished. Erratic electricity, lack of petrol and vehicles, and simply staff overwork can make the local monitoring visits that NGO brokers are supposed to do nearly impossible. Nonetheless, the brokers have to write monthly, quarterly, and annual reports to send up the chain to the development professionals, who are responsible for producing a glossy report for the donor, a report that must convince the donor that they deserve further funding. Butterfly altruists who visit their projects sometimes find themselves greeted by legions of dancers, joyous children, and others eager to assure them that their help has been gratefully received. Development professionals, whose projects take years to complete, find gratification delayed, if ever delivered.

Freelance altruists and professionals share yet another problem: it is impossible for either to know whether the orphans they are feeding are the chief's nieces and nephews, whether the youth group they are funding meets after the visitor leaves, or whether the broker left in charge of the project is doing what she promised. Sometimes, because of cultural rather than physical distance, they may not understand what they are seeing, even when it is right in front of them.

IMAGINATION AND FANTASY

In discussing the romance of AIDS altruism, we have said much about imagination and fantasy. In doing so, we are not pointing to some pathology of those who are moved to do good in faraway places, but to something essential and universally human. People could not survive without fantasy, without imagining the larger meanings of their actions. We imagine our children going to college or having children of their own; we imagine ourselves in a beautiful new outfit; we fantasize about the pleasure we will derive from a movie or a good meal. These subjective experiences *are* the joys of life, not false substitutes for joys. Fantasy and imagination are how we animate our lives with meaning.[1]

The drawback of fantasy is that it can distort perceptions of reality, as when we see our children only as fulfilling our aspirations rather than as separate people with struggles and triumphs of their own. In altruism, sometimes donors' fantasies inhibit dealing effectively with African realities. African brokers' fantasies—both about the donors and about poor villagers—shape what altruists imagine can be accomplished, and what they do accomplish. Altruists need to imagine that their efforts are desperately needed, that a small investment, such as a pair of goats, can transform a family's life, or that a short training of village volunteers in "decision-making" can create "AIDS competent communities." Altruists, brokers, and villagers are all moved by the fantasies they have about one other. The interplay of those imaginings has been a central theme of this book.

What are their major fantasies? For all parties, one of the deepest is about connection. Altruists seek a sense of human connection with those whom they want to help. "Before" photographs of skeletal orphans and "after" photographs of laughing children at play create a sense of connection. Freelance altruists who volunteer in a village and development professionals who discuss projects with elite brokers often find that such personal connections fulfill their longings for deep encounters across boundaries of geography, wealth, or culture.[2]

Malawians also develop fantasies of the material gains that foreigners may bring. As foreigners seek brokers, so Malawians seek patrons. To the altruist, an acquaintance's wistful request for an iPad, a poor villager's hope for capital to start a business, a pastor's appeal to support his church, or an elite broker's presumption that international conference invitations, job advice, or even a laptop will be forthcoming, can be jarring. But these requests, like those for an e-mail address or a phone number, express Africans' fantasies of connection.

As we have repeatedly emphasized, patron-client relationships are at the core of the political economy of Africa; patrons and clients need one another.[3] Anthropologist China Scherz has beautifully described, in work on Uganda, how many African societies value dependence, not independence.[4] In Malawi, too, village life rests on a social safety net woven by ties of reciprocal dependence. Ties of unequal dependence—of the poor on their wealthier kin, of all sorts of clients on their patrons—are integral to full personhood.[5] Thus, both villagers and brokers imagine—and try to create—ties of dependence to foreign donors.

MORAL IMAGINATIONS

We have shown how powerfully imagination animates—and bedevils—relationships among brokers, donors, and villagers. For example, local brokers often imagine not human rights or women's empowerment, which international donors see as critical to fighting AIDS, but rather fulfilling their duties as town fathers, maintaining moral order by controlling mercenary women and shutting down video parlors where young people might be tempted into risky sexual activity.

We are often so deeply committed to our own moral codes that we do not recognize the views of others as "moral."[6] Western donors who want Africans to become self-reliant and fulfill their individual potential are hardly aware that their moral passion emerges from societies very different from African ones. Since African societies value interdependence, resisting "peer pressure," as organizations promoting HIV prevention teach, means risking isolation. Even altruists who feel wounded incomprehension when they discover that brokers are diverting project resources to help their own relatives show how little they understand the moralities of redistribution and reciprocity that make perfect sense in Africa.

Successful African brokers themselves hold conflicting worldviews. On the one hand, many feel deeply committed to their nations and their cultures. On the other hand, they express ambivalence about their own societies. We have heard them romanticize village life as the warm and authentic, if impoverished, world of their "grannies," and then proceed to moral criticism of village life, that backward villagers lack the crucial characteristic that could help them become modern—self-reliance. While brokers themselves rely on patrons and support their less fortunate kin, they often say that villagers need to be taught not to expect "handouts," but to rely on their own resources. This view lines up with the sustainability mantra from abroad, that NGOs will "empower" the villagers to solve their own problems and end dependency.

It follows that villagers must not be paid, since poor African governments cannot (or will not) continue the payments. Instead, villagers are to be volunteers who can be offered only training and modest sums for "income generating activities" like raising chickens or creating a community garden. The commitment to self-reliance leaves donors free to move from project to project, imagining that their modest investments will return huge dividends. Sustainability sounds virtuous, connoting respect for the ecology of the natural world and aspirations to manage agriculture, fisheries, and human population growth so as to preserve the planet.[7] As applied to projects for the Third World's poor, however, sustainability turns out to rest on a powerful moral ethic that embraces self-reliance and abhors dependency.

Malawian brokers who have succeeded in Malawi's demanding school system see villagers not only as poor, but also as morally deficient. They tell us that the poor have failed to exercise the disciplined self-restraint and future orientation that their own sacrifices required. Brokers, who may well be the only ones in their families with a job in the formal economy, resent their many poor relatives' expectations that they will redistribute whatever they have accumulated. Thus, brokers' attitudes toward villagers and toward donor aid programs reflect an extraordinarily complex, sometimes acutely ambivalent, moral imagination—at once protective of their societies' cultural integrity and passionately committed to modernity.

Poor villagers bring their own moral imagination to encounters with donors and potential patrons. For them, all visitors from afar must be rich. Being rich, visitors surely understand the normal obligations of reciprocity and redistribution. Someone who has given us two hours of her time for an interview rightly expects reciprocity, at least a packet of sugar or tea. They imagine most intensely that the rich person will help them meet their families' needs. Whether it is paying a child's school fees so that she may, eventually, become a broker, or an opportunity to earn money on an altruist's project, villagers imagine the possibility, however remote, of a life-transforming encounter with a foreigner. That encounter would almost certainly involve creating a patron-client relationship. If the potential patron does not understand his or her moral responsibilities, some villagers work up the courage to enlighten her. Sometimes, especially for villagers with fluent English, a foreigner does perform a miracle—rushes a sick child to the hospital in his car, helps pay for the roof of a village church, or finances a bright son's education, allowing him to support his extended family far into the future. The stories spread, instilling hope in others.

Might we imagine some better approach that would avoid the clash of donors', brokers', and villagers' moral visions—one that allowed not only the NGO brokers but also the poor villagers to benefit from money for AIDS and other development goals? Of course, villagers did benefit from the crucial information, developed by Western researchers, that HIV was sexually transmitted. But once they learned this fact, they knew from previous experiences with sexually transmitted infections what practices would keep them safe—abstinence, fidelity, and condom use. Villagers also benefit materially now and then, as when an NGO distributes some blankets (never enough for everyone) or distributes maize, beans, and cooking oil during the hunger season.[8] But they have to take what's on offer. A respondent in a survey in rural Malawi complained that in exchange for their time the interviewers gave them soap. He said, like a good economist, "I would like to tell you the truth today. This organization is buying soap for us. Tell them to stop buying soap for us. We cannot appreciate with the soap that you buy for us. But if you give us money like K300, K400, we can thank [you] for that because we know our problems. We can use that money for the problems which we have."[9]

We end up being disheartened by the workings of the AIDS enterprise and yet surprised that, despite constant disappointments, the villagers continue to hope that one day they will benefit from the compassion of the altruists who have come to Malawi to help them. And we hope that altruists will recognize their moral obligations as well.

WHAT CAN BE DONE?

How would we advise altruists to do better in the difficult, sometimes heroic efforts they have undertaken to improve the lives of the poor, the suffering, or the benighted around the world? And although brokers and villagers are unlikely to read our book, we do have thoughts about how their interactions with donors might be made better. In the spirit of the improvements we are urging, our advice is modest and incremental rather than dramatic and transformative. We hope, however, that our suggestions will inspire another moral imagination for altruists, one that is more tentative, respectful, and grounded than soaring and certain.[10]

First, however, we want to acknowledge that sometimes visionaries triumph. Paul Farmer, Jim Kim, and Zackie Achmat succeeded against astounding odds in mobilizing world opinion and in challenging political leaders to make antiretroviral drugs available to poor and marginalized people living with AIDS.[11] Global organizations, such as the WHO, the World Bank, and the Global Fund, along with agencies of Western governments, such as USAID and the UK's DFID, coordinated the efforts of donors, drug companies, foundations, and many other actors. Their efforts produced a workable regimen of antiretroviral drugs available at a reasonable price and funds for labs and clinics that could test for HIV in order to identify those who needed the drugs. Perhaps most important of all, they spread the message all over the world that people living with AIDS could be restored to health. By any measure, these are astounding achievements—fueled by daring, fierce imagination—that challenged existing notions of what was possible or prudent.

These successes, however, were largely due to the scientists in the West who developed antiretroviral therapy and the activists who urged global organizations to make the therapy available in Africa and elsewhere. Despite the dramatic success of antiretroviral treatment, the many failures of efforts to change AIDS-related behaviors and, more generally, the failures of Western-funded development efforts to transform ways of life suggest the need for other approaches.

Knowing Brokers

We begin with the suggestion that the donors who fund foreign aid and the development professionals who design the programs to benefit the villagers try to understand more about the brokers upon whom they rely. Although poor villagers or desperate slum dwellers populate donors' imaginations, brokers fundamentally shape what altruists can accomplish. Despite their deep reliance on brokers, altruists typically are incurious about how the world looks and feels from the brokers' point of view.

Seen up-close, brokers are a mixed lot: some are more educated, some less; some are committed to doing what they can to help the less fortunate in the villages; some want to develop their country but at the same time are strategizing to further their personal development by acquiring the educational credentials that enhance dignity and status, as well as employability.[12] Brokers who work for foreign donors are dependent on the huge, chaotic, frenetic enterprise of foreign aid; they all—even the most elite—aspire to greater social and economic mobility. Adding to the difficulty, they are all more or less subject to irrational forces beyond their control. Their jobs may suddenly vanish when a donor pulls out of their country because of government corruption, or an INGO with an office in their country shuts down the local NGO where the broker works, perhaps because the funding was not renewed. They also have to worry that the donors will announce a new theme, and they will have to position themselves to take advantage of the new funding stream perhaps by getting a new credential showing that they are qualified for the new positions that are

205

advertised.[13] Credentials are not enough, however. NGO brokers have to worry that however qualified they are, the malice of their boss or their co-workers will block a promotion or, worse, lead to their dismissal.

It is not only their professional lives that are insecure, but also their private lives. They have to do their job, but at the same time they have to maintain the entrepreneurial activities that many engage in to buffer their insecurity. Most difficult, however, is maintaining their obligations to their extended families. Besieged by poorer relatives who come to them for aid for school fees or a medical emergency or food during the hunger season, they have to parse carefully whom they can accommodate, and how often, and whom they will refuse.

Lastly, we urge donors to be skeptical about brokers' claims that their projects were successful. They should demand rigorous evaluations rather than testimonials from beneficiaries carefully selected by the NGO and documents describing their activities. And they should expect that some of their fantasies will not come to fruition and try to learn from the failures rather than continue to fund minor variations of those failures.

Relations with Brokers

Being aware that the earliest step is to recruit a broker can help an altruist understand both the welcome he or she receives and the sort of relationship he has entered into.

It is not unusual that the first person a freelance altruist happens to meet—a helpful taxi driver, the manager of a motel, or a friendly seatmate on the flight in—will become the altruist's broker and friend, eager to lead her to an orphanage or invite her to his home village. Similarly, a development professional may be assigned a broker by the relevant ministry, a broker who volunteers critical information about the ministry's enthusiasm for or subtle opposition to the project. The personal relationship may be brief and formal, or may develop into a long-lasting friendship. One piece of advice, then, is that altruists should be aware of just how dependent they are on those first contacts. Altruists must thus be both open and cautious: open in the sense that each relationship has the potential to grow into one of substantial help and attachment, and cautious in the sense that a broker certainly has agendas and needs of her own that a visitor may not perceive. An altruist should also be aware that brokers may feel pressure from their own kin to appropriate project resources, pressure to which they might succumb or which they may resist. The altruist must search for an honest broker, but must also be prepared for the possibility that he may be misled by his guide.

The solution is to not to become disillusioned and turn the broker away. Instead, the altruist, professional or amateur, can adapt. The dominant cultural model for relationships in most of Africa is not the bureaucratic employment contract, but the patron-client tie, which is far different from the formal, contractual understandings of employment in the West. The freelance altruist will inevitably be recruited as a patron, as will the visiting development professional when a member of the Malawian elite helps him or her deal with a visa problem or shows him some of the countryside. Both sorts of altruists could do good better by learning how to be good patrons.[14]

Material help and deep affection go together in African societies. We are sometimes amazed at how often those hired years earlier for two months of temporary work seek us out when they hear we have returned. They come to "greet" us (one of the basic ways that clients reaffirm their relations to patrons), show us their children, tell us about their jobs, or seek our advice. Thinking of ourselves only as short-term researchers, we have been turned into patrons. And we often reciprocate by bringing small gifts for a broker or his or her children or by providing help in an emergency. Westerners are often uncomfortable in the role of patron, as we have been—not knowing when we are being taken advantage of, not knowing in what words to turn away requests for assistance, not eager to have people dropping by unexpectedly to greet us. Nonetheless, understanding that from the brokers' point of view employment relationships are colored by patron-client expectations can make those relationships work better for both parties.

The patron-client situation is obviously somewhat different when the broker is one of many working for an NGO that is implementing a project for a big donor. If a small-scale altruist becomes disillusioned with his or her broker because he steals or drinks on the job, she can decide whether to fire or forgive him. For brokers working for an NGO, there is a formal work contract specifying the tasks of the broker and under what conditions he or she can be fired. In many Africans' understanding, however, the employment relationship is foremost a patron-client relationship.

Many things militate against effective working relationships in postcolonial settings like most countries in Africa. Africans were long expected to defer to those above them in authority and status—to their senior kin, to chiefs and village elders, to teachers, employers, and colonial officials. Deference is compounded when the person in authority is a foreigner. Deference creates a problem for truth telling. Brokers often find it difficult to tell their foreign colleagues that a donor's program is not going according to plan. A broker may have discovered that the village chiefs are irritated with the project and will sabotage it; a broker may already know that nurses who were expected to use an iPad to book appointments for pregnant women will refuse to have anything to do with the electronic gadgets, but not pass on what he knows. As one said, "Aah, it is difficult to speak to those above you."[15]

The Western response to evident inequalities in status has been to insist that everyone is really equal and to talk about local "ownership" of the donor's project. Since both donors and brokers know that the donor provides the resources and is ultimately in charge, talk about "ownership" is just that, talk. The more intimate and trusting partnership that the donor seeks, even in a large development organization with many employees, is more likely to develop if brokers feel tied to their colleagues and superiors by bonds of personal loyalty, in turn cemented by patron-client exchanges. Westerners see patron-client ties as demeaning the subordinate; Africans see them as empowering the subordinate because patrons have obligations to their clients.

The Social Consequences of Altruism

Donors and those elite brokers who receive regular salaries worry that aid makes less fortunate Africans "dependent" and saps their initiative. That is not our worry, both because we see no sign that Africans we know have been slow to try to improve their own lives and also because overcoming the hurdles they face without donor assistance would be almost impossible.

If one looks at what aid projects do, aside from whether they meet specified aims, the most consequential positive effect is that they expand the formal labor market. Donor aid also influences brokers' aspirations and identities. The projects stimulate intense aspirations for credentials that, however costly, might permit rising in the formal job market. For young people who have a high school education but are still living in a village, the existence of NGOs multiplies the possibility of one day leaving subsistence agriculture and, in the shorter term, of per diems from a training or the occasional chicken, goat, or bag of fertilizer donated to an NGO income generating project. One step toward achieving these aspirations is a chance meeting with a visiting foreigner. Another step is participation in a CBO. These CBOs have an elaborate apparatus of committees—for home based care, orphans, youth, PLWAs, and so forth, each committee with an executive committee, treasurer, secretary, and sometimes many more officers. They currently do not receive regular funding, but rather wait for an NGO to arrive bearing benefits.

This elaborate apparatus of ostensibly modern, or modernizing activity, along with the trainings that are the main benefit donors offer to villagers, do not "empower" local communities, as donors wish, but create a capricious, unpredictable, and irrationalizing set of incentives. In rural settings, the development structure offers not jobs and orderly career paths, but extraordinarily unpredictable one-time benefits that arrive without apparent rhyme or reason. A 2015 World Vision advertisement claims "facilitation of community empowerment through advocacy and partnering in which the capacity of district and community groups were built to take advantage of their rights and advocate for change...."[16] As we have shown, this turns out to mean in practice that the relatively elite villagers, selected for a training because they are relatives of the chief or because the NGO wants to train people who already read in English, receive allowances for attending a training on whatever the donor's interest is.

Despite our skepticism about the value of trainings and our continuing amazement that virtually all bold attempts to transform Africa come down to yet more training, there may a broader, yet unanticipated, benefit. The NGO chain, with its hierarchy of trainers, trainers of trainers, and those being trained, creates a career ladder of its own that can anchor at least a fantasy of reward for the immense effort young Malawians invest in education. We sometimes ask rural parents, struggling to cobble together school fees for a bright son or daughter who has had to stop school repeatedly for lack of funds, "but if she is able to finish, will she be able to get a job?" Their answer: "No, but without schooling, there is no hope." That shred of hope comes largely from the NGO world and from the trainings themselves—not only because they offer educated village youth more cosmopolitan identities, but also because the kinds of jobs they might be able to get after repeated rounds of volunteering and training do not require specialized education. The lower-level NGO positions, especially jobs like "Trainer," provide a kind of sheltered labor market for an economy that has yet to produce enough private sector jobs or white-collar positions for the legions of bright, educated, but not technically skilled secondary school graduates. In the end—if, for example, parts of Africa develop enough internet infrastructure to compete with India and the Philippines for call centers, data processing, and other cyber-commerce—it will be the NGO enterprise that has sustained and inspired that labor force, albeit under the guise of "empowering" village communities.

This is, however, a very expensive, roundabout way of accomplishing a worthy goal. As we have repeated many times, large donors and small altruists of all sorts would do better to sustain projects they believe are worthwhile by continuing to fund them and to simply pay villagers as well as higher-level staff to carry out activities that the donors believe are worthwhile.[17]

AFRICANS ALREADY HAVE SOCIAL ARRANGEMENTS THAT WORK

At a more general level, it is important to understand that Africans are not the generic impoverished, helpless unfortunates of the Western donor imagination. Many may be poor, but they have complex social arrangements, some of which have developed over centuries, which in many respects continue to work for their communities. Understanding and appreciating those arrangements is critical to doing effective development work.

Most Africans might well prefer, if it were possible, to live in a developed market economy with ample opportunity and a smoothly functioning labor market. They might also prefer to live in an effective rule-of-law state, with good policing, secure property rights, and uniform, enforceable family law. But these arrangements are not available to most Africans in most contemporary African societies. (Some elements of this complex, like effective policing and economic opportunity, are unavailable in the poorest cities of Western societies as well.) Their absence has implications for those trying to help poor Africans.

As anyone who has worked on the ground in an African country is already aware, chiefs are the locus of village governance and possessors of much power. Simply to get an NGO project started, the chief has to approve. Since one of a chief's responsibilities is to "bring development to the community," the chief rarely refuses a project. The only case we know of a chief rejecting a project occurred when an NGO wanted the chief to command his subjects to mold bricks for a library. He said, "We don't need a library, we need clean water."[18]

Chiefs and other traditional authorities are not democratic in the Western sense. They are normally unelected.[19] Many are corrupt or at least favor their own relatives when they distribute benefits. Nonetheless, chiefs and other traditional authorities—mostly male, often hereditary—maintain basic law and order in their communities and organize villagers to provide the sorts of public goods governments either cannot or will not provide (like repairing paths or boreholes). [20] Most important, chiefs control the allocation of "customary land" as families grow and adjudicate basic claims to property, marriage, children, and other resources. Chiefs resolve disputes and maintain order within their villages. They also have responsibility for funerals, a critical function in societies where continuing connections to ancestors are central.

Donors who want to reach beneficiaries in the villages need to recognize that they are dealing with societies that already have functioning institutions, not only chiefdoms, but also churches and mosques. These institutions have powerful holds on local people. We have been surprised to find projects to transform communities that focus on training those in the modern sector, such as health surveillance assistants and agricultural extension agents, while ignoring traditional leaders—who then may not support the project or may even actively oppose it. Even refusing to hire a chief's son or daughter may imperil a project. Moreover, chiefs normally enforce any lasting improvements in village life, by, for example, assessing small fees to pay for borehole repairs. Finding a way to work with these local authorities is, then, essential to creating effective programs with enduring effects. That is one implication of appreciating the resilience of the existing institutional systems upon which Africans depend. [21]

A second is that trying to change institutions that Westerners consider illegitimate—because they are not gender-egalitarian, nor democratic, nor encouraging of individual autonomy, and so on—is a mistake in the absence of the modern institutional order that such autonomous, democratic, and egalitarian people would require. Our ideals make sense to us because they work in our advanced-capitalist, liberal-democratic institutional order. Without effective modern institutions, Africans quite rightly depend upon and remain attached to the institutions they have.

The same practical logic applies with even greater force to the informal systems of generalized reciprocity upon which most Africans, and above all the African poor, depend. On every front, neither villagers nor elite Malawians are autonomous. A husband has to ask permission of his wife's family before he can take her for medical treatment; a young woman who gets pregnant by a local boy depends on community opinion supporting her family's right to negotiate with the boy's family; a village woman whose sister's goats eat her food crop needs the chief to rule that her sister was wrong (and then she may choose to "forgive" her sister because, in the end, she depends on that very sister).[22] Even cosmopolitan brokers are not free agents. We have pointed out that they are often reluctant to do anything that would disrupt relations with their local peer networks. As one distinguished leader of a Western AIDS project said, in explaining her resistance to donor demands to quickly scale up a project, "I still have to live here."

Donors and NGOs use the term "community" to refer to the poor who live in a village; the term suggests a holistic community. As foreigners who have studied or worked in villages know, relations of interdependence in a village community are not always harmonious.[23] There are factions, people cheat and betray each other, jealousies and rivalries abound, and envy sometimes leads villagers to burn a neighbor's crops or use witchcraft to avenge a grievance. Nonetheless, these relations of interdependence and, above all, reciprocal obligations to kin are the only source of security people have in a very insecure world. Thus, the very image of an autonomous, independent, empowered individual that is so hallowed in the Western imagination is likely to make little sense in the daily lives of Malawians. Perhaps if a fully effective labor market emerges in parts of Africa and people's basic claims to property and person are protected by an effective legal system, some of the traditions of reciprocal interdependence upon which most Africans depend will slowly die out. But until that time, it would be realistic for Western altruists to question the taken-for-granted truths of their own moral imaginations, to question whether they really make sense in such different societies.

A TEMPERED MODESTY

Many of the problems of the AIDS romance in Africa characterize the development enterprise as a whole. To obtain funding from idealistic publics, large donor organizations (such as the US government's USAID) have to promise that they will "transform" the lives of women or of the global poor, UNAIDS has to promise that it will "end AIDS by 2030," and the smaller organizations have to promise that they will "save one child" or that they will uplift the utterly destitute to lives of hope and progress. It is likely, however, that projects that respond to what Africans themselves say are their priorities, such as clean water, are more successful.

Recently, Nobel Prize winner Angus Deaton has mounted a particularly scathing critique of foreign aid. He argues that it has been more harmful than helpful and advises that foreign aid money be spent *on* Africa but not *in* Africa; moreover, he says, "it is unethical for us to try to impose our priorities on them."[24] Although Deaton writes that citizens of the rich world should be persuaded that aid can be harmful, we think it unlikely that foreign aid from rich countries to poor ones will end. The moral commitment to help will remain, and, more pragmatically, rich countries have other motives for spending money abroad. Our strongest advice for institutional altruists is that they not try to transform the lives of others. Instead, offer modest help to advance goals that those in need of your help actually want.

This means, of course, learning what they do want. It may not be what you think they should want. The 2008 University of Pennsylvania survey in rural Malawi asked respondents to rank five policy priorities in order of importance: agricultural development, clean water, education, health services, and HIV/AIDS programs: clean water came out on top and more AIDS services was last, with nearly half of respondents ranking HIV/AIDS services as the least important policy intervention.[25] A 2005 Afrobarometer survey in eighteen African countries, a much larger study, asked if the government should devote many more resources to AIDS, "even if this means that less money is spent on things like education." Fewer than half of the respondents agreed.[26] Interviews with fifty village headmen in Malawi suggest their logic. Headmen said that if there were clean water, they would not need health services, and pointed out that even the HIV+ need clean water to stay healthy.[27]

Providing boreholes for clean water and paying technicians to repair them, paving rural roads so that men and women can more easily access a market, assuring regular deliveries to health facilities of something as simple, but critical, as soap—these are realistic goals. Utterly unrealistic goals, such as transforming communities, are a sure recipe for being fooled by those you want to help, having to fool your funders by "creating success," and in the end, having to fool yourself.

Another unrealistic goal is "sustainability." Research convincingly shows that a project a distant organization has decided will benefit poor villagers will not be sustained by volunteers after the donor decamps. Poor people want to work for money, not for free, and are likely to quickly abandon a project once they find that there are no more benefits after the training.[28] Yet development professionals, convinced (or constrained) by the false promise of "sustainability," continue to rely on poor villagers to voluntarily give their time to implement projects. Instead, they should spend money on employing local people. Villagers desperately want jobs, and there are jobs that they can do that really need to be done.

More modest goals—and a greater interest in the actual lives both of the recipients of one's altruism and of the intermediaries on whose help one relies—might also allow more realistic evaluation of what programs work in what settings. Realistic evaluations in turn might lead to a more cumulative model, not of universal "best practices" (truly a mirage), but of incremental improvements that build on local institutions and local capacities. A greater willingness to take risks, not on outlandish, transformative projects (the scandalously over-promoted Millennium Villages embody this over-the-top rhetoric), but on modest ones might make a modest difference. This should be accompanied by a real commitment to collect realistic evidence about what projects cost, who benefits from the donor funds, and what their effects actually are. Experimenting with different approaches to helping beneficiaries might in the end allow improvements in how aid is allocated and what altruists can try to do. Many of the problems with the altruistic enterprise are the inevitable result of having aspirations that far exceed our knowledge or capacity, of being forced by the funding environment, and ultimately by the imaginations of distant publics, to promise more than can possibly be delivered, thus disappointing donors, brokers, and villagers alike.

Lastly, accept that what local people really want may be prosaic things like clean water and school fees for their children. Providing those things, even on a small scale, may do more than all the soaring ambition of programs that promise transformation on the cheap.

ACKNOWLEDGMENTS

WE BEGIN, AS IS CONVENTIONAL, by thanking the many visiting altruists, development workers and volunteers, and especially the Malawians, who shared their lives with us. In our case, we mean it. Malawi's national motto is "The Warm Heart of Africa," and indeed, Malawians are remarkably open, warm, generous, and eager to talk with outsiders. As we walk in local markets, people who speak English want to chat about everything from American politics (a source of particular fascination during the Obama era), to soccer, to their curiosity about us—where we "go to church," our ages, how many children we have, and of course where we are from. Malawians we meet eagerly describe their own schooling, the younger siblings for whom they are responsible, their career successes and frustrations, or, for villagers, their efforts to farm successfully, rotating crops between groundnuts and maize, or hauling jerry cans of water from the river to irrigate their crops. All these conversations, both formal interviews and casual conversations in minibuses, over meals, or in the rural motels where we stayed, have deepened our understanding of AIDS in Malawi and of the ways Malawians experience the global AIDS enterprise. Our debt, both to close friends and to many acquaintances and generous strangers, is immense.

We are also enormously grateful to all the international development workers, some Americans or others working in Malawi or elsewhere in Africa, who consented to be interviewed about their work and their lives. We quote many of them here, but since we have made every effort to keep their identities anonymous, we must thank them in this impersonal way, although our debt to them is a very personal one. We and our students interviewed many others, whose experiences and views of the world inform this book. We are grateful for their time and for the many insights they shared with us.

We especially want to thank our extraordinarily helpful Malawian friends and colleagues: McDaphton Bellos, Violet Boillo, Abdul Chilungo, Agnes Chimbiri, Wyson Chimesya, Angela Chimwaza, Davie Chitenje, the late Fanizo George, Jonathan Kandodo, Pilirani Kunkwenzu, Christopher Manyamba, Janepher Matenje, James Mkandawire, Esnat Sanudi, Lonnie Tchunga, and especially Dr. Eliya Zulu, a former graduate student, who first introduced us to Malawi.

To make our way in the thicket of the global AIDS enterprise, we have sought advice from those with long-time involvement the aid world. Development professionals familiar with the chaotic world of aid organizations tried to keep us from losing our way: Agnes Chimbiri, Shanti Conley, Jamaica Corker, Tsetsele Fantan, Gabi Gahn, Peter Godwin, Daniel Halperin, Peter Jones, Jonathan Kandodo, Peter Kilmarx, Carol Lancaster, Boemo Sekgoma, Sharon Stash, Rand Stoneburner, Linda Tawfik, and Susan Zimicki. We are grateful to Mary Mahy of UNAIDS for providing us with the most recent data on HIV in Malawi.

We also learned much from the dozens of undergraduate and graduate students, as well as postdoctoral fellows and faculty members at the University of Pennsylvania and other academic institutions, who were exceptionally generous in sharing their unpublished research on Malawi with us: jimi adams, Phil Anglewicz, Nicole Angotti, Jere Behrman, Julia Behrman, Crystal Biruk, Jennifer Browning, Sahai Burrowes, David Chilongozi, Yael Danovitch, Kim Yi Dionne, Kate Dovel, Anne Esacove, Emily Freeman, Maggie Frye, Hannah Furnass, Patrick Gerland, Monica Grant, Tom Hannan, Stéphane Helleringer, Will Jackson, Amy Kaler, Hans-Peter Kohler, Iliana Kohler, Tara McKay, Eleanor Meegoda, Erin Mitchell, Tyler Myroniuk, Oleosi Ntschebe, Francis Obare Onyango, Samantha Page, Fiona Parrott, Michelle Poulin, Georges Reniers, Rachel Sullivan Robinson, Enid Schatz, Kirsten Smith, Valerie Paz Soldan, Sahra Suleiman, Iddo Tavory, Rebecca Thornton, Jenny Trinitapoli, Cathy van den Ruit, Janneke Verheijen, Joanna Watkins, Alex Weinreb, Anika Wilson, and Sara Yeatman.

Lindsay Bayham provided invaluable research assistance. She prepared the graphs we use to track global AIDS funding and tracked down much other information that we did not know or were doubtful about, thus keeping us from embarrassing mistakes. Ugur Yildrim ably prepared the bibliography and provided a judicious analysis of issues in the literature. Sarah Gilman prepared the original version of the "Categories of Institutional Actors in the Global AIDS Enterprise" figure in chapter 3.

Other colleagues, students, and friends read chapters of the manuscript or the entire manuscript, offering valuable suggestions and saving us from many errors. We thank Adam Ashforth, Marie Berry, Michael Bracher, Diana Cammack, Jamaica Corker, Juan Delgado, Paul DiMaggio, Kim Yi Dionne, Leydy Diossa, Matías Fernández, Peter Godwin, Tom Hannan, Arlie Hochschild, Dennis Hodgson, Ben Jones, Dick Madsen, Saskia Nauenberg, Lant Pritchett, Peter Roberts, Gigi Santow, Jeremy Shiffman, Bill

Sullivan, Jeff Swindle, Sylvia Tesh, Steve Tipton, Jenny Trinitapoli, Nicolas van de Walle, Daniel Wroe, Viviana Zelizer, Amy Zhou, and two anonymous reviewers.

We are grateful for feedback from colleagues who have responded to our work at talks and seminars at the University of California, Berkeley, UCLA, University of Pennsylvania, University of North Carolina, University of North Texas, Harvard University, Duke University, the American Sociological Association, Population Association of America, the World Bank, Pennsylvania State University, University of Malawi College of Medicine, Cornell University, and Tulane University.

The book could not have been written without the support of sabbaticals from the Russell Sage Foundation (Swidler), the Guggenheim Foundation and the Center for Advanced Studies in the Behavioral Sciences (Watkins), and support from the Center for Health Research, the Committee on Research, and the Center for African Studies at Berkeley (Swidler), to all of which we are very grateful. The Canadian Institute for Advanced Research (CIFAR) is a remarkable organization supporting groups of scholars in a variety of fields to pursue innovative, interdisciplinary questions. CIFAR stimulated Swidler's initial interest in AIDS in Africa and supported her while she made a career-changing, and as it turned out life-changing, turn to a new research area. The stimulation provided by the members of CIFAR's Successful Societies Program, and its co-chairs, Peter Hall and Michèle Lamont, have been invaluable. Watkins' career-changing turn from the historical demography of Europe to population growth and AIDS in Africa was supported by funding for survey research from the Rockefeller Foundation and the National Institute of Child Health and Human Development (NICHD), which permitted her to spend many months in Africa, first in Kenya, then Malawi.

Meagan Levinson went far beyond what one expects from a senior editor, carefully reading the entire manuscript and offering incisive comments on virtually every page. The immensely dedicated, patient, professional staff at Princeton University Press dealt beautifully with the unique challenges of a book about difficult but important issues and one that relies on unusual sorts of evidence: Samantha Nader, the creative-solver-of-all-problems Debbie Tegarden, the brilliant illustration guru Dimitri Karetnikov, and Doreen Perry, among others, did a superb job.

Jerry Cotts, the brother of Susan Watkins, and his wife (Ann Garneau, a long-time friend of Susan's) came to Malawi to visit us: Jerry took some of the wonderful photos in our book. Our friends Carol Heimer and Sylvia

Tesh also joined us in Malawi, enriching our research and generally making life more enjoyable. We are also indebted to Donald Treiman, who visited us in 2016 and enriched the book with additional photographs.

Claude Fischer is due very special thanks. In the final months of revising the book, he repeatedly took time away from his own work to edit chapter after chapter of the manuscript. In addition, in his role of husband (to Ann Swidler) and father (of Avi and Leah Fischer), he did double duty while Ann was away on repeated visits to Africa; he coped with the anxiety of having a wife who was often outside range of phone or internet; and he offered a loving embrace when she returned. Leah Fischer deserves special thanks for accompanying her mother on their first adventure in Africa.

Anne Esacove's wonderful new book, *Modernizing Sexuality: U.S. HIV Prevention in Sub-Saharan Africa*, reached us just as our book was going to press. We would have loved to include her valuable insights into the issues we address.

Susan Watkins would like to thank her siblings, children, and grandchildren for making her life happier during the writing of this book: Jerry Cotts, Virginia Cotts, Ann Garneau, David Shaw, Nina Shaw, Richard Shaw, Kimika Tashima, Emma Watkins, Kate Watkins, Robbie Watkins, and Tim Watkins.

NOTES

PREFACE

1. Boseley, "Saving Grace."
2. http://www.theguardian.com/values/getinvolved/story/0,,2135661,00.html [accessed 12/19/15].
3. *Congressional Record*, p. 7875.
4. http://www.hopeformalawi.com/Hope_for_Malawi/About.html [accessed 5/18/12].
5. The phrase "working misunderstandings" appeared originally in Laura Bohannan's (pen name Eleanore Smith Bowen) anthropological novel *Return to Laughter*, and was then taken up by later anthropologists. See http://h-net.msu.edu /cgi-bin/logbrowse.pl?trx=vx&list=H-Africa&month=0408&week=a&msg=HqsY /bB3EI76fcLu4U5Xpw&user=&pw= [accessed 4/24/14].
6. Chabal, *Africa*, p. 48. Important recent discussions of dependence in African societies are Ferguson, "Declarations of Dependence" and *Give a Man a Fish* and Scherz, *Having People, Having Heart*.
7. The classic reference is Bayart, *The State in Africa*; on corruption in Nigeria, see D. Smith, *A Culture of Corruption*; for Kenya, Odhiambo, "Determinants of Corruption in Kenya"; and for Malawi, Robinson and Seim, "Who Is Targeted in Corruption?"
8. K. Smith and Watkins, "Perceptions of Risk."
9. Chimwaza and Watkins, "Giving Care to People."
10. An example of such a project, suggesting the level of commitment required, is Bwengu Projects. http://www.bwenguprojects.co.uk/ [accessed 1/16/16]. The retired British couple that founded the organization live six months a year in a Malawian village where they directly supervise the building projects and feeding programs their organization sponsors. We met them at the modest motel where they had stopped over for a night to purchase supplies.
11. They are not unlike the depictions of cruelty by nineteenth-century American reform movements, such as abolitionism, meant to arouse emotions and sympathy from bourgeois audiences—what Karen Halttunnen ("Humanitarianism and the Pornography of Pain") has called the "pornography of pain."

CHAPTER 1. INTRODUCTION: ALTRUISM FROM AFAR

1. For critical views of aid, see Kristoff, "Aid: Can It Work?"; van de Walle, "Aid's Crisis of Legitimacy"; Easterly, *The White Man's Burden*; Moyo. *Dead Aid*; Deaton, *The Great Escape*.
2. http://countrymeters.info/en/Malawi [accessed 4/3/16].
3. http://www.thegaia.org/news/archives/june2004.htm [accessed 11/22/04].

4. Myroniuk, Press, and H.-P. Kohler, "Why Rely on Friends Instead of Family?"

5. Details on the extent of intra-familial transfers of money and assistance in rural Malawi can be found in Weinreb, "Substitution and Substitutability"; I. Kohler et al., "Intergenerational Transfers"; Davies, "What Motivates Gifts?"

6. Some Malawian businesses practice occasional small-scale altruism, such as providing funds for scholarships or blankets for orphans in a village.

7. Recent work on the history of humanitarianism includes: Adam Hochschild, *Bury the Chains*; Calhoun, "The Imperative to Reduce Suffering"; Stamatov, *The Origins of Global Humanitarianism*. Manji and O'Coill, "The Missionary Position," describe similarities between contemporary NGOs and earlier missionary efforts.

8. Watkins, Swidler, and Hannan, "Outsourcing Social Transformation."

9. This may include appearing the way altruists imagine them. Duncan McNicholl contrasted photos of Malawians looking the way donors expect them to look with photos of them dressed up, giggling about dressing down to look needy: http://waterwellness.ca/2010/04/28/perspectives-of-poverty/ [accessed 6/16/10].

10. Krause, *The Good Project*.

11. The small but important literature on the role of local brokers and translators in development includes: Olivier de Sardan, "A Moral Economy of Corruption in Africa?" and his *Anthropology and Development*; Pigg, "Globalizing the Facts of Life"; Lewis and Mosse, *Development Brokers and Translators*; Merry, *Human Rights and Gender Violence*; Anders, *In the Shadow of Good Governance*; Mosse, *Adventures in Aidland*.

12. See Bleiker and Kay, "Representing HIV/AIDS in Africa."

13. See Garrett, "The Challenge of Global Health."

14. Wallace, *The Aid Chain*.

15. National AIDS Commission, "National HIV/AIDS Response," and accompanying spreadsheet.

16. See, for example, the World Vision workshop, "Empowered Biblical Worldview and Farmer Managed Natural Regeneration (FMNR) Conference for Church Leaders," Lilongwe, Malawi, August 11–13, 2015. http://beatingfamine.com/malawi-gains-momentum-at-world-vision-workshop/ [accessed 8/8/16].

17. On the relation between poverty and HIV, see Shelton, Cassell, and Adetunji, "Is Poverty or Wealth"; Mishra et al., "HIV Infection Does Not Disproportionately Affect the Poorer in Sub-Saharan Africa." This pattern varies across countries and contexts (see Gillespie, Kadiyala, and Greener, "Is Poverty or Wealth Driving HIV Transmission?") and may be reversing in more recent data (for Zimbabwe, see Lopman et al., "HIV Incidence and Poverty"); Parkhurst, "Understanding the Correlations."

18. Morfit, "'AIDS Is Money.'"

19. Morfit, "'AIDS Is Money,'" p. 74.

20. Whether development aid stimulates overall economic growth is intensely debated. Marren, "Overseas Development Aid," provides a recent overview.

21. D. Smith, "Patronage, Per Diems."

22. According to OECD estimates, overseas development assistance is 31.5 percent of Malawi's gross national income. https://public.tableau.com/views/AidAtAGlance_Recipients/Recipients?:embed=n&:showTabs=y&:display_count=no?&:showVizHome=no#1 [accessed 1/13/16].

23. *HIV prevalence*: the most recent estimate is 10.04 percent prevalence for those in the age group 15–49—giving Malawi the ninth highest HIV prevalence in the world. https://www.cia.gov/library/publications/the-world-factbook/rankorder /2155rank.html [accessed 1/27/16]. A new Malawi Demographic and Health Survey was conducted in 2015–16, but as of August 2016, the data on HIV prevalence had not been analyzed. *Donor dependence*: In 2010–11, donors provided 98 percent of Malawi's AIDS budget. See Government of Malawi, "2012 Global AIDS Response Progress Report," p. 26. *Size:* 45,560 square miles [Wikipedia "Malawi," accessed 8/7/16]. *Population*: 17,785,430. http://countrymeters.info /en/Malawi [accessed 8/7/16]. *Proportion rural*: approximately 84 percent. http:// faostat.fao.org/CountryProfiles/Country_Profile/Direct.aspx?lang=en&area =130 [accessed 8/7/16]. *Peacefulness*: Unlike some other countries seeking independence from colonial powers, Malawi (then the British protectorate of Nyasaland) transitioned to independence without widespread violence; similarly, in 1994, the dictatorship of Hastings Banda gave way to multiparty politics, accompanied by only sporadic outbreaks. Since then there have been occasional and highly localized religious/ethnic protests, strikes by university lecturers or civil servants, some that have provoked tear gas, but these were all in urban areas and only one, in July 2011, largely driven by the poor state of the economy, occasioned any deaths (nineteen in total). See Power, *Political Culture and Nationalism*; Malawi Human Rights Commission (MHRC), "Report on the Demonstrations."

24. Jackson and Rosberg, "Why Africa's Weak States Persist"; Herbst, *States and Power in Africa*. For analysis of Malawi's failures of governance, see Booth and Cammack, *Governance for Development*; Cammack, "Malawi's Political Settlement."

25. Callaghy, "The State as Lame Leviathan."

26. On the important role local chiefs play in much of Africa, see Baldwin, *The Paradox of Traditional Chiefs*. On the role of chiefs in Malawi see: Dionne, "Local Demand for a Global Intervention"; Cammack, "Understanding Local Forms of Accountability"; Cammack, Kanyongolo, and O'Neil, " 'Town Chiefs' in Malawi"; Swidler, "Cultural Sources of Institutional Resilience." Logan, "The Roots of Resilience," points to the broad support for traditional leaders in contemporary Africa. This paragraph and the next draw on these sources and on our own fieldwork.

27. Gross National Income Per Capita, Atlas method, in 2015 US dollars, World Bank. http://data.worldbank.org/country/malawi [accessed 8/7/16:]; Malawi's rank among countries: Sixth poorest in 2014 IMF rankings, third poorest in World Bank rankings, and fourth poorest in CIA ranking based on purchasing power GDP per capita. https://en.wikipedia.org/wiki/List_of_countries_by _GDP_%28PPP%29_per_capita#List_of_countries_and_dependencies [accessed 1/4/16].

28. For a recent description of life in a Malawian village, see Verheijen, *Balancing Men, Morals, and Money*.

29. See, for example, Johnson-Hanks, *Uncertain Honor*; Chabal, *The Politics of Suffering and Smiling*.

30. Serieux et al., "The Impact of the Global Economic Crisis."

31. Lieberman, *Boundaries of Contagion*.
32. We are grateful to Mary Mahy, Division Chief, Strategic Information and Monitoring, UNAIDS, for providing the UNAIDS 2016 estimates of HIV incidence from 1970–2015. While these estimates rely on complex epidemiological modeling, they suggest no change in the rate at which HIV incidence declined from its peak in 1992–93, either as HIV-prevention programs ramped up or as antiretroviral drugs became widely available.
33. Tavrow, *Family Planning Knowledge*.
34. Several studies have found stronger support for the behavior change hypothesis than the heterogeneity hypothesis. See Hallett et al., "Declines in HIV Prevalence."
35. Vermund, "Massive Benefits of Antiretroviral Therapy."
36. Donnell et al., "Heterosexual HIV-1 Transmission."
37. Padian et al., "Weighing the Gold in the Gold Standard," conducted a review of HIV prevention interventions. They found thirty-seven studies that met the "gold standard" for assessing the effect of an intervention: randomized controlled trials. Only six demonstrably reduced HIV incidence, all of which were biomedical (male circumcision, treatment of sexually transmitted infections, one vaccine trial).
38. A recent study compared African countries with PEPFAR-supported programs promoting abstinence and fidelity to countries without such programs and found no differences in reported sexual behaviors (Lo, Lowe, and Bendavid, "In Sub-Saharan Africa Abstinence."
39. Studies that claim to show that HIV-prevention programs work rely on self-reports of behavior change, which have again and again been shown to be unrelated to actual HIV incidence. On the unreliability of self-reports when compared to biomarkers, see Plummer et al., "A Bit More Truthful"; Helleringer et al., "The Reliability of Sexual Partnership Histories."
40. Epstein, Helen, *The Invisible Cure*.
41. Watkins, "Navigating the AIDS Epidemic."
42. Simon Bato journal, June 2002.
43. The rich trove of research produced by the original University of Pennsylvania project (originally, the "Malawi Diffusion and Ideational Change Project") and its successors can be found at Google Scholar Profile: Malawi Longitudinal Study of Families and Health (MLSFH). https://scholar.google.com/citations ?user=dNEAH3YAAAAJ.
44. See Watkins and Swidler, "Hearsay Ethnography." The anonymized ethnographic journals are available online at http://deepblue.lib.umich.edu/handle /2027.42/113269.

CHAPTER 2. FEVERED IMAGINATIONS

1. This paragraph draws on thoughtful comments from Dennis Hodgson.
2. http://www.who.int/features/factfiles/hiv/facts/en/index3.html [accessed 8/7/16]. The figures are not precise. The number of those living with AIDS could be as low as 34 million and as high as 39.8 million.

3. Mary Mahy, Division Chief of Strategic Information and Monitoring, UNAIDS, Geneva, Switzerland. Email to Watkins, March 17, 2016.

4. http://projectavalon.net/lang/en/jim_humble_2_interview_transcript_en .html [accessed 1/8/2014]. We did not interview Jim Humble, and we have not protected his anonymity. In 2010, Jim Humble's "Miracle Mineral Solution" was condemned by the FDA: http://www.fda.gov/Safety/MedWatch/SafetyInforma tion/SafetyAlertsforHumanMedicalProducts/ucm220756.htm [accessed 1/16/16]. Although he was eventually run out of Balaka, the ability of this dignified-looking quack to promote his "AIDS cure" to Malawians provides another instance of how unregulated the world of visiting altruists really is.

5. See https://www.bestzapper.com/what-is-a-zapper/ [accessed 3/12/14].

6. NGOs in Malawi and other AIDS-stricken countries play a particularly important role in influencing the visualization of the "real epidemic": In the *Columbia Journalism Review*, Karen Rothmyer ("Hiding the Real Africa") writes that these organizations "understandably tend to focus not on what has been accomplished but on convincing people how much remains to be done. As a practical matter, they also need to attract funds."

7. http://www.hosannalc.org/pdfs/Malawi_Journal.pdf [accessed 3/2/10].

8. Interview with head of Malawi office of a large USAID-supported INGO, June 2008.

9. Given the pervasive accessibility of information on the web, to protect the anonymity of those we interviewed from this organization, we do not provide a link to the website. We have also made minor changes to the language from the website (changing the grammar, moving phrases around, occasionally using synonyms) so that it is not traceable.

10. This passage and the next are from personal communication with William Rankin, a co-founder of GAIA, e-mail to Watkins January 28, 2014, used with permission.

11. Wallace, *The Aid Chain*.

12. Ebrahim, *NGOs and Organizational Change*, p. 67.

13. Epstein, Helen, "The Lost Children of AIDS," p. 1. See Hope's response and Epstein's reply at http://www.nybooks.com/articles/2005/12/15/the-lost-children -of-aids-an-exchange/.

14. Krause, *The Good Project*.

15. Chabal and Daloz, *Africa Works*; Swidler and Watkins, "Ties of Dependence"; Chabal, *Africa*.

16. Colson, "The Search for Healing," p. 114.

17. This quote and those that follow describing an NGO visit are from Thomas Hannan's fieldnotes, July 21, 2009. See also Hannan, "World Culture and Small-Scale Altruism."

18. http://www.malawiproject.org/index.php?module=pagemaster&PAGE_user_ op=view_page&PAGE_id=95&M MNposition=85:84 [accessed 5/26/05].

19. Stories of backward, superstitious villagers frequently accompany nation-building, colonial, or modernizing projects (see chapter 8). The Jewish "Chelm Stories," immortalized by Isaac Bashevis Singer in *The Fools of Chełm and Their History*, are a classic example.

20. Trueman Uyezani journal, October 6, 2006.

CHAPTER 3. LUMBERING BEHEMOTHS AND
FLUTTERING BUTTERFLIES

1. "Addressing Multiple and Concurrent Sexual Partnerships in Generalized HIV Epidemics, PEPFAR General Population and Youth HIV Prevention, Technical Working Group and AIDSTAR-One," October 29–30, 2008. Watkins attended and interviewed PEPFAR and AIDSTAR officials.

2. Data for Figures 3.1 and 3.2 were compiled by Lindsay Bayham from multiple sources: for The Gates Foundation, from Funders Concerned About AIDS (FCAA) Annual Reports, available online at http://www.fcaaids.org/Resources /Publications/tabid/197/Default.aspx; for bilateral donors (US, UK, France, Germany, Netherlands, Canada, and Sweden), The Kaiser Family Foundation, "Financing the Response to AIDS in Low- and Middle-Income Countries," Annual reports from 2005–14, available online at http://kff.org/global-health-policy /report/financing-the-response-to-aids-in-low-and-middle-income-countries -international-assistance-from-donor-governments-in-2014/; for the Global Fund, from the yearly disbursements in Annual Reports available online at http://www .theglobalfund.org/en/publications/annualreports/; for UNAIDS, from http:// www.unaids.org/en/ourwork/managementgovernancebranch/planningfinance accountability/programmeplanningperformancemeasurement; for The World Bank, http://datatopics.worldbank.org/hnp/worldbanklending; and for the WHO, from multiple sources, including WHO Annual Workplans and for data from 2010–14, the WHO's 2012–13 HIV Operational Plan, available online at http://whqlibdoc.who.int/publications/2012/9789241503709_eng.pdf. Figures reflect actual disbursements, not enactments. Further details are available from the authors.

   Of course, as with other foreign aid, not all the money—or even a majority of the money—budgeted for AIDS in Africa is spent in Africa, or even for such goods as food and medicines that directly benefit Africans. For US aid, see Oxfam America, "Foreign Aid 101."

3. Initially focused on saving the lives of the HIV+, it subsequently expanded to include prevention and care, as well transitioning from an emergency response to promoting sustainable country programs. http://www.pepfar.gov/about/.

4. AVERT.org, an AIDS NGO based in Britain, provides an excellent description of the way money flows through the aid chain: AVERT.org, "Funding for HIV and AIDS," http://www.avert.org/funding-hiv-and-aids.htm [accessed 1/16/14]. Avert estimates that for the HIV response in low- and middle-income countries, including domestic sources of AIDS funding (57 percent of the total), there was "$20.2 billion made available in 2014 and a projected $21.7 billion by the end of 2015": http://www.avert.org/professionals/hiv-around-world/global-response /funding [accessed 3/29/16]. An examination of the determinants of donor generosity finds that a strong predictor is inertia: aid budgets evolve slowly (Fuchs, Dreher, and Nunnenkamp, "Determinants of Donor Generosity," p. 190).

5. Calculated from Burrowes et al., What Explains the Geographic Distribution," sheet 2.

6. Putzel, "The Global Fight against AIDS," pp. 1129–30.

7. UNAIDS is the Joint United Nations Programme on HIV/AIDS. UNAIDS consists of eleven co-sponsors: United Nations Children's Fund (UNICEF), World Food Program (WFP), United Nations Development Programme (UNDP), United Nations Office on Drugs and Crime (UNODC), United Nations Educational, Scientific and Cultural Organization (UNESCO), International Labor Organization (ILO), World Health Organization (WHO), The World Bank, and UN Women. The goals of UNAIDS are leadership and advocacy, mobilizing resources, engaging civil society, tracking, monitoring, and evaluation of the epidemic and responses to it, and providing information and technical support (Wikipedia, accessed 2/28/14).

8. The WHO shapes global health policy more broadly, but for AIDS, that function falls largely to UNAIDS and the Global Fund. Nitsan Chorev (*The World Health Organization*) offers a sophisticated history of the WHO's evolving strategies for managing pressures from its member states (most from the global south), which dominate its governing body, the World Health Assembly (WHA), and the wealthy countries of the global north, which provide the bulk of its funding. See also Heimer, "Old Inequalities, New Disease" and Lieberman, *Boundaries of Contagion* for good overviews of the global AIDS enterprise.

9. Oomman, Rosenzweig, and Bernstein, "Are Funding Decisions Based on Performance?" p. 20, describe these Country Coordinating Mechanisms: "Grant proposals are developed and submitted to the Global Fund by country-level partnerships called Country Coordinating Mechanisms, which include representatives of the government, multilateral and bilateral agencies, businesses, groups affected by the diseases, and other private and public sector stakeholders. They are evaluated by an independent technical review panel, which recommends approval or rejection."

10. http://www.theglobalfund.org/en/ccm/

11. Interview with the pastor of a rural church who was also an elected representative to the Country Coordinating Mechanism, March 23, 2009.

12. The Millennium Development Goals (MDGs) and reports on progress toward each goal can be found at http://www.un.org/millenniumgoals/ [accessed 1/22/14]. In 2015, the United Nations adopted a much broader set of seventeen Sustainable Development Goals: http://www.un.org/sustainabledevelopment/sustainable-development-goals/ [accessed 5/9/16].

13. Thomas Weiss ("The MDGs and the UN's Comparative Advantage," p. 1) describes the MDGs: "The MDGs represent a consensus on development policies and targets, even in the absence of a common understanding of what constitutes development or agreement on the best strategies. In that sense, they are a quintessentially UN achievement by setting aside disagreements on contested concepts in favor of an accord about shared goals and milestones."

14. Countries report their progress on a host of measures in biannual reports to the United Nations General Assembly Special Session (UNGASS) on AIDS. Scanning the recent reports, http://www.unaids.org/en/dataanalysis/knowyourresponse/countryprogressreports/2012countries, suggests that while compliance with reporting is not universal, a large majority countries report data on at least some measures (168 countries out of a possible 192).

15. Weiss, "The MDGs and the UN's Comparative Advantage," p. 3.
16. http://www.unaids.org/sites/default/files/media_asset/JC2686_WAD2014 report_en.pdf [accessed 3/28/2016].
17. Nagaraj, "'Beltway Bandits' and 'Poverty Barons,'" p. 589. Cooley, "Outsourcing Authority," discusses the destructive consequences of competition among NGO contractors. He also points out "how deeply institutionalized contracting has become across all aspects of domestic and global governance" (p. 265). See also Cooley and Ron, "The NGO Scramble."
18. McKee, Bertrand, and Becker-Benton, *Strategic Communication in the HIV/AIDS Epidemic*, give a sense of the complex partnerships and funding flows that link these various actors. See, for example, the many funded reports cited in the bibliography, pp. 312–32.
19. Interview with Chief of Party of a USAID-funded project in Malawi, July 28, 2010; interview with staff member of PSI-Botswana, October 2010.
20. On the global explosion of NGOs, see Watkins, Swidler, and Hannan, "Outsourcing Social Transformation." In the mid-1980s, international donor policy shifted from funding governments to funding non-profits. Because Malawi's first post-colonial leader, Hastings Banda (ruled 1961–94), was firmly opposed to the entry of foreign organizations, the shift to NGOs was delayed until multiparty elections in 1994, after which the new government welcomed them (see Forster, "AIDS, the Local Community"; Power, *Political Culture and Nationalism*.
21. According to UNAIDS, HIV prevalence was 11.8 percent in 1995, which was fifth highest in the world. Malawi's highest prevalence was 13.8 percent from 2000–2002. See http://www.unaids.org/en/dataanalysis/tools/aidsinfo/?subject =AIDSINFO11-WORLD. By 2014, prevalence had fallen to 10.0 percent, the ninth highest in the world. See http://www.unaids.org/en/dataanalysis/data tools/aidsinfo/.
22. This count excludes government ministries and donor organizations. There are no reliable current lists of AIDS organizations in Malawi. The National AIDS Commission (NAC) stopped maintaining a systematic list after 2006, and although NGOs are supposed to register with the Council on Non-Governmental Organizations, it is likely that many do not, since this requires that the organization pay dues. The difficulties of getting reliable counts of NGOs are discussed in Watkins, Swidler, and Hannan, "Outsourcing Social Transformation." Among other problems, many NGOs that exist on paper turn out to have become defunct (or, as in the case of "briefcase NGOs," never to have had programs or activities in the first place), while many other small altruists may operate without being formally registered. See Barr, Fafchamps, and Owens, "The Governance of Non-Governmental Organizations."
23. For example, the Southern African AIDS Trust, a regional NGO, supports indigenous community organizations to transform themselves into a registered NGO with a professional staff that can write funding proposals and produce the paperwork that donors require for governance, finance management, reporting, and auditing. http://www.satregional.org/about-sat/who-are-we/ [accessed 4/5/16].
24. Of the $58 million, $42 million was disbursed. Of this, 10.3 percent was directed to the NAC's community mobilization project. Browning, "The Difficulty of Monitoring."

25. Browning, "The Difficulty of Monitoring"; Swidler and Watkins, " 'Teach a Man to Fish.' "
26. See, for example, Walsh et al., " 'The Problem Is Ours.' "
27. NAC allowed CBO proposals only from the "Group Village Headman" administrative level, not from individual villages. A Group Village Headman can have from a handful of villages to fifty or more in his area. NAC also systematized the process of training representatives from each of these Group Village CBOs to write proposalws that met NAC's guidelines.
28. Trinitapoli and Vaisey, "The Transformative Role."
29. Hannan, "World Culture at the World's Periphery."
30. A version of the diagram appeared in a 2005 UN report, "aids2031: Evolution and Future of Donor Assistance," as an image of donor assistance in Tanzania, along with a color key and a list of acronyms. A slightly neater version was published in Cohen, "The New World of Global Health," p. 166.

The key to the acronyms is:

CCM: Country Coordinating Mechanisms
CF: Clinton Foundation
CIDA: Canadian International Development Agency
CTU: Central Technical Unit
DAC: Development Assistance Committee
GFATM: Global Fund for AIDS, Tuberculosis, and Malaria
GFCCP: Global Fund Country Coordinating Plan
GTZ: German Agency for Technical Cooperation
HSSP: Health Sector Support Plan
NAC: National AIDS Council
NGO: Non-Governmental Organization
NORAD: Norwegian Agency for Cooperative Development

NCTP: National Care and Treatment Plan [HCTP]
NSF: National Strategic Framework
PEPFAR: President's Emergency Plan for AIDS Relief
PMO: Prime Minister's Office
PRSP: Poverty Reduction Strategy Papers
RNE: Royal Netherlands Embassy
Sida: Swedish International Development Agency
SWAp: Sector-wide Approach
TACAID: Tanzania National AIDS Commission
USAID: United States Agency for International Development
UNICEF: United Nations Children's Fund
WB: The World Bank
WHO: World Health Organization

31. http://www.fhi.org/en/HIVAIDS/country/Namibia/res_namibiapresidentini tiative.htm.
32. Putzel, "The Global Fight against AIDS."
33. Figures for NAC's "Grants Approved for the January to June 2010 Cycle" are from *The Nation*, Friday, July 23, 2010, p. 14. While the value of the Malawi kwacha fluctuates widely, at the time, the two grants were worth roughly $800,000 and $1 million (with the Malawi kwacha at roughly 150 to the dollar).
34. Swidler and Watkins, " 'Teach a Man to Fish.' "
35. The variation in whether the largest funders pay attention to performance in making grants is discussed in Oomman, Rosenzweig, and Bernstein, "Are Funding Decisions Based on Performance?"
36. The most notable of these was the 2005 Paris Declaration on Aid Effectiveness. http://www.oecd.org/dac/effectiveness/parisdeclarationandaccraagendafor action.htm [accessed 2/3/14].

37. The classic discussion of competition among aid organizations is Cooley and Ron, "The NGO Scramble."
38. Krause, *The Good Project*.
39. Brokers also play a critical role for multinational business firms seeking to navigate the political and regulatory hurdles of other countries' political systems, as Peter Evans (*Embedded Autonomy*) describes for Brazil.
40. Declaration of Commitment on HIV/AIDS, p.6.
41. Annan, preface, http://www.unaids.org/bangkok2004/GAR2004_html/GAR 2004_01_en.htm#.
42. Interview with director of large USAID-funded NGO in Malawi, July 27, 2008.
43. For the continuities between the family planning movement and responses to AIDS, see Cleland and Watkins, "Sex without Birth or Death"; Robinson, *Intimate Interventions*.
44. UNAIDS initiated a Best Practices Collection in 1996. See Funnell, "An Evaluation of the UNAIDS Best Practices Collection."
45. U.S. Government Accountability Office (GAO). *HIV/AIDS*.
46. Development interventions are notoriously difficult to evaluate (see Easterly, "Can the West Save Africa?").
47. In 2002, the Global HIV Prevention Working Group produced the first of several reports, "Global Mobilization for HIV Prevention: A Blueprint for Action." Backed by the Bill & Melinda Gates Foundation and the Henry J. Kaiser Family Foundation, and with an all-star membership of influential AIDS researchers, government leaders, and representative of major NGOs, the Working Group's message was, in essence, "we know what works; just give us the money."
48. USAID, "An Overview of Combination Prevention." https://aidsfree.usaid.gov /resources/pkb/combination/overview-combination-prevention [accessed 5/13/16]; see also Hankins and de Zalduondo, "Combination Prevention."
49. Interview with the director of a large USAID-funded NGO in Malawi, July 27, 2008.
50. Watkins fieldnotes, meeting on "Addressing Multiple and Concurrent Sexual Partnerships in Generalized HIV Epidemics, PEPFAR General Population and Youth HIV Prevention, Technical Working Group and AIDSTAR-One": October 29–30, 2008.
51. Cooley and Ron, "The NGO Scramble."
52. Piot et al., "AIDS: Lessons Learnt."

CHAPTER 4. CULTURAL PRODUCTION

1. In Malawi, the answer to what the AIDS organizations could do was very little until President Banda left office in 1994. Although Banda acknowledged the presence of AIDS in the country in 1985, the first two interventions addressed AIDS only indirectly: blood screening was introduced in the two central hospitals and a program was developed to address tuberculosis and other sexually transmitted diseases. For the early period of HIV prevention, see Wangel, "AIDS in Malawi."

2. There is a large literature on culture. Particularly relevant for this chapter is the literature on the culture of organizations, which recognizes that culture is constitutive of organizational routines, such as rituals, structures, and rules. See, for example, Meyer and Rowan, "Institutionalized Organizations"; Weber, "A Toolkit for Analyzing"; Thornton, Ocasio, and Lounsbury, "The Institutional Logics Perspective." For development examples, see Bebbington et al., "Of Texts and Practices"; Benzecry and Krause, "How Do They Know?"

3. "The (Red)™ Manifesto" offered the staggering claim that "as first world consumers, we have tremendous power. What we collectively choose to buy, or not to buy, can change the course of life and history on this planet" (see http://brandaidworld.wordpress.com/ [accessed 2/17/14]). See also Richey and Ponte, *Brand Aid*; de Waal, "The Humanitarian Carnival."

4. On cancer and AIDS in the twentieth century, see Sontag, *Illness as Metaphor*.

5. See, for example, Bayer and Edington, "HIV Testing, Human Rights."

6. See Calhoun, "The Imperative to Reduce Suffering."

7. See, for example, Trinitapoli and Vaisey, "The Transformative Role"; Lasker, *Hoping to Help*.

8. See, for example, the views of Evangelical leader Rick Warren: http://www.pewforum.org/2009/11/13/the-future-of-evangelicals-a-conversation-with-pastor-rick-warren/ [accessed 4/20/16].

9. See Lancaster, *George Bush's Foreign Aid*; Hindman and Schroedel, "U.S. Responses to HIV/AIDS."

10. On culture in the response to AIDS see Barz and Cohen, *The Culture of AIDS in Africa*. O'Toole ("Fighting AIDS with Pictures and Words") surveys the enormous array of AIDS symbols and images in South Africa, from T-shirts and AIDS ribbons to dramas and billboards, and describes the branding strategies of the major AIDS campaigns: the Treatment Action Campaign, Soul City, and loveLife.

11. There is a large literature on pressures for both innovation and homogenization in culture industries (see Peterson and Berger, "Cycles in Symbol Production"; Lopes, "Innovation and Diversity"; Dowd, "Concentration and Diversity Revisited"). Paul Hirsch ("Processing Fads and Fashions") argues that culture-producing organizations, like all organizations, seek to reduce uncertainty. Nonetheless, they are driven by "fads and fashions" because it is difficult to predict what culture consumers will want. The AIDS culture industry is also driven by fads and fashions, but since its ultimate consumers are funding organizations rather than unpredictable teenagers, its dynamics are somewhat different. Organizations want innovative-sounding programs to justify a continuing flow of funding, but they need not innovate in ways that fundamentally challenge their control over organizational processes and procedures. Thus they "innovate" by churning projects, recycling themes and practices in new packages.

12. Kerongo, "Kenya: Durex Sponsors."

13. *The Herald,* Zimbabwe. January 24, 2014 http://allafrica.com/stories/2014012 40708.html [accessed 1/24/14].

14. Blog by "Malawi Mel," "It's a Lilongwe to Malawi!" http://malawimel.blogspot .com/2012/01/sister-2-sister.html [posted January 14, 2012, accessed 3/5/14].

The camp was built around an HIV-prevention curriculum created by Grassroot Soccer, http://www.grassrootsoccer.org/ ([accessed 3/6/14]), which has attracted a wide array of sponsors to a program that "uses the power of soccer to educate, inspire, and mobilize communities to stop the spread of HIV."

15. Makaniki, "Malawi: BLM Launches."

16. This creative re-appropriation of the female condom is recounted in McDonnell, "Cultural Objects as Objects." McDonnell cites a similar report from Zimbabwe: Vickers, "Zimbabweans Make Condom Bangles."

17. *The Daily Mirror* (Accra), "High Demand for Female Condoms."

18. Interview with District AIDS Coordinator about "2009 World AIDS Day," December 20, 2009.

19. In chapter 10, we explain why, despite their appearance of precision, it is unlikely that these detailed counts are accurate.

20. The Names Project began the AIDS Memorial Quilt in 1987. See http://www.aidsquilt.org/about/the-aids-memorial-quilt [accessed 5/3/16]. Activism came both from an increasingly assertive gay community (see Shilts, *And the Band Played On*; Gamson, "Silence, Death"; Altman, *Power and Community*; Epstein, Steven, *Impure Science*) and from public campaigns by celebrities like Magic Johnson and Elizabeth Taylor.

21. There is an extensive literature on "AIDS exceptionalism"—the public health focus on a single disease rather than on strengthening overall health systems, and on the shift, following the success of AIDS activists, to mobilization around single diseases. See, for example, Garrett, "The Challenge of Global Health."

22. Wikipedia offers an extensive list of "awareness ribbons" for various conditions: http://en.wikipedia.org/wiki/List_of_awareness_ribbons [accessed 3/14/14].

23. Best, "Disease Politics."

24. Gamson, "Silence, Death"; D'Emilio, *Sexual Politics*; Armstrong, *Forging Gay Identities*.

25. Among Lewis' many speeches and press releases is "Notes from UN Press Briefing by Stephen Lewis, Special Envoy for HIV/AIDS in Africa, at Noon, January 8, 2003," in which he suggests that those who ignore the epidemic might someday be prosecuted for "crimes against humanity." He describes a pediatric ward in a Zambian hospital: "infants were clustered, stick-thin, three and four to a bed, most so weakened by hunger and ravaged by AIDS (a prevalence rate in the nutrition section of the ward of 56 % ... in the respiratory section of the ward, 72 %), that they really had no chance. We were there for forty-five minutes. Every fifteen minutes, another child died, awkwardly covered with a sheet, then removed by a nurse, while the ward was filled with the anguished weeping of the mothers. A scene from hell." http://data.unaids.org/Media/Speeches01/sp_lewis_december-2002-trip_08jan03_en.pdf.

26. The range of advocates' arguments—and fears—is evident in the work of a prestigious advocacy group: Global HIV Prevention Working Group, "Global Mobilization for HIV Prevention," and its successor reports. See also de Waal, "How Will HIV/AIDS." The larger question of what drives fads in global public health policy has received remarkably little attention. For an exception, see Shiffman, "A Social Explanation"; Shiffman and Sultana, "Generating Political Priority"; Hafner and Shiffman, "The Emergence of Global Attention."

27. "Breaking the Silence" has been a consistent theme of AIDS-prevention efforts. In 2000, it was the official theme of the XIII International AIDS Conference in Durban, South Africa, and it remains a major focus of prevention interventions around the world. See the discussion of "confessional technologies" in Nguyen, *The Republic of Therapy*.

28. See Cleland and Watkins, "The Key Lesson of Family Planning"; Robinson, "From Population to HIV"; Robinson, *Intimate Interventions*.

29. Even a biologically effective antiretroviral vaginal gel will face enormous obstacles if women won't use it. See, Marrazzo et al., "Tenofovir-Based Pre-Exposure Prophylaxis." Similarly, using condoms requires changes in behavior that many people have been unwilling to make. See, Hearst and Chen, "Condoms for AIDS Prevention"; Potts et al., "Reassessing HIV Prevention."

30. Watkins' fieldnotes, 2006. Reports dictated by local interviewers, 2006.

31. Watkins' fieldnotes, 2006. Reports dictated by local interviewers, 2006.

32. This excerpt and the two following are from Patuma Nagalande journal, July 11, 2004.

33. Patuma Nagalande journal, July 11, 2004.

34. Foucauldian analysis would note that this "incitement to desire" is an aspect of much moralizing discourse. See Stoler, *Race and the Education of Desire*.

35. UNESCO Institute for Statistics, Statistics in Brief for Malawi 2007: http://stats.uis.unesco.org/unesco/TableViewer/document.aspx?ReportId=121&IF_Language=eng&BR_Country=4540. In chapter 6, we provide a diagram illustrating the dramatic drop-off as students ascend the educational ladder, particularly as they reach secondary school, which requires paying school fees and often living away from home. While about 30 percent of those who enter primary school begin secondary school, only 4 percent manage to graduate.

36. Watkins, "Navigating the AIDS Epidemic."

37. Kaler, "When They See Money."

38. Kamlongera, "Theatre for Development."

39. Alice Chawake journal, December 31, 2002.

40. John Lwanda ("Poets, Culture and Orature," p. 79) describes the changing role of drama in Malawi between independence and the beginning of multiparty rule in 1994: "With education, drama became urban and scripted, as distinct from the rural oral. The impetus for this included: the needs of writers, school students, and the MBC [Malawi Broadcasting Corporation]. By the 1980s, script-based or partly-scripted drama had become a more significant part of public entertainment and education." The Story Workshop produces a variety of AIDS dramas for radio (http://www.storyworkshop.org/our_issues/hiv_aids/index .html [accessed 3/27/14]). For detailed descriptions of their programs, see: http://www.storyworkshop.org/our_approach/radio/soap_operas/index.html [accessed 3/26/10].

41. We are grateful to Anika Wilson, then a graduate student, for locating and copying broadcasts, which we then had transcribed.

42. The Media Monitoring Project was funded by NAC and conducted by the Media Council of Malawi (Lilongwe, Malawi, P.O. Box 30916). We are grateful to Anika Wilson for locating and copying the monthly reports of the project for January, February, and March 2004.

43. http://www.jica.go.jp/english/news/announcements/jica_archive/2006 /0604_4.html [accessed 4/8/14]. For other examples of AIDS songs see Lwanda, "The [In]visibility of HIV/AIDS." Song, like drama, is an important part of Malawian culture, and songs have been used for a variety of purposes. During the authoritarian reign of President Banda, songs often had social themes with sometimes shocking humor in the lyrics (Lwanda, "Poets, Culture and Orature").

44. See Barz and Cohen, *The Culture of AIDS*.

45. Treichler, *How to Have Theory*, p. 226.

46. The videos, along with a host of posters, radio spots, and other materials, are available in PSI's online catalog of BCC (Behavior Change Communications) materials [all accessed 2/25/14]: http://misaccess.psi.org/bcc_catalog/web /search.html. The nightclub-themed videos are: Côte d'Ivoire ("T'es Yere T'es Cool"): http://misaccess.psi.org/bcc_catalog/web/files/T%27es%20Yere,%20T %27es%20Cool%201_small.mpg; Kenya ("Hi, I'm Mary"): http://misaccess .psi.org/bcc_catalog/web/files/hi_im_mary_1_1.mpg; Mali ("Mali Restaurant TV Spot"): http://misaccess.psi.org/bcc_catalog/web/files/mali%20restaurant _small%283%29.mpg.

47. Hearst and Chen, "Condoms for AIDS Prevention."

48. UNAIDS, *Report on the Global AIDS Epidemic* , pp. 66–68.

49. See Mosse, *Adventures in Aidland*.

50. Lamont, Beljean, and Clair ("What Is Missing?") offer an interesting sociological analysis of the creation of categories as a fundamental way culture shapes social life.

51. In Malawi, pregnant women who attend HIV services are tested for HIV. The official policy is that they can choose to opt out, but in practice, the health providers insist. See Angotti, Dionne, and Gaydosh, "An Offer You Can't Refuse?"

52. See van den Borne, *Trying to Survive*, ch. 9.

53. Nguyen, "Ties that Might Heal," pp. 130; 131.

54. Meyer and Rowan, "Institutionalized Organizations."

55. Patuma Nglande journal, June 29, 2004.

CHAPTER 5. GETTING TO KNOW BROKERS

1. Ntonya, George, "So, AIDS Is Money?" quoted in Morfit, "'AIDS Is Money.'"

2. Nyoni, "Canada Grants K700m for Aids"; Times Reporter, "UNFPA, BLM Launch"; Phalula, "MSF Assists Orphans"; Reuters, "Bush Pledges $500m"; Somanje,"GAIA Launches K42.6m Project."

3. For other typologies of brokers, see Gould and Fernandez, "Structures of Mediation"; Stewart, "A Tale of Two Communities."

4. On the importance of international conferences for connecting elite brokers and donors, see Mindry, "Nongovernmental Organizations, 'Grassroots,'"; Merry, *Human Rights and Gender Violence*.

5. Merry, *Human Rights and Gender Violence*, pp. 10–11.

6. Merry, *Human Rights and Gender Violence*, p. 17.

7. Burrowes, "Development Aid, Social Capital."

8. Thomas Hannan fieldnotes, June 2009.

9. Thomas Hannan fieldnotes, June 2009.
10. Interview with Crisis Corps volunteer in the office of a district AIDS coordinator, June 10, 2009.
11. Interview with financial officer of an NGO in Mangochi District, July 2011.
12. Interview with district-level NGO manager, June 2013.
13. Frye, "Bright Futures," Figure 3, p. 1578.
14. Grant, "Education in the Context of the HIV/AIDS Epidemic," p. 50.
15. Interview with two male participants in an NGO training, June 22, 2006.
16. The new, globally authoritative development goals adopted by the United Nations in 2015 to replace the Millennium Development Goals are called the Sustainable Development Goals. See http://www.un.org/sustainabledevelopment/sustainable-development-goals/ [accessed 2/21/16].
17. On flexible opportunism in African settings, see Johnson-Hanks, "When the Future Decides"; *Uncertain Honor.*
18. Daniel Haji interview with former member of an AIDS youth club in Balaka District, 2005.
19. Global development experts, perhaps recognizing the limitations of training, have more recently upped the ante, now claiming to teach "capacity development": "capacity development has evolved from its original understanding as being synonymous with education and training to a system of intervention that fosters the knowledge base and the capacity of individuals and organizations by creating learning opportunities and assisting with the generation and acquisition of new knowledge and skills and aiming to facilitate systemic and lasting change" (Vallejo and Wehn, "Capacity Development Evaluation," p. 10).
20. The following paragraphs are based on multiple interviews with a village CBO volunteer, later NGO employee and volunteer, July 2004 and July 2006.
21. http://mtvstayingalive.org/about-us/.
22. This paragraph is based on visits to the organization and on multiple interviews with Bashil Kunthani, between 2004 and 2013.
23. See Englund, *Prisoners of Freedom.*
24. See, for example, Munthali, "Scary Budget," which features a graph, "Decline in Grants," on the front page, and reports that the finance minister "largely blames the decline in total revenue and grants as a share of GDP entirely on the continued decrease in donor grants, which amounted to K132.8 billion in 2014/15, but are projected to decline to K97.1 billion in 2015/16" (pp. 2–3).
25. Anderson, "Ephemeral Development Agendas."
26. Interview with NGO monitoring and evaluation officer, July 1, 2014.
27. Castel, Phiri, and Stampini, "Education and Employment in Malawi."
28. Frye, "Bright Futures."
29. Interview with district project manager for a humanitarian relief NGO, June 21, 2014.
30. Group interview with Frank and friends, July 17, 2014.
31. Anders, *In the Shadow of Good Governance,* p. 83.
32. Multiple interviews with an NGO monitoring and evaluation specialist, June and July 2009, and June 2010.
33. Multiple interviews in 2009 with Moira, the board member, and with Teresa, the local broker. In 2011, a student interviewed Moira again.

34. Interview with Moira, a Good Futures board member, 2009.
35. To protect anonymity, in this excerpt and the one below, we do not provide a link to the website. We have made minor changes to the language from the website (changing the grammar, moving phrases around, occasionally using synonyms) so that the language is not traceable.
36. Interview with Teresa, July 2011.
37. Hannan ("World Culture at the World's Periphery") has shown how the globalized rhetoric of World Society penetrates local imaginations.

CHAPTER 6. BROKERS' CAREERS

1. Interview with mid-level district government employee, October 2015.
2. Writing of South African schools, Lam, Ardington, and Leibbrandt ("Schooling as a Lottery," p. 125) note that "In addition to the fact that crowded schools with poor infrastructure and weak administration do not teach well, they are also likely to do a worse job evaluating students than better-equipped and better managed schools. While students everywhere tend to rationalize failure to be the result of bad luck, there may be more truth to these perceptions in poor schools with high failure rates."
3. Frye, "Bright Futures."
4. Ministry of Education, Science and Technology (Malawi), "Education Management Information System (EMIS)," Table 2.11, p.39.
5. Interview, deputy program director of a large INGO, July 2010.
6. Interview, survey interviewer for an INGO, June 2008.
7. Interview, former data manager, National Statistical Office of Malawi, August 2004.
8. See D. Smith, *A Culture of Corruption*, on corruption in university admissions in Nigeria.
9. See Chabal, *Africa*, on "everyday arbitrariness" due to the "dereliction of the state" in many African countries, p. 151.
10. Interview of program manager for a large INGO, June 13, 2013.
11. Among many other sources, see: Englund, "Witchcraft, Modernity and the Person"; Whyte, *Questioning Misfortune*; Ashforth, *Madumo*; J. Smith, *Bewitching Development*; Geschiere, *Witchcraft, Intimacy and Trust*.
12. Group interview with the NGO monitoring and evaluation officer, Frank, and his friends, July 21, 2014.
13. Ashforth, "Reflections on Spiritual," p. 6. See also Ashforth, *Witchcraft, Violence, and Democracy*, p. 63.
14. Multiple interviews with a CBO volunteer, June 2008. All interview excerpts in the section on Maxwell Honde are from these interviews.
15. Interview with a program manager for a large INGO, June 2008. All interview excerpts in the section on Estele Zgambo are from these interviews.
16. Sharra, "Solving the Study Leave Conundrum."
17. Njiragoma, "Macro Staff Go 3 Mths without Pay."
18. Multiple interviews with a trainer employed by a faith-based NGO, June 13–17, 2009.

19. See Kaler and Watkins, "Disobedient Distributors."
20. SACCODE-Trust, http://www.globalgiving.org/projects/orphaned-children-in -malawi/#progressReports [accessed 12/9/09].
21. Green, *The Development State*, p. 10.

CHAPTER 7. THEMES THAT MAKE EVERYONE HAPPY

1. As Thomas Spear writes, http://h-net.msu.edu/cgi-bin/logbrowse.pl?trx=vx&list =H-Africa&month=0408&week=a&msg=HqsY/bB3EI76fcLu4U5Xpw&user= &pw= [accessed 4/24/14], the term "working misunderstanding" appeared first in Laura Bohannan's novel *Return to Laughter*, then in Dorward's "Ethnography and Administration." See also Spear, "Neotraditionalism and the Limits."
2. Kamiyala, "Giving Women Power."
3. The role of practices and concepts in bridging differences at more conscious levels has been a major theme in the sociology of science. In this sense, our perspective resonates with Latour's actor-network theory, and with the larger study of "practice" as the ground on which apparently irreconcilable differences become reconciled (see Schatzki, Knorr Cetina, and von Savigny, *The Practice Turn*). The literature on colonial Indirect Rule provides another example (see, Mamdani, *Citizen and Subject*). Despite overwhelming superiority in military might, colonial rulers simply could not keep the peace, let alone govern, if they did not find ways to accommodate local rule.
4. Centers for Disease Control, "Stigma Major Barrier."
5. In nearly twelve years of ethnographic journals (1999–2008) we found only two incidents of families refusing care for a relative with the symptoms of AIDS, and both of these were because the sick person had abdicated his or her filial responsibility of sharing his wealth with the family. One was a prostitute who was said to have spent all her money on clothes and lotions, the other a man who worked in South Africa for several decades, remarried there, never sent money to his family and wife in Malawi, and returned because he was dying.
6. Agence France-Presse, "African Churches Urged."
7. Hunter, *Love in the Time of AIDS*; Hirsch et al., *The Secret*; Poulin, Dovel, and Watkins, "Men with Money."
8. Trinitapoli, "AIDS and Religious Life in Malawi"; Trinitapoli and Weinreb (*Religion and AIDS in Africa*, pp. 170–73) find that across Africa, those who are religious—especially Christians—are less likely to stigmatize those living with AIDS. Using data from Malawi they suggest why: Christian churches organize their members to visit and provide for those who are ill, and this sense of reciprocal obligation extends to those with AIDS.
9. Chimwaza and Watkins, "Giving Care to People."
10. Peters, Walker, and Kambewa, "Striving for Normality."
11. Durham and Klaits, "Funerals and the Public Space."
12. Watkins, "Navigating the AIDS Epidemic."
13. Klaits, *Death in a Church of Life*.
14. Kaler et al., "Walking Corpses and Kindly Neighbours."
15. Kaler et al., "Walking Corpses and Kindly Neighbours," p. 179.

16. Alice Chawake journal, October 10, 2002. All the excerpts below describing this meeting are from the same journal. The seed multiplication groups were an initiative of the Malawi Government. See Ng'ambi and Maliro, "Seed Security in Malawi."

17. Angotti et al.,"Popular Moralities," p. 459.

18. Descriptions of responses to AIDS elsewhere in Africa suggest that Malawi is not unusual. For Botswana, see Klaits, *Death in a Church of Life*; for Tanzania, see Desmond, "'Ni kubahatisha tu!'"; for Kenya, see Shipton, *The Nature of Entrustment*; for Zambia, see Colson, "The Search for Healing."

19. Ashforth and Watkins, "Narratives of Death."

20. See http://en.wikipedia.org/wiki/Miss_HIV [accessed 5/8/14].

21. Watkins ("Navigating the AIDS Epidemic") describes Malawian villagers' own strategies for avoiding infection, such as seeking social support from religious communities for resisting temptation, divorcing a partner believed to be infected, or selecting less attractive women as sexual partners.

22. In the gay communities of Europe, Australia, North America, and Brazil, the moral mobilization of the community at risk was critical for prevention efforts. In these cases, fighting stigma may have been central to motivating behavior change (See: Gamson, "Silence, Death"; Altman, *Power and Community*; Parker, "Sexuality, Culture, and Power").

23. Donnelly, *A Twist of Faith*, p. 5.

24. Maia Green ("Calculating Compassion," p. 45) notes that the category orphans and vulnerable children (OVC) "is not merely an emotionally compelling category. It has become part of the 'built moral environment' of the international development order in which it is materially embedded. Situated within documents, frameworks, policy instruments, and departments, the OVC is a key word and a budget line. OVC action plans drive programming in affected countries where teams within ministries and AIDS Commissions are responsible for achieving OVC outcomes."

25. Richter and Norman, "AIDS Orphan Tourism", pp. 223; 224.

26. Rosenthal, "Raising our Children," p. 139.

27. Rosenthal, "Raising our Children," p. 144.

28. Ainsworth and Filmer ("Poverty, AIDS, and Children's Schooling") analyzed data for twenty-eight African countries, finding that "several country surveys, particularly Cote d'Ivoire 2005, Malawi 2004, Namibia 2006/7, and Zambia 2005/6, show evidence that orphans tend to be placed in households that promote education, even after adjusting for household wealth" (p. 26). See also Nyamukapa, Foster, and Gregson, "Orphans' Household Circumstances"; Government of Malawi and UNICEF, *Orphanhood in Malawi 2004–2006*.

29. Firm estimates of the numbers of orphaned children in institutional care in Africa are very hard to come by. A UNICEF report on South Africa echoes many others, noting the "lack of comprehensive data on children in formal care" ("South Africa: Protection for Orphans and Vulnerable Children." http://www .unicef.org/southafrica/protection_6633.html [accessed 3/13/16]).

30. Richter and Norman, "AIDS Orphan Tourism," p. 221. Richter and Norman cite reports by the Firelight Foundation and UNICEF concluding that, "Resi-

dential care facilities have expanded, perversely driven by the availability of funds available for them." See Firelight Foundation, *The Promise of a Future*; UNICEF, *Improving Protection*.

31. The quote is from the second *Children on the Brink* report: Hunter and Williamson, *Children on the Brink*, p. 1. The report has been updated several times, for example: UNAIDS (Joint United Nations Programme on HIV/AIDS), UNICEF, and USAID, *Children on the Brink 2004*.

32. Government of Malawi and UNICEF. *Orphanhood in Malawi 2004–2006*, n.d., authors' files, p. 8.

33. Meintjes and Giese, "Spinning the Epidemic," p. 409.

34. Chirwa, "Social Exclusion and Inclusion," p. 96; see also van de Ruit, "The Institutionalization of AIDS Orphan Policy."

35. Henderson, "South African AIDS Orphans," p. 307.

36. Henderson, "South African AIDS Orphans."

37. Henderson, "South African AIDS Orphans," p. 308; see also, for Ethiopia, Abebe, Tatek, and Aase, "Children, AIDS"; for urban South Africa, Meintjes and Geise, "Spinning the Epidemic."

38. Meintjes and Giese, "Spinning the Epidemic," pp. 420–22.

39. Meintjes and Giese, "Spinning the Epidemic," p. 421.

40. Timberg and Halperin, *Tinderbox*.

CHAPTER 8. THEMES THAT MAKE EVERYONE ANXIOUS

1. Since the 1970s when households headed by a female became seen as a development problem (see Pearce, "The Feminization of Poverty"), the development enterprise has been preoccupied with the situation of women: their economic vulnerability, their social powerlessness, and their physical vulnerability to repeated childbearing, to AIDS, and to sexual violence.

2. UNAIDS, *Global Report 2012*, pp. 66, 11; UNAIDS, *Empower Young Women*. In sub-Saharan Africa, women typically become infected at earlier ages than men, a consequence of patterns of sexual relationships in which men are expected to provide resources to women and women are expected to reciprocate by agreeing to have sex. Thus, until boys become able to earn money, they cannot afford much sex. As their earning power increases, they are more likely to have multiple partners, including sex workers, and to become HIV+. There is a large literature on what is called "transactional sex" in Africa, which emphasizes the economic inequality of men and women. The exchange of money and sex is not, however, devoid of emotion and significance (see Poulin, "Sex, Money, and Premarital Partnerships"). Transfers of money or goods also allow men to fulfill their moral obligations of redistribution and reciprocity and to establish patron-client ties with women that often persist beyond any single exchange (see Swidler and Watkins, "Ties of Dependence").

3. On the rumor and its sources, see Fassin, *When Bodies Remember*, pp. 95–96.

4. LaFraniere, "AIDS Now Compels Africa."

5. Malamula, "Culture Source of Violence."

6. Mosse, "Is Good Policy Unimplementable," has written that development policies are adopted not because they work on the ground, but because they embody a persuasive narrative that can appeal to multiple constituencies.
7. See also Ferguson, *The Anti-Politics Machine* and also his *Expectations of Modernity*.
8. Scholars studying the United States and Europe have also found that a sense of moral order is central to personal and political commitments. See Lamont, *The Dignity of Working Men*.
9. http://www.unaids.org/en/aboutunaids/unitednationsdeclarationsandgoals/2001declarationofcommitmentonhivaids [accessed 8/13/16].
10. The full history of the movement of women to the center of the broader development agenda has yet to be written. The victory of feminists in redefining population policy at the 1994 UN population conference in Cairo was one important turning point (see Luke and Watkins, "Reactions of Developing-Country Elites"). The emphasis in micro-finance and conditional-cash transfer programs on directing money to women (who are understood to use the money for the benefit of their families) rather than to men (who would, it is believed, use the money on alcohol and girlfriends) is another indicator of change.
11. On the relation between poverty and HIV, see Shelton, Cassell, and Adetunji, "Is Poverty or Wealth at the Root"; Mishra et al., "HIV Infection Does Not Disproportionately"; Parkhurst, "Understanding the Correlations."
12. Daniel Haji journal, July 2005.
13. On the different perspectives of global elites, national elites, and rural Malawians, see Tawfik and Watkins, "Sex in Geneva, Sex in Lilongwe."
14. Patuma Nagalande journal, July 2004. This journal is the source of both this quote and the next.
15. Simon Bato journal, February 2004. A longer excerpt from the diary describing the fight in the bar can be found in Swidler and Watkins, "Ties of Dependence," p. 155.
16. Mizere, "Govt to Help Victimised Girls."
17. Chandilanga, "Kaliati Accused of Abuse."
18. Mlozi, "Law Will Not Spare Celebrities."
19. Watkins fieldnotes, meeting in Pretoria, South Africa, May 8, 2012.
20. Mpaka, "Malawi-Rights."
21. The case went to the High Court in Blantyre, which ruled in favor of the sex workers and ordered that the women should be compensated. Following the judgment, a lawyer representing the women said, "This judgement is a big contribution to Malawi, as it will give parliament guidelines on how to deal with issues to do with mandatory HIV test [*sic*] when members will be discussing the HIV Management Bill," adding that he hoped that the case would be discussed at the international level as a step towards respecting the human rights for sex workers (Malikwa, "Sex Workers Win Forced HIV Test Case").
22. Interview with director of the Malawi Human Rights Commission, October 2009.
23. Balaka District Assembly. 2000. "HIV/AIDS Plan 2000–2002."
24. The meetings were held in 2005; the minutes were provided to Watkins by one of the consultants for NAC.
25. Daniel Haji journal, January 2006.

26. Daniel Haji journal, August 2005.
27. Angotti, Dionne, and Gaydosh, "An Offer You Can't Refuse."
28. Describing the dilemmas faced by "Monica," a Ugandan NGO broker, Erin Moore ("Translating Girls' Empowerment," p. 79) writes, "part of her professionalism as a cultural broker rested in the careful signaling of her cultural identity as an African woman, an identity that carried with it the authorization to represent the needs of other African women and girls. Yet as much as Monica participated in her own self-presentation as an indispensable local expert, her Northern supervisors also continually reworked her presentations to ensure she represented 'grassroots' rather than 'global' interests."
29. Some are pure inventions, or—as apparently happens with some frequency—ripped from headlines in other African countries. See below on the claim that Malawians believe that having sex with a virgin will cure AIDS.
30. E-mail in possession of the authors.
31. See Fassin, *When Bodies Remember*.
32. See the account in Epstein, *The Invisible Cure*.
33. There is little, or very mixed, evidence about whether any of these standard interventions actually decrease HIV transmission. The global AIDS enterprise, however, has large constituencies committed to the standard interventions: condom distribution, behavior change, voluntary counseling and testing, along with sexual transmitted infection (STI) treatment. See Potts et al., "Reassessing HIV Prevention."
34. Shelton, "Why Multiple Sexual Partners?"; Halperin and Epstein, "Concurrent Sexual Partnerships."
35. Kornfield and Namate, "Cultural Practices Related to HIV/AIDS." See also Page, "'Narratives of Blame.'"
36. Anthropologists have spent a generation criticizing the use of the term "culture." Merry in *Human Rights and Gender Violence*, p. 10, nicely describes the assumptions built into this use of the term.
37. Malawi Human Rights Commission (MHRC), "Cultural Practices and Their Impact."
38. The report appears to have involved consultation that reached beyond the MHRC offices to the district level. The acknowledgements thank district commissioners, chiefs, and NGO officials for "giving pointers to the areas where culture was believed to be deeply entrenched and for assisting in many other ways" (p. 6.).
39. Simon Bato journal, September 2003. We can't know what the trainers actually said about each practice, but we can take the neighbor's notes as an indication of what those being trained thought important enough to write down.
40. The term "civic education" is used in Malawi to refer to teaching that does not occur in school, (e.g., when an NGO or a government official talks about AIDS at a community meeting). See Englund, *Prisoners of Freedom*.
41. Simon Bato journal, September 2003.
42. One of the few sexual practices whose effects on HIV transmission have interested researchers is "dry sex," the practice of women using various herbs, powders, or leaves to dry and tighten the vagina in order to enhance their partners' pleasure. Systematic studies of this practice have been inconclusive, with most studies showing no greater HIV risk among women who practice dry sex than

among those who do not. See, for example, Lopman et al., "HIV Incidence in 3 Years."

43. The best estimates for Africa come from a long-term cohort study in Rakai, Uganda (Gray et al., "Probability of HIV-1 Transmission"). During the long, asymptomatic, "latency" phase of HIV infection, which lasts about eight years on average, the likelihood of transmission for one act of unprotected heterosexual intercourse with an infected partner is less than 1 in 1,300 (Boily et al., "Heterosexual Risk of HIV-1 Infection." Transmission is twenty-six times more likely during the first three months after infection, and seven times more likely in the last 9–10 months before death, though transmission is negligible during the last months of illness when people are too ill to have sex (Hollingsworth, Anderson, and Fraser, "HIV-1 Transmission, by Stage of Infection"). Nonetheless, because the period of latency is so much longer, it contributes more to transmission than the other phases.

44. National AIDS Commission, *National Strategic Plan for HIV and AIDS (2011–2016)*. Estimates are based on modeling transmission of new infections.

45. In Malawi, the most recent Demographic and Health Survey, in 2010, shows HIV prevalence for those age 15–49 as 17.4 in areas categorized as urban, 8.9 in rural areas, for an average of 10.6 for the total population 15–49. National Statistical Office and IFC Macro, Malawi Demographic and Health Survey 2010, p. 198, table 14.5.

46. See, for example, Pigg, "Constructing Social Categories."

47. See, for example, *Daily Times*, "Let's Revisit Our Cultural Beliefs," p. 2.

48. A "chiefs' campaign" might well be seen as a benefit for the chiefs, who would have opportunities to attend workshops or trainings, with attendant per diems and travel allowances.

49. World Bank, "Project Appraisal Document."

50. USAID-Malawi. "HIV/AIDS Strategy 2002–2006."

51. A 2006 Monitoring and Evaluation report for NAC reflects the same gap between local priorities and global action. In the document, combating harmful cultural practices ranks fourth in a list of ten objectives. But despite the relatively high priority given to harmful cultural practices, the least amount of money is allocated to it (Malawi National AIDS Commission, "Technical Progress Report").

52. Evan Lieberman, in *Boundaries of Contagion*, has written persuasively of the way that sharp ethnic boundaries undermine political commitment to fighting AIDS. Where ethnic boundaries make AIDS seem to be one group's problem, dominant groups may neglect AIDS because it is not "their" problem, or, as in Mbeki's South Africa, the politically dominant group may avoid the topic because it threatens to stigmatize their own people.

53. The details of how this remarkable campaign was put together come from interviews with participants in 2010. Its history exemplifies the complex tangle of influences we outline in chapter 2. We observed banners, advertisements, and bumper stickers everywhere throughout the month we spent in Malawi in June and July 2008. According to an informant who participated in designing the campaign, the original impetus was a UN report on violence against children as a global problem and a subsequent UNICEF report on child rights also fo-

cusing on violence against children. Then in 2006, the Permanent Secretary for Gender put together a technical working group on child protection, which involved UNICEF and several Malawian NGOs. Drawing partly on the 2006 Human Rights Commission's report on harmful cultural practices, the Malawian brokers, our informant claimed, suggested the specific messages.

CHAPTER 9. A PRACTICE THAT MAKES EVERYONE HAPPY

1. There is a large literature on the role of "practices" (as opposed to cultural "symbols") in organizing social life. Bourdieu, *Outline of a Theory of Practice,* has been the most influential (see also Ortner, "Theory in Anthropology"; Schatzki, Knorr Cetina, and von Savigny, *The Practice Turn*; Biernacki, *The Fabrication of Labor*). This perspective has been especially influential in science studies, in the work of Bruno Latour (Latour and Woolgar, *Laboratory Life*), among others.
2. See Scherz, *Having People, Having Heart*, for an analysis of the deep commitment of NGOs to sustainability, despite its incompatibility with many aspects of African cultural practices.
3. As many NGO have found, even clean water and school classrooms are often not sustainable. They have to be maintained or repaired, and without incentives to do so, or without a government that bears this responsibility (as Western governments do), communities may see such infrastructure fall into disrepair (see Booth and Cammack, *Governance for Development in Africa*).
4. Englund, *Prisoners of Freedom*.
5. Englund, *Prisoners of Freedom,* p. 91, makes a similar observation about a training he observed: "The impact was to make Chichewa seem like a language that lacked the vocabulary used in 'conflict resolution,' with even 'discussing' (*kukambirana*) becoming a technical procedure that could be performed only by those who were specifically trained."
6. Interview with a participant in an AIDS training, June 6, 2007.
7. Kendall, "Global Policy and Practice."
8. Multiple interviews with a facilitator for an AIDS training, June 17 and 18, 2006.
9. Interview with the chief of party of a USAID-funded NGO, June 2010.
10. Interview with a trainer at an AIDS-prevention training, June 2005.
11. Verheijen, *Balancing Men, Morals, and Money*, p. 233.
12. Frank and Meyer ("University Expansion and the Knowledge Society," p. 294) point to the global prestige of such abstract knowledge: "To make the knowledge grade, practical skills must be at least nominally supplemented by general principles, i.e., linked to universal and educationally certified truths transcending any particular local situation ..."
13. Rossi, "Aid Policies and Recipient Strategies," p. 37.
14. See Green, "Participatory Development."
15. Global Fund to Fight AIDS, Tuberculosis and Malaria, Annual Report 2002/ 2003, p. 73. The grant covered activities other than HIV prevention.
16. Oxford Policy Management, "Local Perceptions, Participation and Accountability," p. 59.
17. To manage the selection process, NAC hired INGOs that had, or created, district offices; the proposals, often hand-written and filed in thick binders, are

public documents. We were permitted to read and scan them by the officials in the office of the district where we were staying.

18. Costs as of 2008, taken from the report of the National Statistics Office's collection of market data.

19. Handwritten document, "Nsamanyada Community Based Organization Project Proposal, No. 0020," 41 pp., 2008, scan in authors' files. If the 120,000 kwacha budgeted for ten bicycles, justified by the need for those trained to travel to other villages to transmit what they had learned, are moved to the training side of the ledger, then training ate up even more of the proposed budget.

20. Singini, "FYF Project to Empower Households."

21. Swidler and Watkins, " 'Teach a Man to Fish.' " James Ferguson (*Give a Man a Fish*) has sharply criticized the slogan as expressing "a core belief that the object of development work is transformation, not charity, and that recipients of aid should get productive skills and the opportunity to work, not handouts and dependency" (p. 35). He and others point out that the slogan suggests that the poor are poor because they are ignorant, rather than that they lack boats, motors, etc. Ferguson also points to a "kind of horror among those who make it their business to 'uplift and develop' the poor at the idea of giving money to the poor" (pp. 38–39).

22. In one of the only systematic surveys of a broad population of NGOs, Barr, Fafchamps, and Owens ("The Governance of Non-Governmental Organizations," p. 667) find that in Ugandan NGOs, "the large share of total costs represented by wages and allowances is consistent with earlier observations that the sector focuses more on 'talking' than on the delivery of physical goods and services."

23. Adapting a manual can, but should not be, expensive. The NGO PSI revised its manual for training youth from age 15–24 to be used in a new project for youth age 10–14; this took three full-time staff members nearly a year, for a cost of $36,000 (Interview with PSI trainer, June 22, 2006).

24. Keen, *Complex Emergencies*; Calhoun, "The Imperative to Reduce Suffering."

25. Interview with district-level NGO manager, November 2013.

26. Halema, "Poor Malawians Do Not Know."

27. Interview with the national executive director of a faith-based youth organization, July 2005.

28. Interview with an African physician stationed in Malawi with a major INGO, July 2011.

29. Colson, "The Search for Healing."

30. Brown and Green, "At the Service of Community Development."

31. Interview with research supervisor for a large health project, July 17, 2011.

32. Interview with member of a rural youth support organization, July 2004.

33. http://www.satregional.org/country_programmes/malawi [accessed 12/20/13].

34. Virtually all the reviews of projects that depend on community volunteers note that it is a "challenge" (the euphemism for "problem") to motivate volunteers if they are not paid (see Maes, "Volunteerism or Labor Exploitation?"; Kalofonos, " 'All They Do Is Pray' "; Gibbs et al., "Mismatches between Youth Aspirations"). A relatively comprehensive review by the World Bank of community home based care said that there were "insufficient incentives for volunteers" and "burn

out, lack of motivation, and commitment on part of volunteers" (see Moham-mad and Gikonyo, "Operational Challenges," p. 11, table 7). They recom-mended, however, that "the volunteers should be from the community, and therefore, the community can determine ways to compensate and motivate the volunteers" (p. 17).

35. Jones, "Pentecostalism, Development NGOs and Meaning," p. 182. James Pfeiffer ("Civil Society, NGOs, and the Holy Spirit") writes of an NGO pro-gram in Mozambique that struggled to sustain volunteer participation amid the changing expectations and demands of local participants. He contrasts this with churches that stimulated and maintained large-scale involvement in the same communities.

36. Interview with a facilitator for a youth PSI training, 2006.

37. See D. Smith, "Patronage, Per Diems."

38. See Johnson-Hanks, "On the Modernity of Traditional Contraception"; *Uncertain Honor*.

CHAPTER 10. CREATING SUCCESS

1. Maes, "Volunteerism or Labor Exploitation?"

2. Mthawanji, "Losing Money, Saving Life."

3. USAID has a website devoted to "Telling Our Story," http://blog.usaid.gov/2010/08/telling-our-story [accessed 2/23/15] and offers explicit guidance about how to construct such narratives (see: https://www.google.com/url?sa=t&rct=j&q=&esrc=s&source=web&cd=2&ved=0CCUQFjAB&url=https%3A%2F%2Fwww.k4health.org%2Fsites%2Fdefault%2Ffiles%2Fusaid_ghana_communications_guidelines_10_july_2013.pdf&ei=4Y_rVPPlOdLVoASB64CADw&usg=AFQjCNE9jAMej3oqXrCQ4-KP40et8JwZXA&bvm=bv.86475890,d.cGU&cad=rja [accessed 2/23/15], produced not directly by USAID, but by a subcontractor, K4Health). The example we quote here can be found in USAID, "AFRICA Health Sector Results Reporting," Bureau for Africa, Office of Sustainable De-velopment (AFR/SD), May 2006, p. 62, http://www.google.com/url?sa=t&rct=j&q=&esrc=s&source=web&cd=1&ved=0CB4QFjAA&url=http%3A%2F%2Fpdf.usaid.gov%2Fpdf_docs%2FPdacp137.pdf&ei=74nrVJKRGYmWoQT4yoFA&usg=AFQjCNFEVpcvck81PAImajkmWK5Lj15Eyg&bvm=bv.86475890,d.cGU [accessed 2/23/15].

4. Nguyen, "Ties That Might Heal," pp. 130–31.

5. Comaroff, "Beyond Bare Life," p. 204.

6. Nguyen 2002, "Ties That Might Heal," p. 130.

7. Temudo, "Western Beliefs and Local Myths," p. 261.

8. Krause, *The Good Project*.

9. See Mohan, "The Disappointments of Civil Society"; Swidler, "Dialectics of Pa-tronage"; Leonard et al., "Does Patronage Still Drive Politics."

10. See also https://www.usaid.gov/vietnam/tools-usaid-partners [accessed 12/20/15] for USAID's instructions on how to write success stories, e.g., "Success Story Guidelines" and "Guidelines for interviewing beneficiaries."

11. Interview, monitoring and evaluation officer, international faith-based NGO, July 2010.

12. Krause, *The Good Project*. See also Vallejo and Wehn, "Capacity Development Evaluation."
13. Krause, *The Good Project*, p. 71.
14. Browning, "The Difficulty of Monitoring."
15. Plummer et al.," 'A Bit More Truthful' "; Minnis et al., "Biomarker Validation of Reports"; Pool et al., "Assessing the Accuracy of Adherence."
16. See, for example, the randomized trial of an ambitious community-driven development intervention reported in Casey, Glennerster, and Miguel, "Reshaping Institutions." A recent experimental trial in Malawi demonstrated that giving female secondary school students and their parents money kept the students in school and reduced HIV incidence (see Baird et al., "Effect of a Cash Transfer Programme").
17. Padian et al. ("Weighing the Gold," p. 627) conducted a systematic review of behavioral change and biomedical interventions to select those that used randomized controlled trials (RCTs) or a quasi-experimental design to assess the causal impact of interventions to prevent the sexual transmission of HIV in low and middle income countries. Of the eight non-biomedical interventions (seven for behavior change, one microfinance), they found none with statistically significant differences between intervention and control groups. Of the thirty-nine biomedical interventions, thirty-three had no statistically significant results, five had positive results (three of these were male circumcision), and one had a negative result.
18. Hallett et al., "Declines in HIV Prevalence."
19. Angus Deaton ("Instruments, Randomization, and Learning") has provided a compelling critique of the use of randomized trials to evaluate development interventions.
20. Interview with the expatriate director of a multi-year USAID-funded AIDS-prevention project, June 2013.
21. Interview with the expatriate director of a large USAID-funded NGO in Malawi, July 27, 2008.

CHAPTER 11. CONCLUSIONS

1. Arlie Hochschild (*The Time Bind*) and Peter Stromberg (*Caught in Play*) provide rich analyses of the role of fantasy and imagination in modern experience. Mosse ("Is Good Policy Unimplementable?") also highlights the role of brokers in translating among the imaginations of different actors in the policy enterprise, noting that creating policy also "requires the constant work of *translation* (of policy goals into practical interests; practical interests back into policy goals), which is the task of skilled brokers (managers, consultants, fieldworkers, community leaders) who read the meaning of a project into the different institutional languages of its stakeholder supporter," p. 647 [emphasis in original].
2. On the presentation of vulnerability and the search for connection, see Rothmyer, "Hiding the Real Africa"; Freidus and Ferguson, "Malawi Orphans."
3. Chabal and Daloz, *Africa Works*; Swidler and Watkins, "Ties of Dependence."

4. Scherz, *Having People, Having Heart*.
5. Chabal, *Africa*, p. 48.
6. Lamont (*The Dignity of Working Men*) has emphasized the importance of keeping "the world in moral order" to the lives of middle- and working-class men in France and the United States.
7. Ebrahim (*NGOs and Organizational Change*) describes the origins of the global discourse on sustainability.
8. Recent approaches promoting cash grants or unconditional cash transfers speak to this problem. Except in wealthier African countries like South Africa, however, government grants that would reach broad populations are unaffordable. Donor-sponsored cash-transfer programs targeting the very poor have usually not reached their targets. It is unclear how much sense it makes to target the poorest 15 or 20 percent of households in communities where most people are very poor (see Ferguson, *Give a Man a Fish*; Stoeffler, Mills, and del Ninno, "Reaching the Poor"; Olivier de Sardan et al., "Cash Transfers in Niger").
9. Field notes from a focus group conducted in April 2008 with respondents in the University of Pennsylvania survey. We are grateful to Kim Yi Dionne who permitted us to quote from her interviewer's notes.
10. The development enterprise has attracted more than its share of analysts who offer sweeping remedies: brashly confident, scathingly negative, or sharply critical. Jeffrey Sacks is probably the best known (most recently his *The Age of Sustainable Development*). See also Dambisa Moyo (*Dead Aid*), who argues that all aid to Africa should be ended because it creates dependency; Deaton, *The Great Escape*; Easterly, *The Tyranny of Experts*.
11. This effort involved many more actors and organizations, including Oxfam, Paulo Texiera and the government of Brazil, James Love (the director of the NGO Knowledge Ecology International), and a global social movement under the umbrella of the Campaign for Essential Medicines (see Kapstein and Busby, *AIDS Drugs for All*).
12. See Maia Green's (*The Development State*) excellent study of the meaning of "development" in Tanzania as a personal project. In rural Malawi, a villager who has a brick house with a metal roof rather than a mud hut with a thatch roof is considered "developed."
13. For many years, AIDS was the dominant global health priority. A study by Norma Anderson ("Ephemeral Development Agendas") of NGO brokers in Malawi, found that by between 2008 and 2010, the dominant priority had become climate change. By 2014, however, this had faded but had not been replaced by a new dominant priority. Her respondents complained that they were "currently spinning their wheels" and that they were "unable to strategize or plan for the next big development agenda, because there was no clear development agenda."
14. Our perspective has affinities with the "developmental patrimonialism" recommended by scholars such as David Booth and Diana Cammack (see Booth and Golooba-Mutebi, "Developmental Patrimonialism?"; Booth and Cammack, *Governance for Development in Africa*).
15. Interview with district-level NGO manager, June 2013.
16. *The Nation* (Malawi), World Vision Advertisement.

17. A very small number of NGOs, among them GAIA, discussed in chapter 1, have adopted such a model. Their core funding goes to pay local women in twenty-five villages to run programs for these villages. Rather than being committed to whatever their current project is and in essence using villagers to carry out the project, GAIA is committed to these villages and the wellbeing of their people (providing an emergency supply of grain during the desperate famine of 2004, for example). Nonetheless, even GAIA, when it seeks large-scale funding from big foundations, rather than relying simply on private donations, is driven to propose "innovative projects" that big donors are interested in supporting.
18. Interview with a group village headman, December 14, 2013.
19. On elected town chiefs, see Cammack, Kanyongolo, and O'Neil, " 'Town Chiefs' in Malawi"; Cammack, "Understanding Local Forms of Accountability."
20. See Baldwin, *The Paradox of Traditional Chiefs,* for a persuasive analysis of the role of chiefs and of African governance more generally.
21. The greatest sources of local institutional capacity are reciprocal interdependence of family and neighbors, traditional authorities such as chiefs, and religious congregations (see Swidler, "Cultural Sources of Institutional Resilience"). Among the many studies of African religious communities, see Trinitapoli and Weinreb, *Religion and AIDS in Africa.*
22. All these incidents are from our field notes: the first in May 2015, the second in June 2006, and the third from a chief's court we observed in June 2012.
23. See, for example, Foster, "Peasant Society"; Cleaver, "Paradoxes of Participation"; Mohan and Stokke, "Participatory Development and Empowerment"; Mansuri and Rao, *Localizing Development.*
24. Deaton, *The Great Escape,* p. 317.
25. Dionne, Gerland, and Watkins, "AIDS Exceptionalism."
26. Dionne, "Local Demand for a Global Intervention," p. 2470.
27. Dionne, "Local Demand for a Global Intervention," p. 2472.
28. Mansuri and Rao, "Localizing Development; Maes, " 'Volunteerism or Labor Exploitation?' "

REFERENCES

Abebe, Tatek, and Asbjorn Aase. "Children, AIDS and the Politics of Orphan Care in Ethiopia: The Extended Family Revisited." *Social Science & Medicine* 64.10 (2007): 2058–69.

Agence France-Presse. "African Churches Urged to Fight Stigmatization of AIDS." *CDC HIV/Hepatitis/STD/TB Prevention News Update,* May 3, 2003. http://www .thebody.com/content/art27900.html?ic=4003

Ainsworth, Martha, and Deon Filmer. "Poverty, AIDS, and Children's Schooling: A Targeting Dilemma." World Bank Policy Research Working Paper No. 2885, 2002. http://elibrary.worldbank.org/doi/pdf/10.1596/1813–9450–2885

Altman, Dennis. *Power and Community: Organizational and Cultural Responses to AIDS.* London: Taylor and Francis, 1994.

Anders, Gerhard. *In the Shadow of Good Governance: An Ethnography of Civil Service Reform in Africa.* Leiden, The Netherlands: Brill, 2010.

Anderson, Norma J. "Ephemeral Development Agendas and the Process of Priority Shifts in Malawi." *Journal of Asian and African Studies.* Published online February 18, 2016. DOI: 10.1177/0021909616630567.

Angotti, Nicole, Kim Yi Dionne, and Lauren Gaydosh. "An Offer You Can't Refuse? Provider-Initiated HIV Testing in Antenatal Clinics in Rural Malawi." *Health Policy and Planning* 26.4 (2011): 307–15.

Angotti, Nicole, Margaret Frye, Amy Kaler, Michelle Poulin, Susan Cotts Watkins, and Sara Yeatman. "Popular Moralities and Institutional Realities in Malawi's Struggle Against AIDS." *Population and Development Review* 40.3 (2014): 447–73.

Armstrong, Elizabeth A. *Forging Gay Identities: Organizing Sexuality in San Francisco, 1950–1994.* Chicago: University of Chicago Press, 2002.

Ashforth, Adam. "Reflections on Spiritual Insecurity in a Modern African City." *African Studies Review* 41.3 (1998): 39–67.

Ashforth, Adam. *Madumo: A Man Bewitched.* Chicago: University of Chicago Press, 2000.

Ashforth, Adam. *Witchcraft, Violence, and Democracy in South Africa.* Chicago: University of Chicago Press, 2005.

Ashforth, Adam, and Susan Cotts Watkins. "Narratives of Death in Rural Malawi in the Time of AIDS." *Africa* 85.2 (2015): 245–68.

Auvert, Bertran, Dirk Taljaard, Emmanuel Lagarde, Joëlle Sobngwi-Tambekou, Rémi Sitta, and Adrian Puren. "Randomized, Controlled Intervention Trial of Male Circumcision for Reduction of HIV Infection Risk: The ANRS 1265 Trial." *PLOS Medicine* 2.11 (2005): e298.

Bailey, Robert C., Stephen Moses, Corette B. Parker, Kawango Agot, Ian Maclean, John N. Krieger, Carolyn F. M. Williams, Richard T. Campbell, and Jeckoniah O Ndinya-Achola. "Male Circumcision for HIV Prevention in Young Men in Kisumu, Kenya: A Randomised Controlled Trial." *The Lancet* 369 (2005): 643–56.

Baird, Sarah, Richard S. Garfein, Craig McIntosh, and Berk Özler. "Effect of a Cash Transfer Programme for Schooling on Prevalence of HIV and Herpes Simplex Type 2 in Malawi: A Cluster Randomised Trial." *The Lancet* 379 (2012): 1320–29.

Balaka District Assembly. "HIV/AIDS Plan 2000–2002." 2000. Accessed at the Office of the Balaka District Assembly.

Baldwin, Kate. *The Paradox of Traditional Chiefs in Democratic Africa.* New York: Cambridge University Press, 2015.

Barr, Abigail, Marcel Fafchamps, and Trudy Owens. "The Governance of Non-Governmental Organizations in Uganda." *World Development* 33 (2005): 657–79.

Barz, Gregory, and Judah M. Cohen. *The Culture of AIDS in Africa: Hope and Healing through Music and the Arts.* Oxford: Oxford University Press, 2011.

Bayart, Jean François. *The State in Africa: The Politics of the Belly.* New York: Longmans Publishing, 1993.

Bayer, Ronald, and Claire Edington. "HIV Testing, Human Rights, and Global AIDS Policy: Exceptionalism and Its Discontents." *Journal of Health Politics, Policy and Law* 34.3 (2009): 301–23.

Bebbington, Anthony, David Lewis, Simon Batterbury, Elizabeth Olson, and M. Shameem Siddiqi. "Of Texts and Practices: Empowerment in Organisational Cultures in World Bank-Funded Rural Development Programmes." *Journal of Development Studies* 43 (2007): 597–621.

Benzecry, Claudio, and Monika Krause. "How Do They Know? Practicing Knowledge in Comparative Perspective." *Qualitative Sociology* 33.4 (2010): 415–42.

Best, Rachel Kahn. "Disease Politics and Medical Research Funding: Three Ways Advocacy Shapes Policy." *American Sociological Review* 77.5 (2012): 780–803.

Biernacki, Richard. *The Fabrication of Labor: Germany and Britain, 1640–1914.* Berkeley: University of California Press, 1995.

Bleiker, Roland, and Amy Kay. "Representing HIV/AIDS in Africa: Pluralist Photography and Local Empowerment." *International Studies Quarterly* 51.1 (2007): 139–63.

Boily, Marie-Claude, Rebecca F. Baggaley, Lei Wang, Benoit Masse, Richard G. White, Richard J. Hayes, and Michel Alary. "Heterosexual Risk of HIV-1 Infection per Sex Act: Systematic Review and Meta-Analysis of Observational Studies." *Lancet Infectious Disease* 9 (2009): 118–29.

Booth, David, and Diana Cammack. *Governance for Development in Africa: Solving Collective Action Problems.* London: Zed Books, 2013.

Booth, David, and Frederick Golooba-Mutebi. "Developmental Patrimonialism? The Case of Rwanda." Africa Power & Politics Working Paper No. 16, Africa Power and Politics Programme (APPP), Overseas Development Institute, London, 2011.

Boseley, Sarah. "Saving Grace: Grace Mathanga, Shoe Seller." *The Guardian,* February 18, 2003. Accessed December 19, 2015. http://www.theguardian.com/world/2003/feb/18/aids.sarahboseley5

Bowen, Elenore Smith. *Return to Laughter: An Anthropological Novel.* New York: Doubleday, 1964.

References

Bourdieu, Pierre. *Outline of a Theory of Practice.* Cambridge, UK: Cambridge University Press, 1977.

Brown, Hannah, and Maia Green. "At the Service of Community Development: The Professionalization of Volunteer Work in Kenya and Tanzania." *African Studies Review* 58.2 (2015): 63–84.

Browning, Jennifer. "The Difficulty of Monitoring: HIV/AIDS Community-Based Organizations in Rural Malawi." Senior Thesis, Development Studies, University of California, Berkeley, 2006.

Burrowes, Sahai. "Development Aid, Social Capital and Patronage in Sub-Saharan Africa." Doctoral dissertation, HSPA Doctoral Program, University of California, Berkeley, 2012.

Burrowes, Sahai, Augustine Harawa, Xiuzhe Mai, Katie Greenberg, James Willard, and Sherly Sarkizzadeh. "What Explains the Geographic Distribution of Community-Based Health Organizations in Malawi? An Analysis of 15-Year Trends [data file and codebook-VERSION 1]." Vallejo, CA: Touro University California, 2015.

Calhoun, Craig. "The Imperative to Reduce Suffering: Charity, Progress, and Emergencies in the Field of Humanitarian Action." In *Humanitarianism in Question: Politics, Power, Ethics*, edited by M. Barnett and T. G. Weiss, 73–97. Ithaca and London: Cornell University Press, 2008.

Callaghy, Thomas. "The State as Lame Leviathan: The Patrimonial Administrative State in Africa." In *The African State in Transition*, edited by Z. Ergas, 87–116. New York: St. Martin's Press, 1987.

Cammack, Diana. "Understanding Local Forms of Accountability: Initial Findings from Ghana and Malawi." In *Accountable Government in Africa: Perspectives from Public Law and Political Studies*, edited by D. M. Chirwa and L. Nijzink, 256–73. Tokyo: United Nations University Press, 2012.

Cammack, Diana. "Malawi's Political Settlement: Crafting Poverty and Peace, 1994–2014." African Studies Association Meetings, San Diego, CA, November 2, 2015.

Cammack, Diana, Edge Kanyongolo, and Tam O'Neil. "Town Chiefs' in Malawi." Africa Power and Politics Working Paper No. 3, Africa Power and Politics Programme, Overseas Development Institute, London: 2009.

Casey, Katherine, Rachel Glennerster, and Edward Miguel. "Reshaping Institutions: Evidence on Aid Impacts Using a Pre-Analysis Plan." *Quarterly Journal of Economics* 127.4 (2012): 1755–812.

Castel, Vincent, Martha Phiri, and Marco Stampini. "Education and Employment in Malawi." African Development Bank Group Working Paper Series No. 110, 2010.

Centers for Disease Control, "Stigma Major Barrier to Fighting AIDS, Says Piot." CDC National Prevention Information Network, Dec. 2, 2002. Accessed May 14, 2016. http://www.thebody.com/content/art21856.html

Centre for Social Research. *Directory of AIDS Service Organizations in Malawi.* Zomba, Malawi: Centre for Social Research Documentation Unit, 1997.

Chabal, Patrick. *The Politics of Suffering and Smiling.* London, New York, and Pietermaritzburg, South Africa: Zed Books and University of KwaZulu-Natal Press, 2009.

Chabal, Patrick, and Jean-Pascal Daloz. *Africa Works: Disorder as Political Instrument.* Oxford and Bloomington: James Curry and Indiana University Press, 1999.

Chandilanga, Herbert. "Kaliati Accused of Abuse." *Saturday Nation,* June 23, 2007. Accessed June 22, 2015. https://groups.yahoo.com/neo/groups/MALAWIANA /conversations/topics/16211

Chimwaza, Angela F., and Susan Cotts Watkins. "Giving Care to People with Symptoms of AIDS in Rural Sub-Saharan Africa." *AIDS Care* 16.7 (2004): 795–807.

Chirwa, Wiseman Chijere. "Social Exclusion and Inclusion: Challenges to Orphan Care in Malawi." *Nordic Journal of African Studies* 11 (2002): 93–113.

Chorev, Nitsan. *The World Health Organization between North and South.* Ithaca: Cornell University Press, 2012.

Cleaver, Frances. 1999. "Paradoxes of Participation: Questioning Participatory Approaches to Development." *The Journal of International Development.* 11.4 (1999): 597–612.

Cleland, John, and Susan C. Watkins. "The Key Lesson of Family Planning Programmes for HIV/AIDS Control." *AIDS* 20 (2006): 1–3.

Cleland, John, and Susan C. Watkins. "Sex without Birth or Death: A Comparison of Two International Humanitarian Movements." In *Social Information Transmission and Human Biology*, edited by J.C.K. Wells, S. Strickland, and K. Laland, 205–21. London: Taylor and Francis, 2006.

Cohen, Jon. "The New World of Global Health." *Science* 311 (2006): 162–67.

Colson, Elizabeth. "The Search for Healing: The AIDS Epidemic in Gwembe Valley." In *The HIV/AIDS Epidemic in Sub-Saharan Africa in a Historical Perspective*, edited by P. Denis and C. Becker, 113–25. Online edition, October 2006. http://www.rag.sn/sites/rds.refer.sn/IMG/pdf/12COLSON.pdf

Comaroff, Jean. "Beyond Bare Life: AIDS, (Bio)Politics and the Neoliberal Order." *Public Culture* 19.1 (2007): 197–219.

Congressional Record–House, vol. 146, pt. 6, May 10–23, 2000.

Cooley, Alexander. "Outsourcing Authority: How Project Contracts Transform Global Governance Networks." In *Who Governs the Globe?*, edited by D. D. Avant, M. Finnemore, and S. K. Sell, 238–65. New York: Cambridge University Press, 2010.

Cooley, Alexander, and James Ron. "The NGO Scramble: Organizational Insecurity and the Political Economy of Transnational Action." *International Security* 27.1 (2002): 5–39.

Danovich, Yael. Interview with NGO Monitoring and Evaluation Officer, July 2010.

Davies, Simon. "What Motivates Gifts? Intra-Family Transfers in Rural Malawi." *Journal of Family and Economic Issues* 32.3 (2010): 473–92.

Deaton, Angus. *The Great Escape: Health, Wealth and the Origins of Inequality.* Princeton and Oxford: Princeton University Press, 2013.

Deaton, Angus. "Instruments, Randomization, and Learning about Development." *Journal of Economic Literature* 48 (2010): 424–55.

"Declaration of Commitment on HIV/AIDS." United Nations General Assembly, Special Session on HIV/AIDS, 25–27, June 2001.

D'Emilio, John. *Sexual Politics, Sexual Communities: The Making of a Homosexual Minority in the United States, 1940–1970*, 2nd ed. Chicago: University of Chicago Press, 1998.

Desmond, Nicola. 2009. "Ni kubahatisha tu!' It's Just a Game of Chance!' Adaptation and Resignation to Perceived Risks in Rural Tanzania." PhD Dissertation, Medical Research Council, Social and Public Health Sciences Unit, University of Glasgow, 2009.

de Waal, Alex. "How Will HIV/AIDS Transform African Governance?" *African Affairs* 102 (2003): 1–23.

de Waal, Alex. "The Humanitarian Comedy: A Celebrity Vogue." *World Affairs* 171.2 (2008): 43–56.

Dionne, Kim Yi. "Local Demand for a Global Intervention: Policy Priorities in the Time of AIDS." *World Development* 40.12 (2012): 2468–77.

Dionne, Kim Yi, Patrick Gerland, and Susan Watkins. "AIDS Exceptionalism: Another Constituency Heard From." *AIDS and Behavior* 17.3 (2013): 825–31.

Donnell, Deborah, Jared M. Baeten, James Kiarie, Katherine K. Thomas, Wendy Stevens, Craig R. Cohen, James McIntyre, Jairam R. Lingappa, and Connie Celum. "Heterosexual HIV-1 Transmission after Initiation of Antiretroviral Therapy: A Prospective Cohort Analysis." *The Lancet* 375.9731(2010): 2092–98.

Donnelly, John. *A Twist of Faith: An American Christian's Quest to Help Orphans in Africa*. Boston: Beacon Press, 2012.

Dorward, David. "Ethnography and Administration: A Study of Anglo-Tiv 'Working Misunderstanding.'" *Journal of African History* 15 (1974): 457–77.

Dowd, Timothy J. "Concentration and Diversity Revisited: Production Logics and the U.S. Mainstream Recording Market, 1940–1990." *Social Forces* 82.4 (2004): 1411–55.

Durham, Deborah, and Frederick Klaits. "Funerals and the Public Space of Sentiment in Botswana." *Journal of Southern African Studies* 28.4 (2002): 777–95.

Easterly, William. "Can the West Save Africa?" *Journal of Economic Literature* 47 (2009): 373–447.

Easterly, William. *The Tyranny of Experts: Economists, Dictators, and the Forgotten Rights of the Poor*. New York: Basic Books, 2013.

Easterly, William. *The White Man's Burden: West's Efforts to Aid the Rest Have Done So Much Ill and So Little Good*. New York: Penguin Press, 2006.

Ebrahim, Alnoor. *NGOs and Organizational Change: Discourse, Reporting, and Learning*. New York and Cambridge, UK: Cambridge University Press, 2005.

Englund, Harri. "Witchcraft, Modernity and the Person: The Morality of Accumulation in Central Malawi." *Critique of Anthropology* 16.3 (1996): 257–79.

Englund, Harri. *Prisoners of Freedom: Human Rights and the African Poor*. Berkeley: University of California Press, 2006.

Epstein, Helen. *The Invisible Cure: Africa, the West, and the Fight Against AIDS*. New York: Farrar, Straus and Giroux, 2007.

Epstein, Helen. "The Lost Children of AIDS." *The New York Review of Books*, November 3, 2005. http://www.nybooks.com/articles/18399

Epstein, Helen, and Julia Kim. "AIDS and the Power of Women." *The New York Review of Books*, February 15, 2007. http://www.nybooks.com/articles/2007/02/15/aids-and-the-power-of-women/

Epstein, Steven. *Impure Science: AIDS, Activism, and the Politics of Knowledge*. Berkeley: University of California Press, 1996.

Evans, Peter. *Embedded Autonomy: States and Industrial Transformation*. Princeton: Princeton University Press, 1995.

Fassin, Didier. *When Bodies Remember: Experiences and Politics of AIDS in South Africa*. Berkeley: University of California Press, 2007.

Ferguson, James. *The Anti-Politics Machine: "Development," Depoliticization, and Bureaucratic Power in Lesotho*. Minneapolis: University of Minnesota Press, 1994.

Ferguson, James. *Expectations of Modernity: Myths and Meanings of Urban Life on the Zambian Copperbelt*. Berkeley: University of California Press, 1999.

Ferguson, James. *Give a Man a Fish: Reflections on the New Politics of Distribution*. Durham, NC: Duke University Press, 2015.

Ferguson, James. "Declarations of Dependence: Labour, Personhood, and Welfare in Southern Africa." *Journal of the Royal Anthropological Institute (N.S.)* 19 (2013): 223–42.

Firelight Foundation. *The Promise of a Future: Strengthening Family and Community Care for Orphans and Vulnerable Children in Sub-Saharan Africa*. Santa Cruz, CA: Firelight Foundation, 2005.

Forster, Peter G. "AIDS, the Local Community and Traditional Health Practitioners in Malawi." Unpublished paper, archives of the Centre for Social Research, Zomba, Malawi, 1994.

Foster, George. "Peasant Society and the Image of Limited Good." *American Anthropologist* 67.2 (1965): 293–315.

Frank, David John, and John W. Meyer. "University Expansion and the Knowledge Society." *Theory and Society* 36 (2007): 287–311.

Freidus, Andrea, and Anne Ferguson. "Malawi Orphans: The Role of Transnational Humanitarian Organizations." In *Vulnerable Children: Global Challenges in Education, Health, Well-Being, and Child Rights*, edited by D.J.J. Johnson, D. L. Agbényiga, and R. K. Hitchcock, 203–15. New York: Springer Press, 2013.

Frye, Margaret. "Bright Futures in Malawi's New Dawn: Educational Aspirations as Assertions of Identity." *American Journal of Sociology* 117.6 (2012): 1565–624.

Fuchs, Andreas, Axel Dreher, and Peter Nunnenkamp. "Determinants of Donor Generosity: A Survey of the Aid Budget Literature." *World Development* 56 (2014): 172–99.

Funnell, Susan. "An Evaluation of the UNAIDS Best Practices Collection: Its Strengths and Weaknesses, Accessibility, Use and Impact." Performance Improvement Pty Ltd, Australia, November 1999. Accessed February 4, 2014. https://www.google.com/#q=UNAIDS+best+practices+1998

Gamson, Joshua. "Silence, Death, and the Invisible Enemy: AIDS Activism and Social Movement 'Newness.'" *Social Problems* 36.4 (1989): 351–67.

Garrett, Laurie. "The Challenge of Global Health." *Foreign Affairs* 86.1 (2007): 14–38.

Geschiere, Peter. *Witchcraft, Intimacy and Trust: Africa in Comparison*. Chicago: University of Chicago Press, 2013.

Gibbs, Andrew, Catherine Campell, Sbongile Maimane, and Yugi Nair. "Mismatches between Youth Aspirations and Participatory HIV/AIDS Programmes in South Africa." *African Journal of AIDS Research* 9.2 (2010): 153–63.

Gillespie, Stuart, Suneetha Kadiyala, and Robert Greener. "Is Poverty or Wealth Driving HIV Transmission?" *AIDS* 21 (2007): Suppl. 7, S5-S16.

Global HIV Prevention Working Group. "Global Mobilization for HIV Prevention: A Blueprint for Action." July 1, 2002. Accessed March 14, 2014. http://www.issuelab.org/resource/global_mobilization_for_hiv_prevention_a_blueprint_for_action

Gould, Roger, and Roberto Fernandez. "Structures of Mediation: A Formal Approach to Brokerage in Transaction Networks." *Sociological Methodology* 19 (1989): 89–126.

Government of Malawi. "2012 Global AIDS Response Progress Report: Malawi Country Report for 2010–2011." Lilongwe, Malawi: Government of Malawi, 2012.

Government of Malawi and UNICEF. *Orphanhood in Malawi 2004–2006*. Lilongwe, Malawi: UNICEF, 2009.

Grant, Monica. "Education in the Context of the HIV/AIDS Epidemic: Three Essays on the Case of Malawi." PhD Dissertation, Departments of Demography and Sociology, University of Pennsylvania, 2009.

Gray, Ronald H., Gregory Kigozi, David Serwadda, Frederick Makumbi, Stephen Watya, Fred Nalugoda, Noah Kiwanuka, Lawrence H. Moulton, Mohammad A. Chaudhary, Michael Z. Chen, Nelson K. Sewankambo, Fred Wabwire-Mangen, Melanie C. Bacon, Carolyn F. M. Williams, Pius Opendi, Steven J. Reynolds, Oliver Laeyendecker, Thomas C. Quinn, and Maria J. Wawer. "Male Circumcision for HIV Prevention in Men in Rakai, Uganda: A Randomised trial." *The Lancet* 369 (2007): 657–66.

Gray, Ronald H., Maria J. Wawer, Ron Brookmeyer, Nelson K. Sewankambo, David Serwadda, Fred Wabwire-Mangen, Tom Lutalo, Xianbin Li, Thomas vanCott, and Thomas C. Quinn. "Probability of HIV-1 Transmission per Coital Act in Monogamous, Heterosexual, HIV-Discordant Couples in Rakai, Uganda." *The Lancet* 357 (2001): 1149–53.

Green, Maia. "Calculating Compassion: Accounting for Some Categorical Practices in International Development." In *Adventures in Aidland: The Anthropology of Professionals in International Development*, edited by D. Mosse, 33–56. New York: Berghahn Books, 2011.

Green, Maia. "Participatory Development and the Appropriation of Agency in Southern Tanzania." *Critique in Anthropology* 20.1 (2000): 67–89.

Green, Maia. *The Development State: Aid, Culture and Civil Society in Tanzania*. Suffolk, UK: James Currey, 2014.

Gwaladi, Joe. From the album *Zakanika*, Tempest, Blantyre, 2006, cited in John Lwanda. "Poets, Culture and Orature: A Reappraisal of the Malawi Political Public Sphere, 1953–2006." *Journal of Contemporary African Studies* 26 (2008): 71–101, p. 90.

Hafner, Tamara, and Jeremy Shiffman. "The Emergence of Global Attention to Health Systems Strengthening." *Health Policy and Planning* 28 (2013): 41–50.

Halema, Innocent. "Poor Malawians Do Not Know of Their Poverty." *The Nation* (Malawi), June 27, 2013. Accessed September 28, 2013. http://mwnation.com /poor-malawians-do-not-know-of-their-poverty/

Hallett, T. B., J. Aberle-Grasse, G. Bello, L. M. Boulos, M.P.A. Cayemittes, B. Cheluget, J. Chipeta, R. Dorrington, S. Dube, A. K. Ekra, C. Maurice, J. M. Garcia-Calleja, G. P. Garnett, S. Greby, S. Gregson, J. T. Grove, S. Hader, J. Hanson, W. Hladik, S. Ismail, S. Kassim, W. Kirungi, L. Kouassi, A. Mahomva, L. Marum, M. Nolan, T. Rehle, J. Stover, and N. Walker. "Declines in HIV Prevalence Can Be Associated with Changing Sexual Behaviour in Uganda, Urban Kenya, Zimbabwe, and Urban Haiti." *Sexually Transmitted Infections* 82 (2006): i1-i8.

Halperin, Daniel T., and Helen Epstein. "Concurrent Sexual Partnerships Help to Explain Africa's High HIV Prevalence: Implications for Prevention." *The Lancet* 364.9428 (2004): 4–6.

Halttunen, Karen. "Humanitarianism and the Pornography of Pain in Anglo-American Culture." *American Historical Review*, 100 (1995): 303–34.

Hankins, Catherine A., and Barbara O. de Zalduondo. "Combination Prevention: A Deeper Understanding of Effective HIV Prevention." *AIDS* 24 (2010): S70–S80.

Hannan, Thomas. "World Culture and Small Scale Altruism." MA Thesis, Department of Sociology, University of California, Los Angeles, 2010.

Hannan, Thomas. "World Culture at the World's Periphery: Non-Elite Mechanisms of Diffusion and Maintenance in Rural Malawi." Department of Sociology, University of California, Los Angeles, 2010.

Harries, Anthony D., Rony Zachariah, Joep J. van Oosterhout, Steven D. Reid, Mina C. Hosseinipour, Vic Arendt, Zengani Chirwa, Andreas Jahn, Erik J. Schouten, and Kelita Kamoto. "Diagnosis and Management of Antiretroviral-Therapy Failure in Resource-Limited Settings in Sub-Saharan Africa: Challenges and Perspectives." *Lancet Infectious Diseases* 10.1 (2010): 60–65.

Hearst, Norman, and Sanny Chen. "Condoms for AIDS Prevention in the Developing World: Is It Working?" *Studies in Family Planning* 35.1 (2004): 39–47.

Heimer, Carol. "Old Inequalities, New Disease: HIV/AIDS in Sub-Saharan Africa." *Annual Review of Sociology* 33 (2007): 551–77.

Helleringer, Stéphane, Hans-Peter Kohler, Linda Kalilani-Phiri, James Mkandawire, and Benjamin Armbruster. "The Reliability of Sexual Partnership Histories: Implications for the Measurement of Partnership Concurrency during Surveys." *AIDS* 25.4 (2011): 503–11.

Henderson, Patricia C. "South African AIDS Orphans: Examining Assumptions around Vulnerability from the Perspective of Rural Children and Youth." *Childhood: A Global Journal of Child Research* 13.3 (2006): 303–27.

Herbst, Jeffrey. *States and Power in Africa: Comparative Lessons in Authority and Control.* Princeton: Princeton University Press, 2000.

Hindman, Alex, and Jean Reith Schroedel. "U.S. Responses to HIV/AIDS in Africa: Policies and Perceptions of the Bush Administration." *Human Rights Global Focus* 5 (2010): 3–10.

Hirsch, Jennifer S., Holly Wardlow, Daniel Jordan Smith, Harriet M. Phinney, Santi Parikh, and Constance A. Nathanson. *The Secret: Love, Marriage and HIV.* Nashville, TN: Vanderbilt University Press, 2009.

Hirsch, Paul M. "Processing Fads and Fashions: An Organization-Set Analysis of Cultural Industry Systems." *American Journal of Sociology* 77.4 (1972): 639–59.

Hochschild, Adam. *Bury the Chains: Prophets and Rebels in the Fight to Free an Empire's Slaves.* New York: Houghton Mifflin, 2005.

Hochschild, Arlie. *The Time Bind: When Work Becomes Home and Home Becomes Work.* New York: Metropolitan Books, 1997.

Hollingsworth, T. Déirdre, Roy M. Anderson, and Christophe Fraser. "HIV-1 Transmission, by Stage of Infection." *Journal of Infectious Diseases* 198 (2008): 687–93.

Hunter, Mark. *Love in the Time of AIDS.* Bloomington: Indiana University Press, 2010.

Hunter, Susan, and John Williamson. *Children on the Brink: Executive Summary, Updated Estimates and Recommendations for Intervention.* Washington, DC: United States Agency for International Development, 2000.

Jackson, Robert H., and Carl Rosberg. "Why Africa's Weak States Persist: The Empirical and the Juridical in Statehood." *World Politics* 35.2 (1982): 1–24.

Johnson-Hanks, Jennifer. "When the Future Decides: Uncertainty and Intentional Action in Contemporary Cameroon." *Current Anthropology* 46.3 (2005): 363–85.

Johnson-Hanks, Jennifer. "On the Modernity of Traditional Contraception: Time and the Social Context of Fertility." *Population and Development Review* 28.2 (2002): 229–49.

Johnson-Hanks, Jennifer. *Uncertain Honor: Modern Motherhood in an African Crisis.* Chicago: University of Chicago Press, 2006.

Jones, B. "Pentecostalism, Development NGOs and Meaning in Eastern Uganda." In *Pentecostalism and Development: Churches, NGOs, and Social Change in Africa,* edited by D. Freeman, 181–202. New York: Palgrave-Macmillan, 2012.

Kakhongwe, Paul. *Directory of AIDS Service Organizations in Malawi.* Zomba: Centre for Social Research Documentation Unit, 1997.

Kaler, Amy. "'When They See Money, They Think It's Life': Money, Modernity and Morality in Two Sites in Rural Malawi." *Journal of Southern African Studies* 32.2 (2006): 335–49.

Kaler, Amy, Arif Alibhai, Walter Kipp, Tom Rubaale, and Joseph Konde-Lule. "Walking Corpses and Kindly Neighbours: Retrospective Accounts of AIDS Stigma in Western Uganda." *World Journal of AIDS* 2 (2012): 174–82.

Kaler, Amy, and Susan Cotts Watkins. "Disobedient Distributors: Street-Level Bureaucrats and Would-Be Patrons in Community-Based Family Planning Programs in Rural Kenya." *Studies in Family Planning* 32.3 (2001): 254–69.

Kalofonos, Ippolyotos. "'All They Do Is Pray': Community Labour and the Narrowing of 'Care' during Mozambique's HIV Scale-Up." *Global Public Health* 9.1–2 (2014): 7–24.

Kamiyala, Kondwani. "Giving Women Power." *The Nation* (Malawi), June 19, 2008, Features Section, p. 19.

Kamlongera, Christopher F. "Theatre for Development: The Case of Malawi." *Theatre Research International* 7.3 (1982): 207–21.

Kapstein, Ethan B., and Joshua W. Busby. 2013. *AIDS Drugs for All: Social Movements and Market Transformations*. New York: Cambridge University Press.

Keen, David. *Complex Emergencies*. Cambridge, UK: Polity Press, 2008.

Kendall, Nancy O'Gara. "Global Policy and Practice: The 'Successful Failure' of Free Primary Education in Malawi." PhD dissertation, Stanford Graduate School of Education, 2004.

Kerongo, Grace. "Kenya: Durex Sponsors Sex Health Awareness Party." *Star* (Kenya), July 25, 2013. Accessed July 26, 2013. http://allafrica.com/stories /201307251628.html?aa_source=sptlgt-grid&flv=1

Klaits, Frederick. *Death in a Church of Life: Moral Passion during Botswana's Time of AIDS*. Berkeley: University of California Press, 2010.

Kohler, Iliana, Hans-Peter Kohler, Philip Anglewicz, and Jere R. Behrman. "Intergenerational Transfers in the Era of HIV/AIDS: Evidence from Rural Malawi." *Demographic Research* 27 (2012): 775–834.

Konondo, Davis S. (Balaka District Acting AIDS Coordinator). "2009 World AIDS Day Activity Report." December 12, 2009. Accessed from Balaka District Assembly.

Kornfield, Ruth, and Dorothy Namate. *Cultural Practices Related to HIV/AIDS Risk Behaviour: Focus Group Discussions of Village Leaders in Phalombe*. Lilongwe, Malawi: JSI-STAFH Project, 1997.

Krause, Monika. *The Good Project: Humanitarian Relief NGOs and the Fragmentation of Reason*. Chicago and London: University of Chicago Press, 2014.

Kristoff, Nicholas D. "Aid: Can It Work?" *The New York Review of Books,* October 5, 2006. http://www.nybooks.com/articles/2006/10/05/aid-can-it-work/

LaFraniere, Sharon. "AIDS Now Compels Africa to Challenge Widows' 'Cleansing.'" *The New York Times,* May 11, 2005, p. A1.

Lam, David, Cally Ardington, and Murray Leibbrandt. "Schooling as a Lottery: Racial Differences in School Advancement in Urban South Africa." *Journal of Development Economics* 95.2 (2011): 121–36.

Lamont, Michèle. *The Dignity of Working Men: Morality and the Boundaries of Race, Class, and Immigration*. Cambridge, MA: Harvard University Press, 2000.

Lamont, Michèle, Stefan Beljean, and Matthew Clair, "What Is Missing? Cultural Processes and the Making of Inequality." *Socio-Economic Review* 12 (2014): 573–608.

Lancaster, Carol. *George Bush's Foreign Aid: Transformation or Chaos?* Washington, DC: Center for Global Development, 2008.

Lasker, Judith N. *Hoping to Help: The Promises and Pitfalls of Global Health Volunteering*. Ithaca: Cornell University Press, 2016.

Latour, Bruno, and Steve Woolgar. *Laboratory Life: The Construction of Scientific Facts*. Princeton: Princeton University Press, 1986.

Leonard, David K., Jennifer N. Brass, Michael Nelson, Sophal Ear, Dan Fahey, Tasha Fairfield, Martha Johnson Gning, Michael Halderman, Brendan McSherry, Devra C. Moehler, Wilson Prichard, Robin Turner, Tuong Vu, and Jeroen Dijkman. "Does Patronage Still Drive Politics for the Rural Poor in the

Developing World? A Comparative Perspective from the Livestock Sector." *Development and Change* 41.3 (2010): 475–94.

Lewis, David, and David Mosse, eds. *Development Brokers and Translators: The Ethnography of Aid and Agencies*. Bloomfield, CT: Kumarian Press, 2006.

Li, Tania Murray. *The Will to Improve: Governmentality, Development, and the Practice of Politics*. Durham, NC: Duke University Press, 2007.

Lieberman, Evan S. *Boundaries of Contagion: How Ethnic Politics Have Shaped Government Responses to AIDS*. Princeton: Princeton University Press, 2009.

Lo, Nathan C., Anita Lowe, and Eran Bendavid. 2016. "In Sub-Saharan Africa Abstinence Funding Was Not Associated with Reductions in HIV Risk Behavior." *Health Affairs* 35 (5): 856–63.

Logan, Carolyn. "The Roots of Resilience: Exploring Popular Support for African Traditional Authorities." *African Affairs* 112.448 (2013): 353–76.

Lopes, Paul D. "Innovation and Diversity in the Popular Music Industry, 1969 to 1990." *American Sociological Review* 57.1 (1992): 56–71.

Lopman, Ben, Constance Nyamukapa, Phyllis Mushati, Zivai Mupambireyi, Peter Mason, Geoff P. Garnett, and Simon Gregson. "HIV Incidence in 3 Years of Follow-Up of a Zimbabwe Cohort—1998–2000 to 2001–03: Contributions of Proximate and Underlying Determinants to Transmission." *International Journal of Epidemiology* 37.1 (2008): 88–105.

Lopman, Ben A., James J. C. Lewis, Constance A. Nyamukapa, Phyllis Mushati, Steven Chandiwana, and Simon Gregson. "HIV Incidence and Poverty in Manicaland, Zimbabwe: Is HIV Becoming a Disease of the Poor?" *AIDS* 21(2007): Suppl. 7, S57–S66.

Luke, Nancy, and Susan Cotts Watkins. "Reactions of Developing-Country Elites to International Population Policy." *Population and Development Review* 28.4 (2002): 707–33.

Lwanda, John. "The [In]visibility of HIV/AIDS in the Malawi Public Sphere." *African Journal of AIDS Research* 2.2 (2003): 113–36.

Lwanda, John. "Poets, Culture and Orature: A Reappraisal of the Malawi Political Public Sphere, 1953–2006." *Journal of Contemporary African Studies* 26 (2008): 71–101.

Maes, Kenneth. "Volunteerism or Labor Exploitation? Harnessing the Volunteer Spirit to Sustain AIDS Treatment Programs in Urban Ethiopia." *Human Organization* 71.1 (2012): 54–64.

Makaniki, Chris. "Malawi: BLM Launches 'Manyuchi' Condoms." *The Chronicle* (Malawi), August 29, 2004. Accessed March 21, 2014. http://allafrica.com/stories/200408300296.html

Malamula, Felix. "Culture Source of Violence: CHRR." *The Nation* (Malawi), July 11, 2005, p. 3.

Malawi Human Rights Commission (MHRC). *Cultural Practices and Their Impact on the Enjoyment of Human Rights, Particularly the Rights of Women and Children in Malawi*. Lilongwe, Malawi: Malawi Human Rights Commission, 2006.

Malawi Human Rights Commission (MHRC). *Report on the Demonstrations of 20 July 2011*. Lilongwe, Malawi: Malawi Human Rights Commission, 2011.

Malawi National AIDS Commission. *Malawi National HIV/AIDS Action Framework (2005–2009)*. Lilongwe: National AIDS Commission, n.d. Accessed November 2, 2014. https://www.globalhivmeinfo.org/Gamet/pdf/423_HIV%20response%20logical%20framework%20-%20Malawi.pdf

Malawi National AIDS Commission. "National HIV/AIDS Response: Technical Progress Report for Period up to December 2006: July 2005–June 2006 Financial Year." Spreadsheet. Lilongwe: National AIDS Commission, 2006. Accessed at National AIDS Commission, June 2007.

Malikwa, Mercy. "Sex Workers Win Forced HIV Test Case." *The Nation* (Malawi), May 21, 2015, National Section, p. 1.

Mamdani, Mahmood. *Citizen and Subject: Contemporary Africa and the Legacy of Late Colonialism*. Princeton: Princeton University Press, 1996.

Mansuri, Ghazala, and Vijayendra Rao. *Localizing Development: Does Participation Work?* Washington, DC: International Bank for Reconstruction and Development/The World Bank, 2013.

Marrazzo, Jeanne M., Gita Ramjee, Barbra A. Richardson, Kailazarid Gomez, Nyaradzo Mgodi, Gonasagrie Nair, Thesla Palanee, Clemensia Nakabiito, Ariane van der Straten, Lisa Noguchi, Craig W. Hendrix, James Y. Dai, Shayhana Ganesh, Baningi Mkhize, Marthinette Taljaard, Urvi M. Parikh, Jeanna Piper, Benoît Mâsse, Cynthia Grossman, James Rooney, Jill L. Schwartz, Heather Watts, Mark A. Marzinke, Sharon L. Hillier, Ian M. McGowan, and Z. Mike Chirenje. "Tenofovir-Based Preexposure Prophylaxis for HIV Infection among African Women." *New England Journal of Medicine* 372.6 (2015): 509–18.

Marren, Patrick. "Overseas Development Aid: Is It Working?" In *From the Local to the Global: Key Issues in Development Studies*, 3rd ed., edited by G. McCann and S. McCloskey, 59–77. London and New York: Pluto Press, 2015.

McDonnell, Terrence. "Cultural Objects as Objects: Materiality, Urban Space, and the Interpretation of AIDS Campaigns in Accra, Ghana." *American Journal of Sociology* 115 (2010): 1800–852.

McKee, Neil, Jane Bertrand, and Antje Becker-Benton. *Strategic Communication in the HIV/AIDS Epidemic*. Thousand Oaks, CA: Sage Publications, published by the Johns Hopkins Bloomberg School of Public Health Center for Communication Programs, 2004.

Médecins Sans Frontières (MSF). *No Time to Quit: HIV/AIDS Treatment Gap Widening in Africa*. Brussels: Médecins Sans Frontières, 2010.

Meintjes, Helen, and Sonja Giese. "Spinning the Epidemic: The Making of Mythologies of Orphanhood in the Context of AIDS." *Childhood: A Global Journal of Child Research* 13 (2006): 407–30.

Merry, Sally Engle. *Human Rights and Gender Violence: Translating International Law into Local Justice*. Chicago: University of Chicago Press, 2006.

Meyer, John, and Brian Rowan. "Institutionalized Organizations: Formal Structure as Myth and Ceremony." *American Journal of Sociology* 83.2 (1977): 340–63.

Mindry, Deborah. "Nongovernmental Organizations, 'Grassroots,' and the Politics of Virtue." *Signs: Journal of Women in Culture and Society* 26.4 (2001): 1187–211.

Ministry of Education, Science and Technology (Malawi). "Education Management Information System (EMIS): Education Statistics 2014." Lilongwe: Education Management Information System (EMIS), n.d.

Minnis, Alexandra M., Markus J. Steiner, Maria F. Gallo, L. Warner, M. M. Hobbs, A. van der Straten, T. Chipato, M. Macaluso, and N. S. Padian "Biomarker Validation of Reports of Recent Sexual Activity: Results of a Randomized Controlled Study in Zimbabwe." *American Journal of Epidemiology* 170.70 (2009): 918–24.

Mishra, Vinod, Simona Bignami-Van Assche, Robert Greener, Martin Vaessen, Rathavuth Hong, Peter D. Ghys, J. Ties Boerma, Ari Van Assche, Shane Khan, and Shea Rutstein. "HIV Infection Does Not Disproportionately Affect the Poorer in Sub-Saharan Africa." *AIDS* 21 (2007): Suppl. 7, S17–S28.

Mizere, Agnes. "Gov't to Help Victimised Girls." *The Daily Times* (Malawi), July 3, 2009, p. 3.

Mlozi, Howard. "Law Will Not Spare Celebrities." *The Daily Times* (Malawi), August 2, 2010, p. 2.

Mohammad, N., and J. Gikonyo. "Operational Challenges: Community Home-Based Care (CHBC) for PLWHA in Multi-Country HIV/AIDS Programs (MAP) for Sub-Saharan Africa." African Region Working Paper Series No. 88, World Bank, Washington, DC, 2005.

Mohan, Giles. "The Disappointments of Civil Society: The Politics of NGO Intervention in Northern Ghana." *Political Geography* 21.1 (2002): 125–54.

Mohan, Giles, and Kristian Stokke. "Participatory Development and Empowerment: The Dangers of Localism." *Third World Quarterly* 21.2 (2000): 247–68.

Moore, Erin V. "Translating Girls' Empowerment: Gender, Adolescence, and Transnational NGOs in Urban Uganda." PhD Dissertation, Department of Comparative Human Development, University of Chicago. May 17, 2016.

Morfit, N. Simon "'AIDS Is Money': How Donor Preferences Reconfigure Local Realities." *World Development* 39.1 (2011): 64–76.

Mosse, David. "Is Good Policy Unimplementable? Reflections on the Ethnography of Aid Policy and Practice." *Development and Change* 35.4 (2004): 639–71.

Mosse, David, ed. *Adventures in Aidland: The Anthropology of Professionals in International Development*. New York: Berghahn Books, 2011.

Moyo, Dambisa. *Dead Aid: Why Aid Is Not Working and How There Is a Better Way for Africa*. New York: Farrar, Straus and Giroux, 2009.

Mpaka, Charles. "Malawi-Rights: Police Testing Sex Workers for HIV by Force." *Inter Press Service,* October 10, 2009.

Mthawanji, Dyson. "Losing Money, Saving Life." *The Nation* (Malawi), June 20, 2014, p. 27.

Munthali, Ephraim. "Scary Budget." *Weekend Nation* (Malawi), May 23, 2015, p. 1.

Myroniuk, Tyler, Christina Press, and Hans-Peter Kohler. "Why Rely on Friends Instead of Family? The Role of Exchanges and Civic Engagement in a Rural Sub-Saharan African Context." *African Studies* (forthcoming 2016).

Nagaraj, Vijay Kumar. "'Beltway Bandits' and 'Poverty Barons': For-Profit International Development Contracting and the Military-Development Assemblage." *Development and Change* 46.4 (2015): 585–617.

259

National Statistical Office and ICF Macro. Malawi Demographic and Health Survey 2010. Calverton, Maryland: ICF Macro, 2011, p. 198, Table 4.5.

Ng'ambi, Francis and Moses F. A. Maliro. "Seed Security in Malawi with Emphasis on Food Crops." A draft report prepared for submission to Africa Biodiversity Network (ABN) by Malawi Economic Justice Network (MEJN). Lilongwe, Malawi, April 2003.

Nguyen, Vinh-Kim. *The Republic of Therapy: Triage and Sovereignty in West Africa's Time of AIDS*. Durham, NC: Duke University Press, 2010.

Nguyen, Vinh-Kim. "Ties That Might Heal: Testimonials, Solidarity, and Antiretrovirals in West Africa." In *Unraveling Ties: From Social Cohesion to New Practices of Connectedness*, edited by Y. Elkana, I. Krastev, E. Macamo, and S, Randeria, 117–46. Frankfurt and New York: Campus Verlag, 2002.

Njiragoma, Wycliffe. "Macro Staff Go 3 Mths without Pay." *The Daily Times* (Malawi), August 5, 2011.

"Notes from UN Press Briefing by Stephen Lewis, Special Envoy for HIV/AIDS in Africa, at Noon, January 8, 2003." https://www.google.com/search?q=Notes+from+UN+Press+Briefing+by+Stephen+Lewis%2C+Special+Envoy+for+HIV%2FAIDS+in+Africa%2C+at+Noon%2C+January+8%2C+2003&ie=utf-8&oe=utf-8

Ntonya, George. "So, AIDS is money?" *The Nation* (Malawi), March 14, 2007, p. 25.

Nyamukapa, Constance A., Geoff Foster, and Simon Gregson. "Orphans' Household Circumstances and Access to Education in a Maturing HIV Epidemic in Eastern Zimbabwe." *Journal of Social Development in Africa* 18.2 (2003): 7–32.

Nyoni, S. "Canada Grants K700m for AIDS." *The Daily Times* (Malawi), February 27, 2002, p. 1.

Olivier de Sardan, Jean-Pierre. *Anthropology and Development: Understanding Contemporary Social Change*. London: Zed Books, 2005.

Olivier de Sardan, Jean-Pierre. "A Moral Economy of Corruption in Africa?" *Journal of Modern African Studies* 37 (1999): 25–52.

Olivier de Sardan, Jean Pierre, Oumarou Hamani, Nana Issaley, Younoussi Issa, Hannatou Adamou, and Issaka Oumarou. "Cash Transfers in Niger: The Manna, the Norms and the Suspicions." *Reliefweb*, August 6, 2015. http://reliefweb.int/report/niger/cash-transfers-niger-manna-norms-and-suspicions

Oomman, Nandini, Steven Rosenzweig, and Michael Bernstein. *Are Funding Decisions Based on Performance? A Comparison of Approaches as Practiced by the Global Fund to Fight AIDS, Tuberculosis and Malaria, the U.S. President's Emergency Plan for AIDS Relief, and the World Bank's Multi-Country AIDS Program for Africa in Mozambique, Uganda, and Zambia*. Washington, DC: Center for Global Development, 2010.

Ortner, Sherry. "Theory in Anthropology since the Sixties." *Comparative Studies in Society and History* 26 (1984): 126–66.

O'Toole, Sean. "Fighting AIDS with Pictures and Words: South African Health Campaigns Dominate the Political Landscape." *Eye Magazine*, Summer 2004. Accessed April 23, 2010. http://www.eyemagazine.com/feature.php?id=110&fid=500

Oxfam America. "Foreign Aid 101: A Quick and Easy Guide to Understanding US Foreign Aid." 3rd ed., 2014. Accessed May 8, 2016. http://www.oxfamamerica .org/explore/research-publications/foreign-aid-101/?gclid=Cj0KEQjwx7u5 BRCllePz2biJpIYBEiQA-ZeDmjnrZ0Q6mHQ883eZPDyghbi7CsFVvTsah1VS _SMJ77UaAtb48P8HAQ

Oxford Policy Management. *Local Perceptions, Participation and Accountability in Malawi's Health Sector.* Copenhagen: Norwegian Agency for Development Cooperation (NORAD), 2013.

Padian, Nancy S., Sandra I. McCoy, Jennifer E. Balkus, and Judith N. Wasserheit. "Weighing the Gold in the Gold Standard: Challenges in HIV Prevention Research." *AIDS* 24 (2010): 621–35.

Page, Samantha. "'Narratives of Blame': HIV/AIDS and Harmful Cultural Practices in Malawi: Implications for Policies and Programmes." PhD Dissertation, University of Portsmouth, UK, 2014.

Parker, Richard. "Sexuality, Culture, and Power in HIV/AIDS Research." *Annual Review of Anthropology* 30 (2001): 163–79.

Parkhurst, Justin O. "Understanding the Correlations between Wealth, Poverty and Human Immunodeficiency Virus Infection in African Countries." *Bulletin of the World Health Organization* 88 (2010): 481–560.

Pearce, Diana. "The Feminization of Poverty: Women, Work, and Welfare." *Urban and Social Change Review* 11 (1978): 28–36.

Peters, Pauline, Peter A. Walker, and Daimon Kambewa. "Striving for Normality in a Time of AIDS." *Journal of Modern African Studies* 46.4 (2008): 1–29.

Peterson, Richard A., and David G. Berger, "Cycles in Symbol Production: The Case of Popular Music." *American Sociological Review* 40.2 (1975): 158–73.

Pfeiffer, James. "Civil Society, NGOs, and the Holy Spirit in Mozambique." *Human Organization* 63 (2004): 359–72.

Pfeiffer, James. "International NGOs and Primary Health Care in Mozambique: The Need for a New Model of Collaboration." *Social Science & Medicine* 56 (2003): 725–38.

Phalula, M. "MSF Assists Orphans with Items Worth K130,000." *The Daily Times* (Malawi), July 10, 2010, p. 2.

Pigg, Stacy Leigh. "Constructing Social Categories through Place: Social Representations and Development in Nepal." *Comparative Studies in Society and History* 34.3 (1992): 491–513.

Pigg, Stacy Leigh. "Globalizing the Facts of Life." In *Sex in Development*, edited by S. L. Pigg and V. Adams. Durham, NC: Duke University Press, 2005.

Piot, Peter, Michel Kazatchkine, Mark Dybul, and Julian Lob-Levy. "AIDS: Lessons Learnt and Myths Dispelled." *The Lancet* 374 (2009): 260–63.

Plummer, M. L., D. A. Ross, D. Wight, J. Changalucha, G. Mshana, J. Wamoyi, J. Todd, A. Anemona, F. F. Mosha, A. I. Obasi, and R. J. Hayes. "'A Bit More Truthful': The Validity of Adolescent Sexual Behaviour Data Collected in Rural Northern Tanzania Using Five Methods." *Sexually Transmitted Infections* 80 (2004): 49–56.

Pool, Robert, Catherine M. Montgomery, Neetha S. Morar, Oliver Mweemba, Agnes Ssali, Mitzy Gafos, Shelley Lees, Jonathan Stadler, Andrew Nunn, Angela Crook, Richard Hayes, and Sheena McCormack. "Assessing the

Accuracy of Adherence and Sexual Behaviour Data in the Mdp301 Vaginal Microbicides Trial Using a Mixed Methods and Triangulation Model." *PLoS ONE* 5.7 (2010): e11632. doi: 10.1371/journal.pone.0011632

Potts, Malcom, Daniel T. Halperin, Douglas Kirby, Ann Swidler, Elliot Marseille, Jeffrey D. Klausner, Norman Hearst, Richard G. Wamai, James G. Kahn, and Julia Walsh. "Reassessing HIV Prevention." *Science* 320.5877 (2008): 749–50.

Poulin, Michelle. "Sex, Money, and Premarital Partnerships in Southern Malawi." *Social Science & Medicine* 65.11 (2007): 2383–93.

Poulin, Michelle, Kathryn Dovel, and Susan Watkins. "Men with Money and the 'Vulnerable Women' Client Category in an AIDS Epidemic." *World Development* 85 (2016): 16–30.

Power, Joey. *Political Culture and Nationalism in Malawi: Building Kwacha*. Rochester, NY: University of Rochester Press, 2010.

Pullum, Thomas W. *Orphanhood in Malawi, 2004–2006*. Malawi: Malawi Ministry of Women and Child Development, 2008.

Putzel, James. "The Global Fight against AIDS: How Adequate Are the National Commissions?" *Journal of International Development* 16.8 (2004): 1129–40.

Republic of Malawi and World Bank. *Malawi Poverty and Vulnerability Assessment: Investing in Our Future*. Washington, DC: World Bank, 2007.

Reuters. "Bush Pledges $500m ... to Help Fight HIV/AIDS." *The Daily Times* (Malawi), June 20, 2002, p. 9.

Richey, Lisa Ann, and Stefano Ponte. *Brand Aid: Shopping Well to Save the World*. Minneapolis: University of Minnesota Press, 2011.

Richter, Linda M., and Amy Norman. "AIDS Orphan Tourism: A Threat to Young Children in Residential Care." *Vulnerable Children and Youth Studies* 5 (2010): 217–29.

Robinson, Rachel Sullivan. *Intimate Interventions in Global Health: Preventing Pregnancy and HIV in Sub-Saharan Africa*. Cambridge: Cambridge University Press, 2017.

Robinson, Rachel Sullivan. "From Population to HIV: The Organizational and Structural Determinants of HIV Outcomes in Sub-Saharan Africa." *Journal of the International AIDS Society* 14 (2011): Suppl. 2, S6.

Rosenthal, Anat. "Raising our Children: Community Strategies for Coping with Orphans and Vulnerable Children in Rural Malawi." PhD Dissertation submitted to the Senate of the Hebrew University, Jerusalem, 2008.

Rossi, Benedetta. "Aid Policies and Recipient Strategies in Niger: Why Donors and Recipients Should Not Be Compartmentalized into Separate Worlds of Knowledge." In *Development Brokers and Translators: The Ethnography of Aid and Agencies*, edited by D. Lewis and D. Mosse, 27–49. Bloomfield, CT: Kumarian Press, 2006.

Rothmyer, Karen. "Hiding the Real Africa: Why NGOs Prefer Bad News." *Columbia Journalism Review*, March 21, 2011. http://www.cjr.org/reports/hiding_the_real_africa.php

Sacks, Jeffrey. *The Age of Sustainable Development*. New York: Columbia University Press, 2015.

Schatzki, Theodore R., Karin Knorr Cetina, and Eike von Savigny, eds. *The Practice Turn in Contemporary Theory*. London: Routledge, 2001.

Scherz, China. *Having People, Having Heart: Charity, Sustainable Development, and Problems of Dependence in Central Uganda*. Chicago and London: University of Chicago Press, 2014.

Schmidt, Elizabeth. *Peasants, Traders, and Wives: Shona Women in the History of Zimbabwe, 1870–1939*. Portsmouth, NH: Heineman, 1992.

Serieux, John E., Spy Munthali, Ardeshir Sepehri, and Robert White. "The Impact of the Global Economic Crisis on HIV and AIDS Programs in a High Prevalence Country: The Case of Malawi." *World Development* 40.3 (2012): 501–15.

Sharra, Steve. "Solving the Study Leave Conundrum for Malawian Teachers." Blog "afrika aphukira." June 13, 2013. Accessed June, 22, 2014. http://mlauzi .blogspot.com/2013/06/solving-study-leave-conondrum-for.html

Shelton, James D. "Why Multiple Sexual Partners?" *The Lancet* 374.9687 (2009): 367–69.

Shelton, James D., Michael M. Cassell, and Jacob Adetunji. "Is Poverty or Wealth at the Root of HIV?" *The Lancet* 366 (2005): 1057–58.

Shiffman, Jeremy. "A Social Explanation for the Rise and Fall of Global Health Issues." *Bulletin of the World Health Organization* 87 (2009): 608–13.

Shiffman, Jeremy, and Sharmina Sultana. "Generating Political Priority for Neonatal Mortality Reduction in Bangladesh." *American Journal of Public Health* 103 (2013): 623–31.

Shilts, Randy. *And the Band Played On: Politics, People and the AIDS Epidemic*. New York: St. Martin's Press, 1987.

Shipton, Parker. *The Nature of Entrustment: Intimacy, Exchange, and the Sacred in Africa*. New Haven: Yale University Press, 2007.

Singer, Isaac Bashevis. *The Fools of Chełm and Their History*. New York: Farrar, Straus and Giroux, 1973.

Singini, George. "FYF Project to Empower Households." *The Nation* (Malawi) 20.121 (2013), June 19, 2013, p. 6.

Smith, Daniel Jordan. *A Culture of Corruption: Everyday Deception and Popular Discontent in Nigeria*. Princeton: Princeton University Press, 2006.

Smith, Daniel Jordan. "Patronage, Per Diems and the 'Workshop Mentality': The Practice of Family Planning Programs in Southeastern Nigeria." *World Development* 31.4 (2003): 703–15.

Smith, James Howard. *Bewitching Development: Witchcraft and the Reinvention of Development in Neoliberal Kenya*. Chicago: University of Chicago Press, 2008.

Smith, Kirsten P., and Susan Cotts Watkins. "Perceptions of Risk and Strategies for Prevention: Responses to HIV/AIDS in Rural Malawi." *Social Science & Medicine* 60 (2005): 649–60.

Somanje, C. "GAIA Launches K42.6m Project for Orphans, AIDS Projects." *The Weekend Nation* (Malawi), June 28–29, 2008, p. 3.

Sontag, Susan. *Illness as Metaphor and AIDS and Its Metaphors*. New York: Picador, 2001.

Spear, Thomas. "Neotraditionalism and the Limits of Invention in British Colonial Africa." *Journal of African History* 44 (2003): 3–27.

Stafford, Tom. "Springfield Rotary Helps AIDS Orphans." *Springfield News–Sun*, June 8, 2013. Accessed April 30, 2014. http://www.springfieldnewssun.com /news/news/local/springfield-rotary-helps-aids-orphans/nYDn2/

Stamatov, Peter. *The Origins of Global Humanitarianism: Religion, Empires, and Advocacy*. New York: Cambridge University Press, 2013.

Stewart, Julie. "A Tale of Two Communities: Divergent Development and Embedded Brokerage in Postwar Guatemala." *Journal of Contemporary Ethnography* 41.4 (2012): 402–31.

Stoeffler, Quentin, Bradford Mills, and Carlo del Ninno. "Reaching the Poor: Cash Transfer Program Targeting in Cameroon." *World Development* 83 (2016): 244–63.

Stoler, Laura Ann. *Race and the Education of Desire: Foucault's History of Sexuality and the Colonial Order of Things*. Durham, NC: Duke University Press, 1995.

Stromberg, Peter. *Caught in Play: How Entertainment Works on You*. Palo Alto: Stanford University Press, 2009.

Swidler, Ann. "Dialectics of Patronage: Logics of Accountability at the African AIDS-NGO Interface." In *Globalization, Philanthropy, and Civil Society: Projecting Institutional Logics Abroad*, edited by S. Heydemann and D. C. Hammack, 192–220. Bloomington: Indiana University Press, 2009.

Swidler, Ann. "Cultural Sources of Institutional Resilience: Lessons from Chieftaincy in Rural Malawi." In *Social Resilience in the Neoliberal Era*, edited by P. A. Hall and M. Lamont, 319–45. New York: Cambridge University Press, 2013.

Swidler, Ann, and Susan Cotts Watkins. "Ties of Dependence: AIDS and Transactional Sex in Rural Malawi." *Studies in Family Planning* 38.3 (2007): 147–62.

Swidler, Ann, and Susan Cotts Watkins. " 'Teach a Man to Fish': The Sustainability Doctrine and Its Social Consequences." *World Development* 37.7 (2009): 1182–96.

Tavrow, Paula. *Family Planning Knowledge, Attitudes and Practices: Machinga District, 1993*. Report on a Baseline Survey Commissioned by the Machinga District Health Office and GTZ/Liwonde. Zomba, Malawi: Centre for Social Research, University of Malawi, 1994.

Tawfik, Linda, and Susan Cotts Watkins. "Sex in Geneva, Sex in Lilongwe, and Sex in Balaka." *Social Science & Medicine* Special Edition 64 (2007): 1090–101.

Temudo, Marina Padrão. "Western Beliefs and Local Myths: A Case Study on the Interface between Farmers, NGOs and the State in Guinea-Bissau Rural Development Interventions." In *Between a Rock and a Hard Place: African NGOs, Donors and the State,* edited by J. Igoe and T. Kelsall, 253–78. Durham, NC: Carolina Academic Press, 2005.

The Daily Mirror (Accra). "High Demand for Female Condoms." September 23, 2005. Accessed March 6, 2014. http://www.ghanaweb.com/GhanaHomePage/NewsArchive/artikel.php?ID=90775

The Daily Times (Malawi). "Let's Revisit Our Cultural Beliefs." January 10, 2002, p. 2.

The Global Fund to Fight AIDS Tuberculosis and Malaria. "The Global Fund Annual Report 2002/2003, 22 January 2002 to 31 July 2003." Geneva, Switzerland: The Global Fund to Fight AIDS Tuberculosis and Malaria, 2003.

The Herald (Zimbabwe). January 24, 2014. Accessed January 24, 2014. http://allafrica.com/stories/201401240708.html

The Nation (Malawi), "Grants Approved for the January to June 2010 Cycle." National News, July 23, 2010, p. 14.

The Nation (Malawi). World Vision Advertisement, May 27, 2015, p. 39.

Thornton, Patricia H., William Ocasio, and Michael Lounsbury. *The Institutional Logics Perspective: A New Approach to Culture, Structure and Process.* Oxford: Oxford University Press, 2012.

Timberg, Craig, and Daniel Halperin. 2012. *Tinderbox: How the West Sparked the AIDS Epidemic and How the World Can Finally Overcome It.* London: Penguin Press, 2012.

Times Reporter. "UNFPA, BLM Launch K437.5m Youth Project." *The Daily Times* (Malawi), National Section, June 26, 2006, p. 2.

Treichler, Paula A. *How to Have Theory in an Epidemic: Cultural Chronicles of AIDS.* Durham, NC: Duke University Press, 1999.

Trinitapoli, Jenny. "AIDS and Religious Life in Malawi: Rethinking How Population Dynamics Shape Culture." *Population* 70.2 (2015): 245–72.

Trinitapoli, Jenny, and Alexander Weinreb. *Religion and AIDS in Africa.* New York: Oxford University Press, 2012.

Trinitapoli, Jenny, and Stephen Vaisey. "The Transformative Role of Religious Experience: The Case of Short-Term Missions." *Social Forces* 88.1 (2009): 121–40.

UNAIDS. *Empower Young Women and Adolescent Girls: Fast-Track the End of the AIDS Epidemic in Africa.* 2015. http://www.unaids.org/en/resources/documents/2015/JC2746

UNAIDS. *Global Report: UNAIDS Report on the Global AIDS Epidemic 2012,* 2012. http://www.unaids.org/en/resources/campaigns/20121120_globalreport2012/globalreport

UNAIDS. "HIV Prevention Toolkit: Minimum Requirements for Effective HIV Prevention Programming." 2008. http://hivpreventiontoolkit.unaids.org/Knowledge_Epidemic.aspx

UNAIDS. *Report on the Global AIDS Epidemic.* 2008. http://www.unaids.org

"UNAIDS Statement on South African Trial Findings Regarding Male Circumcision and HIV." WHO, UNFPA, UNICEF, and the UNAIDS Secretariat, July 26, 2005. Accessed June 16, 2014. http://www.who.int/mediacentre/news/releases/2005/pr32/en/

UNAIDS. "The 'Three Ones' in Action: Where We Are and Where We Go from Here." UNAIDS (Joint United Nations Programme on HIV/AIDS), 2005. http://www.unaids.org

UNAIDS (Joint United Nations Programme on HIV/AIDS), UNICEF (United Nations Children's Fund), and USAID (United States Agency for International Development). *Children on the Brink 2004: A Joint Report of New Orphan Estimates and a Framework for Action.* Washington, DC: USAID, 2004. www.unicef.org/publications/index_22212.html

UNFPA. "Joint Statement on Kenyan and Ugandan Trial Findings Regarding Male Circumcision and HIV." December 13, 2006. Accessed June 16, 2014. http://www.unfpa.org/public/News/pid/276

UNFPA. "Safeguarding Young People: UNFPA Regional Initiative." Advertisement, *The Daily Times,* April 23, 2014, p. 25.

UNICEF. *Improving Protection for Children without Parental Care: Care for Children Affected by HIV/AIDS—The Urgent Need for International Standards*. New York: United Nations Children's Fund, 2004.

USAID. "AFRICA Health Sector Results Reporting." Bureau for Africa, Office of Sustainable Development (AFR/SD), May, 2006. Accessed February 23, 2015. http://www.google.com/url?sa=t&rct=j&q=&esrc=s&source=web&cd=1&ved =0CB4QFjAA&url=http%3A%2F%2Fpdf.usaid.gov%2Fpdf_docs%2FPdacp137 .pdf&ei=74nrVJKRGYmWoQT4yoFA&usg=AFQjCNFEVpcvck81PAImajkm WK5Lj15Eyg&bvm=bv.86475890,d.cGU

USAID-Malawi. *HIV/AIDS Strategy 2002–2006*. Lilongwe: USAID, 2003.

US Government Accountability Office (GAO). *HIV/AIDS: USAID and U.N. Response to the Epidemic in the Developing World*. 1998. http://www.gao.gov /products/NSIAD-98-202

Vallejo, Bertha, and Uta Wehn. "Capacity Development Evaluation: The Challenge of the Results Agenda and Measuring Return on Investment in the Global South." *World Development* 79 (2016): 1–13.

van de Ruit, Catherine. "The Institutionalization of AIDS Orphan Policy in South Africa." PhD Dissertation, Department of Sociology, University of Pennsylvania, 2012.

van de Walle, Nicholas. "Aid's Crisis of Legitimacy: Current Proposals and Future Prospects." *African Affairs* 99 (1999): 337–52.

van den Borne, Francine. *Trying to Survive in Times of Poverty and AIDS: Women and Multiple Partner Sex in Malawi*. Amsterdam: Het Spinhuis, 2005.

Vaughan, Megan. *The Story of an African Famine*. Cambridge, UK: Cambridge University Press, 1987.

Verheijen, Janneke. *Balancing Men, Morals, and Money: Women's Agency between HIV and Security in a Malawi Village*. Leiden, The Netherlands: African Studies Center, 2013.

Vermund, Sten H. "Massive Benefits of Antiretroviral Therapy in Africa." *Journal of Infectious Diseases* 209.4 (2014): 483–85.

Vickers, Steve. "Zimbabweans Make Condom Bangles." *BBC News*, February 10, 2005. http://news.bbc.co.uk/2/hi/africa/4250789.stm

Wallace, Tina, Erica Bornstein, and Jennifer Chapman. *The Aid Chain*. Warwickshire, UK: Practical Action Publishing, 2007.

Walsh, Aisling, Chishimba Mulambia, Ruairi Brugha, and Johanna Hanefeld. " 'The Problem Is Ours, It Is Not CRAIDS': Evaluating Sustainability of Community Based Organisations for HIV/AIDS in a Rural District in Zambia." *Globalization and Health* 8.40 (2012). http://www.globalizationandhealth.com /content/8/1/40

Wangel, Ann-Marie. "AIDS in Malawi: A Conspiracy of Silence?" MS in Public Health in Developing Countries, London School of Hygiene and Tropical Medicine, 1985.

Watkins, Susan Cotts. "Navigating the AIDS Epidemic in Rural Malawi." *Population and Development Review* 30.4 (2004): 673–705.

Watkins, Susan Cotts, and Ann Swidler. "Hearsay Ethnography: Conversational Journals as a Method for Studying Culture in Action." *Poetics* 37.2 (2009): 162–84.

Watkins, Susan Cotts, Ann Swidler, and Thomas Hannan. "Outsourcing Social Transformation: Development NGOs as Organizations." *Annual Review of Sociology* 38 (2012): 285–315.

Weber, Klaus. "A Toolkit for Analyzing Corporate Cultural Toolkits." *Poetics* 33 (2005): 227–52.

Weinreb, Alexander. "Substitution and Substitutability: The Effects of Kin Availability on Intergenerational Transfers in Malawi." In *Allocating Public and Private Resources across Generations: Riding the Age Waves*, vol. 2, edited by A. H. Gauthier, C.Y.C. Chu, and S. Tuljapurkar, 13–38. The Netherlands: Springer-Verlag, 2006.

Weiss, Thomas. "The MDGs and the UN's Comparative Advantage in Goal-Setting." *States, Power & Societies* (Newsletter of the Political Sociology Section of the American Sociological Association) 18.1 (2012): 1–4.

White, Landeg. *Magomero: Portrait of an African Village*. Cambridge, UK: Cambridge University Press, 1987.

WHO/UNAIDS. "WHO/UNAIDS Technical Consultation Male Circumcision and HIV Prevention: Research Implications for Policy and Programming: Conclusions and Recommendations." http://www.who.int/hiv/mediacentre/MCrecommendations_en.pdf

World Bank. *Intensifying Action against HIV/AIDS in Africa: Responding to a Development Crisis*. Washington, DC: Africa Region, World Bank, 1999.

World Bank. "Project Appraisal Document on a Proposed IDA Grant in the Amount of SDR 25.4 Million (US$35.0 Million Equivalent) to the Republic of Malawi for a Multi-Sectoral AIDS Project (MAP)." Washington, DC: World Bank, 2003.

Whyte, Susan Reynolds. *Questioning Misfortune: The Pragmatics of Uncertainty in Eastern Uganda*. Cambridge, UK: Cambridge University Press, 1997.

Zuckerman, Ezra. "Construction, Concentration, and (Dis)Continuities in Social Valuations." *Annual Review of Sociology* 38 (2012): 223–45.

INDEX

Note: Page numbers in italic type refer to illustrations or figures.

wife swapping, 156–57
witchcraft, 111, 127, 135, 212
women and girls, 8; development
  enterprise's preoccupation with,
  236n1; empowerment of, 46, 138,
  140–41, 145, 150; harmful cultural
  practices involving, 138–39, 150–65;
  incidence of HIV/AIDS among,
  139, 141, 236n2; mercenary, 138,
  141–48; policies and legislation
  affecting, 146–50; and poverty, 140,
  142, 146; sexual initiation of, 138;
  social gathering of, *144*; as victims,
  139; vulnerable, 138–50, 164–65. *See*
  women and girls: attitudes toward
Women's Legal Resources Centre, 83
working misunderstandings, xi, 123,
  131, 148, 164, 166, 219n5, 235n1
workshops, 7

World Bank, 38–39, 44, 51, 52, 66, 161,
  204, 224n7
World Food Program, 224n7
World Health Organization (WHO),
  39, 204, 224n7, 224n8
World Vision, 6, 20, 43, 51, 52, 66, 83,
  90–91, 114, 115, 135, 181, 209

youth, as target of prevention practices,
  66–72
Youth Alert! Mix, 184
youth clubs. *See* AIDS youth clubs
Youth Impact Organisation, *104*
Youth Net and Counseling
  (YONECO), 94–95

Zakreski, Elaine and Peter, x
Zgambo, Estele, 115–21
Zulu, Eliya, 24

PRINCETON STUDIES IN CULTURAL SOCIOLOGY

Paul J. DiMaggio, Michèle Lamont,
Robert J. Wuthnow, and Viviana A. Zelizer,
Series Editors

Bearing Witness: Readers, Writers, and the Novel in Nigeria by Wendy Griswold

Gifted Tongues: High School Debate and Adolescent Culture by Gary Alan Fine

Offside: Soccer and American Exceptionalism by Andrei S. Markovits and Steven L. Hellerman

Reinventing Justice: The American Drug Court Movement by James L. Nolan, Jr.

Kingdom of Children: Culture and Controversy in the Homeschooling Movement by Mitchell L. Stevens

Blessed Events: Religion and Home Birth in America by Pamela E. Klassen

Negotiating Identities: States and Immigrants in France and Germany by Riva Kastoryano, translated by Barbara Harshav

Contentious Curricula: Afrocentrism and Creationism in American Public Schools by Amy J. Binder

Community: Pursuing the Dream, Living the Reality by Suzanne Keller

The Minds of Marginalized Black Men: Making Sense of Mobility, Opportunity, and Future Life Chances by Alford A. Young, Jr.

Framing Europe: Attitudes to European Integration in Germany, Spain, and the United Kingdom by Juan Dez Medrano

Interaction Ritual Chains by Randall Collins

On Justification: Economies of Worth by Luc Boltanski and Laurent Thévenot, translated by Catherine Porter

Talking Prices: Symbolic Meanings of Prices on the Market for Contemporary Art by Olav Velthuis

Elusive Togetherness: Church Groups Trying to Bridge America's Divisions by Paul Lichterman

Religion and Family in a Changing Society by Penny Edgell

Hollywood Highbrow: From Entertainment to Art by Shyon Baumann

Partisan Publics: Communication and Contention across Brazilian Youth Activist Networks by Ann Mische

Disrupting Science: Social Movements, American Scientists, and the Politics of the Military, 1945–1975 by Kelly Moore

Weaving Self-Evidence: A Sociology of Logic by Claude Rosental, translated by Catherine Porter

The Taylorized Beauty of the Mechanical: Scientific Management and the Rise of Modernist Architecture by Mauro F. Guillén

Impossible Engineering: Technology and Territoriality on the Canal du Midi by Chandra Mukerji

Economists and Societies: Discipline and Profession in the United States, Britain, and France, 1890s to 1990s by Marion Fourcade

Reds, Whites, and Blues: Social Movements, Folk Music, and Race in the United States by William G. Roy

279

280